THE SOUTH
AND THE SECTIONAL CONFLICT

THE SOUTH
AND THE SECTIONAL
CONFLICT

David M. Potter

LOUISIANA STATE UNIVERSITY PRESS

BATON ROUGE 1968

To Richard W. Lyman

Copyright © 1968 by
LOUISIANA STATE UNIVERSITY PRESS

Library of Congress Catalog Card Number: 68–8941
Manufactured in the United States of America by
The Colonial Press Inc.
Designed by Jules B. McKee

Preface

IN ONE OF her incomparable sketches, Frances Gray Patton once observed that no one born in the South later than World War I could remember the Civil War personally. I found this statement most arresting, because though I was born in Georgia in 1910, I have always had a feeling that in an indirect, nonsensory way I could remember what was still called "The War"—as if there had been no other. If I did not see the men in gray march off to battle, I saw great numbers of them march in parades on a Memorial Day which did not fall on the same date that was observed in the North. If I did not experience the rigors of life "behind the lines in the Southern Confederacy," I lived in the long backwash of the war in a land that remembered the past very vividly and somewhat inaccurately, because the present had nothing exciting to offer, and accuracy about either the past or the present was psychologically not very rewarding.

When I completed college at Emory University at the age of twenty-one, I "went North" to study under Ulrich B. Phillips at Yale, and there I began to acquire or try to acquire the perspective which historical studies offer. From that time to this, I have lived in a university environment. Of those thirty-six years, six were spent in the South—two at the University of Mississippi and four at what was then known as Rice Institute. But on balance I have lived longer outside of the South than in it, and hopefully have learned to view it with detachment, though not without fondness. Certainly no longer a Southerner, I am not yet completely denatured.

During this span of academic experience, I have spent a great deal of time teaching about the South and pondering its history, its problems, its evils, its anachronisms, its graces, and its agonizing situation: caught in more ways than one between the past and the present. Apart from concern with the land where I grew up, I have found the subject perennially compelling at a less personal level because the South has been the focus of two of the most profound and most difficult problems in the American experience. In a republic making the transition from a loose confederation of diverse states to a consolidated, homogenized nation, the South presented the spectacle of enduring distinctiveness and combative sectionalism. In a society committed to the principle, if not the practice, of an ever broader equality for all its members, the South has clung to racial distinctions, and thus has become the classic example of a phenomenon that occurs both throughout the nation and throughout the world in such obdurate form as to make it the supreme test of the equalitarian principle.

As a student of the South, I have sometimes tried to explain aspects of the Southern experience to myself by writing about them. The essays in this volume are among the results of this attempt. The first of them was written in 1941; the last in 1967. The John Brown essay has not been published previously, and "The Literature on the Background of the Civil War" has been largely rewritten since it first appeared in William H. Cartwright and Richard L. Watson, Jr., co-editors, *Interpreting and Teaching American History* (31st Yearbook of the National Council for the Social Studies) in 1961. The other nine have been published in various places, but they all now stand in their original form. I am indebted to the publishers who brought them out initially for permission to reprint them:

"The Enigma of the South" was first published in the *Yale Review*, LI (Autumn, 1961), 142–51.

"On Understanding the South" was first published in the *Journal of Southern History*, XXX (1964), 451–62.

"The Historian's Use of Nationalism and Vice Versa" was published in its complete, present form in Alexander V. Riasonovsky and Barnes Riznik, editors, *Generalizations in Historical Writing* (Philadelphia: University of Pennsylvania Press, 1963). The essay was written for the book in question, but it also appeared with some abridgement in the *American Historical Review*, LXVII (1962), 924–50.

"The Lincoln Theme and American National Historiography" was delivered as an inaugural lecture for the Harmsworth Professorship of American History, at Oxford on November 19, 1947, and published by the Clarendon Press at Oxford in 1948.

"Depletion and Renewal in Southern History" was written for a conference in February, 1966, at Duke University, concerning plans for a Center for Southern Studies at Duke, and was first published in Edgar T. Thompson, editor, *Perspectives on the South: Agenda for Research* (Durham: Duke University Press, 1967).

"Horace Greeley and Peaceable Secession" was first published in the *Journal of Southern History*, VII (1941).

"Why Republicans Rejected Both Compromise and Secession" was written for a conference held by the Institute of American History at Stanford University, March 1–2, 1963, and was first published in George H. Knoles, editor, *The Crisis of the Union, 1860–1861* (Baton Rouge: Louisiana State University Press, 1965).

"Jefferson Davis and the Political Factors in Confederate

Defeat" was written for a conference at Gettysburg College in November, 1958, regarding the factors which were decisive in producing Northern victory. It was first published in David Donald, editor, *Why the North Won the Civil War* (Baton Rouge: Louisiana State University Press, 1960).

"The Civil War in the History of the Modern World: A Comparative View" was written for inclusion in a series of essays treating American History in comparative terms. It was first published in C. Vann Woodward, editor, *The Comparative Approach to American History* (New York: Basic Books, 1968).

I have been somewhat apprehensive that the following essays might convey the impression that the history of the South ended at Appomattox. This is by no means my conviction, and to prove it, I was tempted to include the long essay "The Historical Development of Eastern-Southern Freight Rate Relationships," written at the urging of one of my closest friends, the late Brainerd Currie, for *Law and Contemporary Problems* [XII (1947), 416–48], a journal of which he was then the editor. But that essay is, in fact, not quite congruent with the others in this collection, and it was recently reprinted by Richard M. Abrams and Lawrence W. Levine, editors, in *The Shaping of Twentieth Century America* (Boston, 1965). Therefore, after some uncertainty, I decided not to include it here.

The essays which are included, obligingly, almost arranged themselves. Three of them deal with that long-standing riddle: What is the essence of the nature of the South? Three more deal with the evolution of the historical literature, which is not only a matter of "historiography" but also a key to the fascinating changes in the way in which historical interpreters have viewed the South and its past. The last five ask whether Horace Greeley ever intended to let the South secede; what the Republicans thought they were doing when they decided, for the first time in a sectional crisis, not to compromise; whether any of John Brown's best friends were Negroes; how much Jefferson Davis really wanted a Confederate victory; and how we might regard the Civil War if it did not enjoy protected status as an American Iliad, and if its significance had to be measured in the remorseless terms of the dominant forces in the modern world.

DAVID M. POTTER

Stanford University
June, 1968

Contents

xi

THE SOUTH
AND THE SECTIONAL CONFLICT

Part 1

THE NATURE OF SOUTHERNISM

The Enigma of the South

> *Howard Zinn in a recent book,* The Mystique of the South *(1964), has argued that the traditional view of the South as an exotic and unique region is just so much moonshine. The South, he says, is more American than the rest of the United States; it is America in excelsis. Whether he is really talking about the degree of peculiarity of the South or the degree of iniquity of the American society is for his readers to determine. I agree that there has indeed been much nonsense uttered about the distinctiveness of the South—for instance Carl Carmer's assertion, concerning Alabama, that "the Congo is not more different from Massachusetts, or Kansas, or California." But I believe that there are genuine and important features of distinctiveness, and I have attempted to outline them in the following essay.*

*A*MONG THE many flourishing branches of American historical study during the last half-century, one of the most robust has been the history of the South. Fifty years ago, there was already one large body of literature on the Southern Confederacy, especially in its military aspects, and another on the local history of various Southern states, but the history of the South as a region—of the whole vast area below the Potomac, viewed as a single entity for the whole time from the settlement of Jamestown to the present—is largely a product of the last five decades. Today, a multivolume history, a number of college textbooks, a quarterly journal, and a substantial library of monographic studies all serve as measures of the extent of the development in this field.

Anyone who seeks an explanation for this interest in Southern history must take account of several factors. To begin

3

with, the study of American regions is a general phenomenon, embracing not only the South but also New England, the Middle West, and the great physiographic provinces beyond the Mississippi. In a nation as vast and as diverse as ours, there is really no level higher than the regional level at which one can come to grips with the concrete realities of the land. But apart from this regional aspect, the Southern theme has held an unusual appeal for the people of the South because of their peculiarly strong and sentimental loyalty to Dixie as their native land, and for Americans outside the South because of the exotic quality of the place and because it bears the aura of a Lost Cause. Union generals, for some reason, have never held the romantic interest that attached to Stonewall Jackson, Jeb Stuart, George Pickett, Bedford Forrest, and, of course, Robert E. Lee. Today, the predilection of Yankee children for caps, flags, and toys displaying the Rebel insignia bears further witness to the enduring truth that lost causes have a fascination even for those who did not lose them.

But it seems unlikely that either the South as an American region, or the South as Dixieland, or the South as a Lost Cause could hold so much scholarly and popular attention in focus if the South were not also an enigma. To writers for more than half a century the South has been a kind of sphinx on the American land.

To some who viewed it, this sphinx has seemed a great insensate monolith, a vast artifact of the past with no meaning behind its inscrutable expression. Its domain has been just what H. L. Mencken said it was—a cultural desert, a Sahara of the Bozart. But to others this sphinx has seemed to hold a secret, an answer to the riddle of American life.

To many people today, who think of the South in terms of Freedom Riders and lunch-counter sit-ins, of Tobacco Road and Central High School in Little Rock, of robed Klansmen and burning crosses, and perhaps of a Monkey Trial at Dayton, Tennessee, it may seem hard to believe that not long ago the South was regarded by many thoughtful and liberal-minded people as a kind of sanctuary of the American democratic tradition. What is now deplored as the "benighted South," or the "sick South," was, until recently, regarded by many liberals as the birthplace and the natural bulwark of the Jeffersonian ideal—a region where agrarian democracy still struggled to survive, fighting a gallant rearguard action against the commercialism and the industrial capitalism of the Northeast.

It would be a major undertaking to trace the evolution of this concept. The general idea that American democracy is essentially frontier democracy—which closely resembles agrarian democracy—is forever linked with Frederick Jackson Turner, but Turner gave it a Western rather than a Southern orientation. Certainly one of the earliest writers to apply it to the South was William E. Dodd. In 1911, when Dodd had been but recently appointed to the University of Chicago, and twenty-two years before Franklin Roosevelt sent him as our unswervingly democratic ambassador to Hitler's Berlin, he wrote a sketchy little book, now largely forgotten, entitled *Statesmen of the Old South*, with the significant subtitle, *From Radicalism to Conservative Revolt*. The statesmen whom he treated were Jefferson, Calhoun, and Jefferson Davis, and the theme which he developed was that the democratic or radical South of Thomas Jefferson—an equalitarian South of small subsistence farmers—had been subverted by the increasingly aristocratic and hierarchical South of the great slaveholders whose property interests found embodiment in Calhoun and Davis.

In three brief and seemingly artless chapters, Dodd achieved two very subtle effects. First, he defined to suit himself what may be called a normative South—the South of Thomas Jefferson—and thus established an arbitrary basis for identifying all future developments of a Jeffersonian tenor as truly or intrinsically Southern, and for rejecting all conservative or hierarchical developments as aberrations of Southernism. Using this device, he then proceeded to dispose of the whole conservative, slaveholding South of antebellum fame as a kind of deviation or detour in the true course of Southern history. Thus he finessed the basic question whether the true and realistic image of the South might not be a dualism, with as much of Calhoun as of Jefferson in it, or even whether the true South, historically, is not hierarchical and conservative rather than radical and equalitarian.

In justice to Dodd, one must recognize that his version of Southernism was by no means without foundations. Jeffersonianism, as well as Jefferson, did have distinctively Southern origins, and at almost every decisive turning point in the advancement of American democracy—whether at the time of Jackson, or Bryan, or Wilson, or Franklin Rossevelt—the South has thrown crucial weight on the democratic side. Still, there was something of a tour de force about the way in which Dodd reconciled his love for his native South and his commitment to democracy, and, with very little disclosure of the wishful thinking which was involved, identified the land he loved with the values he cherished.

Whether later writers were directly influenced by Dodd or not, the theme of agrarianism has persisted ever since in the literature of the South, sometimes with the most startling implications. Thus when Charles and Mary Beard came to write about the Civil War in their *The Rise of American Civilization* (1927), they pictured it as a conflict between Southern agrarianism and Northern industrialism; in this way, the defenders of slavery were transmuted into democrats, more or less, since agrarianism was, in the Beards' lexicon, by definition democratic, and industrialism was antidemocratic. Again, at the hands of the Beards and of the late Howard K. Beale, in his *The Critical Year*, published in 1930, Reconstruction was not primarily a contest over the rights of Negro freedmen, but rather a series of coups by industrial capitalism to consolidate its ascendancy and to retain its wartime gains, consisting of tariffs, subsidies, and a monetary system favorable to creditors. The Fourteenth Amendment was not a Magna Carta of freedmen's rights, but rather a bulwark for property interests, disguised as a Negro rights measure in order to catch votes. Again, the implications were ironic: for instance, under this formula Andrew Johnson, a onetime slaveowner and an obdurate foe of Negro rights, appeared as a champion of democracy against the predatory capitalists. Thus Johnson received ecstatic praise in a biography (1929) by that archliberal attorney Lloyd Paul Stryker, who later became a crusading spokesman for Negro rights.

Through all of these treatments there runs a persistent implied affirmation of Dodd's cleverly articulated premise: that which is agrarian in the South is truly Southern; anything not in the agrarian tradition is somehow extraneous—a cowbird's egg in the Southern nest. Almost automatically, this formula reduced the factor of biracialism and caste to secondary importance, or even kept it out of sight altogether. Again, some interesting results follow in the literature. For instance, when Howard W. Odum and his associates at Chapel Hill prepared their great compendium *Southern Regions of the United States* (1936), they deployed no less than six hundred maps and charts to show that the agricultural South, despite its rich natural resources, was worse off in almost every measurable respect than the rest of the country. That is, they mapped, measured, and charted the plight of the agricultural South. But not one graph, map, or chart showed the relatively worse plight of the Negroes within the South. In other words, the most careful reader of this encyclopedic survey of Southern economic and social conditions could almost have overlooked the fact that a biracial system prevailed in the South and that under this system the Negroes experienced adverse differentials in almost every respect. No doubt Odum and his associates chose this presentation deliberately, and certainly not because of any blind agrarianism, for they advocated economic diversification for the South. Their purpose may even have been to avoid dulling the concern of white Southerners about differentials by admitting that these differentials fell more heavily upon the Negro than upon the white component in the Southern population. Or, they may have wished to treat Negroes and whites indiscriminately alike as being handicapped by regional differentials. But in any case, their survey of Southern problems left out the greatest problem of all. Like the doctrinal agrarians with whom they disagreed, they presented an image of the South which emphasized the plight of farmers rather than the plight of Negroes.

In quite a different way, the agrarian premise shows itself also in many of the writings of C. Vann Woodward, the foremost historian of the modern South. In Woodward's biography of Tom Watson (1938), for instance, the protagonist of the drama is Watson the agrarian, and the antagonists are the Bourbon Democrats who have betrayed the interests of the South to the forces of industrial capitalism. Or alternatively, one could say, the protagonist is the earlier Watson, who championed Populism and defended Negro rights, while the antagonist is the later Watson, a reactionary racist who betrayed the ideals of his youth. Though Woodward's treatment is deeply subtle and sensitive to complexities, while Dodd's was superficial and grossly oversimplified, both are alike in regarding the agrarian South as, almost a priori, the true South, and any force within the South which runs counter to it as an aberration. This is, of course, quite a different thing from merely favoring the agrarian cause.

Although a whole generation of writers have made this tempting equation between Southernism and agrarianism, it requires only a limited analysis to see that in many respects the Southern economy and the Southern society have not been agrarian at all—in fact, have embodied almost the antithesis of agrarianism. Agrarianism implies an escape from the commercialism of the money economy, but Southern cotton and tobacco and sugar cultivators have consistently been agricultural businessmen producing for market and for cash income. Agrarianism implies production for use rather than production for sale, and therefore diversification rather than specialization, but the Southern agriculturist stuck to his one-crop system in the past as tenaciously as he clings to segregation at the present. It implies the independence of a husbandman who looks to no one else either for his access to the land or for the necessities of his living, but the Southern cultivator has been historically either a slave or a sharecropper, without land and often without opportunity even to grow his own turnip greens in a garden patch. Meanwhile the Southern landowner, whether an absentee planter or a mortgage-holding bank, frequently failed to follow the ennobling agrarian practice of laboring in the earth. To one who is impressed by these aspects, it may seem realistic to regard Calhoun rather than Jefferson as the typical leader of the South; the plantation producing raw materials for the textile industry, rather than the subsistence farm producing for use, as the typical economic unit; hierarchy rather than equality as the typical social condition; and conservatism rather than radicalism as the typical mode of thought.

One man who was long the leading historian of the South saw the region to some extent in these terms. This was Ulrich

B. Phillips, who began his career around the turn of the century with studies of Southern political history and the history of Southern transportation. But wherever his investigations began, they always led him, as he himself said, back to one feature of life in the South which was constant both before emancipation and after, namely the presence of Negroes and whites whose destinies were inextricably intertwined but whose paths in life were separated by a biracial system. Accordingly, Phillips gave only slight attention to the agrarian theme. Instead he concentrated on the staple-crop economy with its plantation units and its slave labor. With supreme thoroughness in research, he made what remains the basic study of slavery as a system of labor (*American Negro Slavery*, 1918). Later he developed an artistry in writing which matched his soundness in research, and he achieved a felicitous conjunction of both talents in a study of the society and economy of the antebellum period (*Life and Labor in the Old South*, 1929).

When Phillips looked at the Southern economy, the image which seemed visible to him was not an independent husbandman laboring in the soil, but a Negro field hand picking cotton. The persistence of this figure, either as a slave or as a sharecropper, and the persistence of the system which kept him in his subordinate role led Phillips, five years before his death in 1934, to write an essay, "The Central Theme of Southern History," in which he stated what he had found at the core of distinctive Southernism. This was not some agrarian ideal, but rather a fixed purpose on the part of the Southern whites to preserve biracialism, or, as he said, in unvarnished terms, to assure that the South "shall be and remain a white man's country."

Although Phillips' stature is still recognized even by his critics, liberal historians have been reluctant to accept his views. Kenneth Stampp has written a new account of slavery

(*The Peculiar Institution*, 1956) which emphasizes, as Phillips never did, the harsh and exploitative aspects of the system; Richard Hofstadter has criticized Phillips for giving too much attention to the plantation, and not enough to the slaves held in small holdings; and at least two writers have questioned the "Central Theme."

It is in some ways ironical for liberals, concerned as they are with the "sick South," to reject a formula which explains so cogently the chronic nature of the illness. But what they found fault with was not in fact the accuracy of Phillips' conclusion; it was rather the lack of moral indignation in his statement of it. By asserting that the policy of biracialism is and will continue to be a central aspect of Southernism, without personally repudiating this policy, he made it difficut for liberals to identify with him. When Harry Ashmore, more recently, said in *An Epitaph for Dixie* (1958) that the South will cease to be the South when it ceases to be segregated, the statement was almost identical with that of Phillips, but liberals could accept Ashmore's because he expects the South, in the old sense, to vanish (hence "an epitaph"), whereas they could not accept Phillips', because he seemingly expected the South to survive, with the implied corollary that efforts at integration must fail. Moreover, in the case of liberals who want to love the South, as some do, but who find it psychologically impossible to love an embodiment of biracialism, the only recourse is a resort to Dodd's original formula: dispose of the factor which is troublesome (in this case the biracialism) by treating it as a great aberration. Here even so excellent a book as Vann Woodward's *Strange Career of Jim Crow* (1955) is a case in point, for though it was intended to emphasize a thoroughly valid observation—namely, that the patterns of biracialism have varied and are not immutable— it lends itself to being read as a statement that caste does not have very deep roots in the South. The preface to the paperback edition (1957) showed that Woodward was himself concerned that his work had been taken too much in this way.

When one considers the degree of hardheadedness and realism which went into Phillips' view that biracialism lay at the core of Southernism, and the vulnerability of the doctrine that agrarianism was the heart of the matter, it seems strange that writers have been so abstinent in accepting the former and so addicted to the latter. Clearly, the agrarian interpretation has drawn its strength from something other than the sheer weight of evidence, and it is worth pondering what the real basis of its acceptance is. In the purely historical literature, this basis is hard to detect, for the historian purports merely to be describing the agrarianism which he finds in the past—not to be advocating it. But in 1930 agrarianism enjoyed open advocacy at the hands of a group of writers, all centered at Vanderbilt University, in the famous manifesto entitled *I'll Take My Stand*. The twelve Southerners who joined in this profession of faith categorically rejected the industrial way of life, which they regarded as the prevailing or American way, and with equal conviction they subscribed to an agrarian way, which they identified as a Southern way. They hoped to carry this Southern way to the nation through "a national agrarian movement."

In the extensive and often heated discussion which followed, attention was focused very heavily upon the operative practicability of their proposals. They were accused of medievalism, and of quixotically renouncing all the benefits of modern science and technology. They were also accused, with somewhat more justice, of being in disagreement among themselves as to whether agrarianism was designed to provide a livelihood for dirt farmers or to restore cultural amenities for the landed gentry. Whether they advocated populism or élitism no one could quite make out. While controversy

raged between them and their assailants, not much attention
was given to the ideological implications of agrarianism, nor
to the question why this particular line of thought had appeared at this particular time. Indeed, the historical significance of agrarian thought has still never been adequately
analyzed.

But it is clearly evident that agrarianism appealed to many
liberals, both before and after the Nashville group, partly because they were looking for an alternative to the prevailing
American way of life. Some writers, like Charles A. Beard,
used agrarianism so enthusiastically as a stick with which to
beat capitalism that it had some of the appearance of a disguised Marxism. But its real significance lay in the fact that
it offered an alternative to Marxism. Here, in fact, was a
way in which a man could renounce industrial capitalism
and all its works without becoming a Marxist. This is perhaps
why the agrarian ideal held so much attraction for such a
large number of social thinkers. It gave them a chance to
express their dissent from the prevailing system without going outside the American tradition in order to do so.

Another significant feature in making agrarianism attractive
was its affirmation that the South had something of value
in its tradition to offer to the nation. The Nashville group
really felt convinced that the Southern sphinx did have an
answer to the riddle, if not of the universe, at least of American life. Their affirmation came at a time when it was being
asserted by critics like Mencken that the Southern tradition
amounted to little more than a sterile, backward-looking
form of ancestor worship. Now suddenly men were saying
in a fresh and arresting way that the Southern tradition was
not merely a pressed flower in the nation's scrapbook of
memories, but rather an urgent message which Americans,
deafened by the roar of progress, had failed to hear. To

Southerners who yearned to believe that there was some element of vitality in the history of their region, this idea seemed immensely appealing.

The continued acceleration of industrial growth and the failure of the Nashville group to rally a popular following soon showed that agrarianism had no future, but it was still widely believed to have a past, and historians continued to apply it to the interpretation of American history. Henry Bamford Parkes made brilliant use of it in his *The American Experience* (1947), and as recently as 1949, Frank L. Owsley, in his *Plain Folk of the Old South*, delineated the structure of antebellum society in terms in which large slaveholders and plain farmers were practically indistinguishable. In these and many other writings, a number of time-honored propositions continued to find acceptance: that American democracy has been nourished primarily from agrarian roots; that agrarian attitudes are inherently democratic; and that the South peculiarly embodies the agrarian tradition.

But of late the first two of these propositions have come under criticism, and the agrarian view has been attacked, for the first time, at its foundations. As long ago as 1945, Arthur Schlesinger, Jr., in his *The Age of Jackson*, offered the then heretical view that Jacksonian democracy owed more to the East and to class-conscious urban workingmen than to the frontier and its coonskin equality. More recently, Richard Hofstadter, in his *Age of Reform* (1955), has gone even further by arguing that Populism had little affinity with liberal democracy, and was in fact a seedbed for such illiberal manifestations as prohibition, nativism, immigration restriction, Red-baiting, and the like. Thus, according to Schlesinger, democracy was not agrarian, and according to Hofstadter, agrarianism was not democratic.

In literal form, the agrarian formula fitted the South remarkably badly. It envisioned a subsistence economy, agricultural diversification, a wide distribution of small landholdings, a large class of independent husbandmen, and an unstratified society. The cold fact is that none of these features has ever been dominant in the South. In the light of these flaws, as well as of recent criticisms, the whole idea of the South as an agrarian society now seems more and more an illusion, nourished by a wish. But once it is discarded, the question reverts to the enigma of the South. All theory aside, is the South, at a purely descriptive level, distinguishable? And if it is, does the distinction lie in anything more than the fact that biracialism takes a form in the South differing from the form it takes elsewhere?

This is a question which the literature of the future will perhaps explore further. Vann Woodward, in *The Burden of Southern History* (1960), has already moved in this direction with incisive and fertile arguments that certain distinctive experiences of the South have put their mark upon the Southern people: the experience of defeat and frustration, in an America of monotonous, taken-for-granted success; the experience of guilt because of the Negro, in an America with a cult of Adamic innocence; the experience of poverty, in an America with abundance which has caused people to confuse life with a standard of living. But though Woodward discusses these factors as experiences impinging upon the Southern culture, we still need a dissection of the culture itself upon which they impinge.

On the face of it, it seems a matter of observation and not of theory to say that the culture of the folk survived in the South long after it succumbed to the onslaught of urban-industrial culture elsewhere. It was an aspect of this culture that the relation between the land and the people remained more direct and more primal in the South than in other parts of the country. (This may be more true for the Negroes than for the whites, but then there is also a question whether the

Negroes may not have embodied the distinctive qualities of the Southern character even more than the whites.) Even in the most exploitative economic situations, this culture retained a personalism in the relations of man to man which the industrial culture lacks. Even for those whose lives were narrowest, it offered a relationship of man to nature in which there was a certain fulfillment of personality. Every culture is, among other things, a system of relationships among an aggregate of people, and as cultures differ, the systems of relationship vary. In the folk culture of the South, it may be that the relation of people to one another imparted a distinctive texture as well as a distinctive tempo to their lives.

An explanation of the South in terms of a folk culture would not have the ideological implications which have made the explanation in terms of agrarianism so tempting and at the same time so treacherous. But on the other hand, it would not be inconsistent with some of the realities of Southern society, such as biracialism and hierarchy, whereas agrarianism is inconsistent with these realities. The enigma remains, and the historian must still ask what distinctive quality it was in the life of the South for which Southerners have felt such a persistent, haunting nostalgia and to which even the Yankee has responded with a poignant impulse. We must now doubt that this nostalgia was the yearning of men for an ideal agrarian utopia which never existed in reality. But if it was not that, was it perhaps the yearning of men in a mass culture for the life of a folk culture which did really exist? This folk culture, we know, was far from being ideal or utopian, and was in fact full of inequality and wrong, but if the nostalgia persists was it because even the inequality and wrong were parts of a life that still had a relatedness and meaning which our more bountiful life in the mass culture seems to lack?

On Understanding the South*

This essay cannot be fully understood without an awareness that it was written during the Goldwater campaign of 1964. At that time, I was especially troubled by what seemed to me the growing ideological separation between the South and the rest of the nation, and the intellectual ostracism the South was incurring because of its conservatism. I felt that divisiveness had never been so acute. I was also distressed by the way in which the generalized feelings of guilt concerning race discrimination were being channelled into denunciations of the South as a scapegoat for all the nation's failures to live according to its ideals. This is a delicate thing to say, for it can be read as a tactical device for diverting attention from the magnitude of the ills that existed in the South, and I did not intend it in that way.

When I wrote, I anticipated that Goldwater would prove politically strong in the South, but I did not anticipate that, with the exception of his home state of Arizona, he would lose every state the Republicans had ever carried since 1876, and carry only states which the Republicans had never won (save that Louisiana had voted once for Eisenhower). Also, I did not anticipate either that the whole idea of racial integration would soon be challenged in some of its aspects by important elements within the black population, or that the guilt feelings throughout the country would cease to be discharged particularly upon the South, as the nationwide character of discrimination came to be better understood.

Although the immediate circumstances which prompted this essay now seem a long time ago, I hope that there is still some applicability in its central point: namely that historians need not justify the South in order to understand it, but that effective historical treatment is impossible without understanding, and that

* This essay was written as a review of Francis Butler Simkins, *The Everlasting South* (Baton Rouge, 1963), and Frank E. Vandiver (ed.), *The Idea of the South: Pursuit of a Central Theme* (Chicago, 1964).

*understanding can never be attained simply by denouncing
Southern society for being what its past has made it, as all societies are.*

*I*N 1847, IN AN article in *De Bow's Review,* J. D. B. De
Bow appealed to his readers, "as Southerners, as *Americans,* as MEN." In this appeal, perhaps unconsciously, he recognized three levels of affiliation and of distinctiveness: a
sectional or regional level, a national level (although the national bond was incomplete), and a human level. While
suggesting implicitly a pluralism and therefore a possible
ambivalence of identities, his invocation also implied that at
each level his readers shared certain commonalities with their
fellow Southerners, their fellow Americans, their fellow men.
What these commonalities were in 1847 would have been a
difficult question, and what they may be more than a century
later is no less difficult, for the homogenizing forces of modern
technology have unquestionably diminished the variety in patterns of human society and thus have reduced the measures
of distinctiveness.

As Southern regional differences have decreased, analytical
writers have grown increasingly preoccupied with the quality
of these differences and with the nature of Southern identity.
Ulrich Phillips' famous essay "The Central Theme of Southern History" defined the problem in 1928 and offered the
answer that Southern white determination to maintain a
biracial system had been at the core of Southernism. Harry
Ashmore, who found the essence of Southernism in the institutions of share-tenancy, one-partyism, and segregation,
seemed to agree with Phillips about the past, but to regard
this past as dying (*An Epitaph for Dixie,* 1958). James W.
Silver, in *Mississippi: The Closed Society* (1964), shows that

the institution of biracialism, although powerfully formative in itself, is perhaps less vital than the Southern psychological commitment to biracialism (if the two can be distinguished). The commitment is so strong that it has led to the erection of the only static and monolithic society in this relatively dynamic and pluralistic nation.

As the issue of integration has grown more transcendent, many recent historians, feeling both a devotion to the South and a sympathy for civil rights, have sought to evade a formula which would compel them to accept either the negation of their principles or the loss of identity of their region. Perhaps it was partly the cruel choice imposed by this dilemma which has stimulated a deeper and more intensive inquiry in recent years concerning the essential meaning of Southernism. Thus we have had Vann Woodward's brooding, questing essays in *The Burden of Southern History* (1960), the gamut of responses which Charles Sellers gathered in *The Southerner as American* (1960), the symposium *The Lasting South* collected by Louis D. Rubin, Jr., and James Jackson Kilpatrick (1957), and, earlier, the sharp insights from literature offered in Rubin's and Robert D. Jacob's *Southern Renascence* (1953) and in Allen Tate's *A Southern Vanguard* (1947). To these we must now add a roundup of essays by Francis B. Simkins under the title *The Everlasting South*, and a symposium from Rice University, *The Idea of the South*, with contributions by George B. Tindall, Richard B. Harwell, Louis D. Rubin, Jr., Frank E. Vandiver, T. Harry Williams, Hugh B. Patterson, Jr., and the late Walter Prescott Webb.

In this latter collection, the writers who address themselves most pointedly to the "pursuit of a central theme" are Vandiver, Rubin, and Tindall. Vandiver entitles his essay "The Southerner as Extremist," and he emphasizes the strain of violence in Southern life. Perhaps violence is the more diagnostic word, for while extremism is not necessarily violent, violence is perhaps invariably somewhat extreme. In developing his analysis, Vandiver suggests the hypothesis that the history of the South is a record of faulty response to challenge, or, as one might say, of failure to make functional adaptations to change, and that a recurrent flaw in the response is an excessive readiness to resort to a policy of "offensive-defense," often too violent in its expression. A very brief summary could hardly do justice to Vandiver's development of this idea, and I will not attempt to recapitulate. Instead, I will confine myself to noting that, although this diagnosis is stated in terms very unlike those of Phillips' "Central Theme," it is not inconsistent with it. Both could be applicable. What Phillips found distinctive was not merely the biracial system, but the determination to maintain the system although it was under challenge. Thus Phillips might have agreed with Vandiver that the "offensive-defense" was a characteristic mode of Southern response, and Vandiver apparently might agree with Phillips that white supremacy has perennially been the obsession that conditioned this response.

Louis Rubin approaches the problem of Southernism from a literary vantage point. He makes a significant distinction between books which are "about the South," in a mere superficial sense of using a locale and stage properties—such as mint juleps, magnolias, decayed mansions—that are commonly identified with the South, and books which are "Southern," in that the values and attitudes of the treatment derive from the Southern experience. Thus, he says, Katherine Anne Porter's *Ship of Fools* is Southern though not about the South, while Sartre's *La Putain respectueuse* is about the South but is not Southern. But though he says that "the way that Miss Porter looks at human beings, the things she thinks are important about them, the values by which she judges their conduct, are quite 'Southern,' " he never does say what this way, these things, these values are. Instead, he turns to deploring the persistent racism of the South and the stubbornness of the "rear-guard action" against human acceptance of the Negro. Few are likely to disagree with these sentiments, but many will wish that, after suggesting that "Southern" books are the key to Southernism, he had turned the key in the lock for us before hastening away to a disquisition on the constructiveness of love and the destructiveness of hate.

Rubin suggests that we can find a criterion of what is intrinsically Southern in those novels that are truly "Southern," instead of merely being about the South. Now if we only had a criterion for knowing which novels are truly Southern, we would be close to an answer. Meanwhile, however, George Tindall invites another approach through the medium of mythology. Tindall's use of the concept of myth is close to that of Henry Nash Smith in *Virgin Land*, or of William R. Taylor in *Cavalier and Yankee*. Tindall invites us to "seek to unravel the tangled genealogy of myth that runs back from the modern Changing South to Jefferson's yeoman and Kennedy's plantation," and along the way to "investigate the possibility that some obscure dialectic may be at work in the pairing of obverse images: the two versions of the plantation [abolitionist and patriarchal], New South and Old, Cavalier and Yankee, genteel and savage, regionalist and agrarian, nativist and internationalist." Projecting his suggestions further, Tindall proceeds to point out some of the psychological as well as the polemical values which make the study of myth a valuable analytical tool. But pointing the way to an answer is not the same as pointing to the answer itself. It is only realistic to recognize that both Rubin and Tindall are concerned with telling where to go to find Southern identity, rather than what it is.

Nearly all of the participants in the Rice symposium are much preoccupied with the present crisis in race relations, and seem, at the moment, more anxious to reform the South than they are to explain it. Consequently, they write more as humanitarians than as historians. At least this is what I think when I read Vandiver's assertion that Jefferson Davis would "certainly loathe" the things which the Confederate flag is now used to defend, or Rubin's surmise that if William Faulkner had lived he would have "stood quietly alongside of James Meredith."

But how can Rubin arrive at this conclusion? It is, to be sure, reliably reported that Faulkner grew increasingly unhappy with the segregationists as time passed, but he was at the same time deeply opposed to the use of force for imposing integration. It was one of the most characteristically Southern things about Faulkner that while he showed strong loyalty to his ideals, he also had an almost compulsive traditional loyalty to place and to people. Thus, while his principles aligned him with one side, his affiliations aligned him with the other. He himself explained this in *Life* (March 5, 1956), and if readers outside the South could not comprehend this dilemma of loyalties, it was not because of any lack of clarity in his statement: "I have been on record," he said, "as opposing the forces in my native country [*sic*] which would keep the condition [segregation] out of which this present evil and trouble has grown. Now I must go on record as opposing the forces outside the South which would use legal or police compulsion to eradicate that evil overnight. I was against compulsory segregation. I am just as strongly against compulsory integration."

Faulkner continued by saying that he and a limited number of other white Southerners had resisted the Citizens Councils partly because they recognized that discrimination was immoral, and partly because "there was another simply human quantity which drew us to the Negro's side: the simple human instinct to champion the underdog. But if we, the (comparative) handful of Southerners I have tried to postulate, are compelled by the simple threat of being trampled if we don't get out of the way, to vacate that middle where we could have worked to help the Negro improve his condition . . . we will have to make a new choice. And this time the underdog will not be the Negro, since he, the Negro, will now be a segment of the topdog, and so the underdog will be that white embattled minority who are our blood and kin." [1]

My purpose in quoting at such length is not to suggest that Faulkner was right, but that whether we would wish it or not, Faulkner clearly suggested that he might stand alongside that white embattled minority whom he recognized as his blood and kin. In any event, I think it is a very tricky business predicting what Jefferson Davis or Faulkner, or any other parties now dead, would be doing if they were still living. This kind of speculation is an old game; it used to be called, "If Lincoln Were Alive Today," and it was played by laymen with axes to grind, who always, by coincidence, found the illustrious dead grinding the right axe. The fact that it is now played by historians, and that the approval of the dead is claimed for no petty, self-serving interest, but for an ideal of the

---

[1] Faulkner was reported by Russell W. Howe as having said in an interview on February 21, 1956: "If it came to fighting I'd fight for Mississippi against the United States even if it meant going out into the street and shooting Negroes" (*Reporter*, March 22, 1956). Soon after, and in several places, Faulkner repudiated this statement as one "which no sober man would make nor any sane man believe" (*Ebony*, September, 1956, p. 70), but he did not directly deny that he had made it. Despite the sensational quality of the phrase about shooting Negroes, perhaps the most revealing aspect of the statement is that the dualism which it poses is not between Negroes and whites nor between equality and inequality nor between right and wrong, but between the United States and Mississippi.

James Silver (*Mississippi: The Closed Society*, xi–xiv), in an authoritative discussion of Faulkner's position, emphasizes his commitment to the cause of Negro equality and integration, but does not deny his acute reluctance to see these objectives imposed by force.

highest moral caliber, does not make it any less a game, and does not bring it any closer to the orbit of history.

The question of the role occupied by history in some of this thinking arises again when one reads Harwell's statement that "as Southerners we are still self-conscious. But we make more and more breakthroughs into being Americans." In terms of De Bow's triad, Harwell seems to reject history written from a Southern position and to sanction history written from an American position. But is majoritarian history essentially more valid than minoritarian? If Harwell means that the defense of integration is superior to the defense of segregation, would he not do better to state it in these con-concrete terms, instead of suggesting that identification with the South is, in itself, discreditable and identification with America is, in itself, meritorious? The most vulnerable aspect of Harwell's statement is its suggestion that the way for the historian to get right is to identify with the right group. But if the historian has any advantage over a layman in attaining reliable results, he gains it not by embracing one group or another but by maintaining a wary skepticism of all groups. Historically, Americanism and Southernism are both just forms of group loyalty, partly irrational and equally an impediment to the historian in his primary task, which is to reconstruct the past with as few biases as possible, whether popular or unpopular.

Perhaps this remark of Harwell's—possibly a passing one by a man who twice asserts, "I am a Southerner"—ought not to be criticized so closely, and it certainly would not deserve such focused attention if it were not symptomatic of a general problem among historians of the South. Historians of this breed are mostly Southern by origin and humanly fond of their native place; also they are mostly liberal by persuasion and humanly wishful that the region they love should embody the cause they love. That is, they yearn for an equation between place and principle. For a long time, beginning as far back as William E. Dodd, they found this equation in the symbolic Southern figure of a great Virginia liberal, Thomas Jefferson. If what Leonard Levy now writes about Jefferson is correct, they improved upon his liberalism considerably, but no matter. The point is that they found Dixie Jeffersonian, and Jeffersonianism liberal. *Ergo* Dixie was liberal. Also to clinch the equation, they found a whole train of other Southerners as understudies for the role of the Sage of Monticello (Andrew Jackson, Andrew Johnson, and Tom Watson of the Populist phase). But since 1954 they have had increasing difficulty in maintaining this view. Today, many Southern historians, keenly sensitive to the adverse national image of the South, feel impelled to protect their credentials as liberals by disavowing any 'self-conscious' or traditionalistic Southernism.

One of the best insights in Francis Simkins' *The Everlasting South* (a collection of five reprinted essays, originally published between 1939 and 1957) is his recognition of the way in which this liberal compulsion has impelled historians to shape Southern history a little closer to their hearts' desire. It has led them, he says, to picture Bacon's Rebellion as a democratic rising, to "give credence to many rumors of slave insurrections," to "often envisage the common people rising against political oligarchies," to predict and to have predicted "for the past ten decades, the breakup of the solid South and the coming of a state of rectitude like that of New York or Illinois," to "honor . . . such nationalists as Andrew Jackson and Andrew Johnson instead of . . . such divisionists as John Randolph and John C. Calhoun." Simkins is suggesting, in a sense, that liberal historians have made not only William Faulkner but all the major figures of the past stand alongside of James Meredith. His indictment is both vigorous and sweeping, and it is summarized in the fighting affirmation that the "chroniclers of Southern history often do not grasp the most elementary concept of sound historiography: the ability to appraise the past by standards other than those of the present." Elaborating this argument, Simkins observes that contemporary Americans, including American historians, generally accept "certain concrete dogmas": that "universal education is better than folk culture; political democracy is better than aristocratic rule; freedom is better than slavery [a truism consorting oddly with these other debatable assertions]; nationalism is better than provincialism; urban standards are better than rural ones." All these dogmas, he recognizes, are bases for action in the world of today, and he does not—or at least says he does not—ask for their abandonment as bases of action. But he does ask that historians refrain either from pretending that men of the past also subscribed to these ideas or from assuming that such men must be repudiated because they did not.

The injunction to appraise the past in the terms which were most relevant to it, rather than in presentist terms, is one which no historian can well dispute, though many historians may nod their heads without enthusiasm. But the implementation of this principle is rendered a great deal more difficult by the fact that when a person objects to the application of presentist, liberal criteria in the evaluation of the past, he may be objecting, as a historian, because the criteria are presentist, or he may be objecting, as a conservative, because they are liberal. When a writer insists that we judge Calhoun by the standards of 1850, is it his sense of historicity or his conservatism that motivates his insistence? This is, of course, not a question to answer cocksurely. But many of Simkins' statements suggest that a strong traditionalist bent rather than a clinical detachment underlies his rejection of presentist attitudes. I would cite, for instance, his comments on the functional value of segregation ("Two biologically aggressive races have dwelt together in large numbers for 340 years without the ruling race losing its integrity of blood"), the merits of an aristocratic system (it generates "a unity of spirit which results in a friendly tie between the masses and the classes"), and the limitations of universal education (a "cure-all" which has "brought us no nearer the millennium than were our ancestors in the eighteenth century").

To appraise the past in its own terms is one thing, but to prescribe for the present in terms of the past is another. Simkins comes very close to the latter when he asks, "Why does the South not divest itself of its democratic pretenses about race and class in order to justify its real passion for social distinctions? Thereby it might be at ease with the compelling forces of its ancient heritage. Thereby it might repel the accusation of hypocritical pose and enjoy the comfort of preaching what it intends to do."

Simkins seems to be almost the only practicing historian of the South who defends the major and historic Southern institution of segregation. As such, he may serve his colleagues better than he serves the South, for liberal historians need to be reminded that segregation has been a functional arrangement even though a harsh and undemocratic one ("the color line was created to sustain the most important fact in Southern history"), and that all values have not been democratic values. It seems to me we ought never to be sorry to see someone marching out of step in the regiment of historians. But the focal question here is whether Simkins' conservative approach may have colored his reading of the past, just as he asserts that the liberals' approach has colored theirs. Do Southerners cling to segregation only because it is part of a pattern of traditionalism, or have they abandoned the best of their traditionalism while clinging to its worst feature? Has the passion of the South really been a generalized "passion for social distinctions," or has it been a specific passion for keeping the Negro in subordination? If the latter, ought not Simkins to face this uncomfortable fact, as he did face it in 1939 when in his essay on "New Viewpoints of Southern Reconstruction" he called for a "rejection of the gloomy generalization that the race, because of its inherent nature, is destined to play forever its present inferior role"?

Simkins' argument loses much of its force because he fails to distinguish between understanding the past and defending or justifying it as a guide for future action. This point seems to me absolutely crucial. Taking Simkins' own example, as between nationalists like Jackson and divisionists like Calhoun, every historian who deals with them will personally prefer one or the other, and it is as arbitrary to impose any obligation on him to honor the divisionist as it would be to honor the nationalist. But no matter which one he honors, he will still have an obligation to understand the other. This obligation to understand is so fundamental to sound history that it may extend to the segregationists of today as much as to the secessionists of a century ago.

To those in the profession who regard history as a weapon in the ideological wars, this may seem a milk-and-water statement, a form of escapism or neutralism or even disguised reactionism at a time when it is every man's obligation to stand up and be counted. But I suggest that understanding what one does not approve is a public virtue, of especial value today, and no mere academic one. We seem, as this is written, to be moving into a period of extremely sharp divisions in American life, where the elements of consensus are seriously eroded. Many of the people in one of our major parties regard the adherents of the other party as bigots, racists, and psychopaths, corroded by bitterness and hatefulness. Yet these characterizations are themselves not made without a certain measure of bitterness and hate. The opposition party, ostracized from contact with the intellectual community, reacts excessively and with an intensity which they might not show if they did not feel themselves cut off. These words are written, admittedly, early in an election campaign which will be over before they are read, but it is not likely that the rancors of this campaign will vanish the morning after the election. In the midst of such sharp divisions, understanding might make the difference between tensions which are strained to the snapping point and those which are not.

It could be and perhaps should be the especial province of historians to provide a measure of such understanding, for their discipline more than any other branch of academic study should have prepared them to understand a society or a movement on its own terms, without at the same time abandoning moral criteria of judgment, as sheer cultural relativism might do. Further, the history of the South may peculiarly need such understanding (real understanding and not that form of condescension which calls itself compassion). For it has become almost a convention of liberal thought to avoid trying to understand the South, and a Mississippian, whether white or Negro, who honestly believes in the social desirability of racial separation, might well feel envy toward a looter in Harlem for the care which is taken to understand how his circumstances have made him what he is. This is, to me, a point which Simkins had in his grasp, but which he permitted to escape: the issue is not whether the ancient ways of the South are to be defended and perpetuated, but whether they are to be understood.

To turn back to the more academic aspect of this review, a question remains as to whether Simkins' conservative approach has assisted him in finding the key to Southern identity. If I read him correctly, his answer to the perennial riddle is that the essence of Southernism has been the South's aristocratic predilection for social hierarchy, its persistent traditionalism. He makes a strong argument that much of the seeming Southern acceptance of democratic, industrialized, urbanized values has been superficial, that it has been, in fact, a mere "democratic pose" adopted reluctantly by people who felt compelled to look as much like other Americans as possible. Advocates of change who believe that the old institutions are already dead and need only to be buried in order to usher in a New Day would be well advised to read Simkins' argument thoughtfully—which they are not likely to do. His view certainly deserves weighing. But I am not persuaded that it brings us any closer to the answer. Like the Jeffersonian picture of the South, it is too simple. The South has been democratic as well as aristocratic, fond of "flush times" and booms as well as of tradition; it has lusted for prosperity, bulldozers, and progress, while cherishing the values of stability, religious orthodoxy, and rural life. Southerners have existed historically in a state of ambivalence, even of dualism, because they could not bear either to abandon the patterns of the Old South or to forego the material gains of modern America.

The logical absurdity and untenability of some of the goals pursued in the South have illustrated the dilemma which the South fell into as it attempted to reconcile the irreconcilable: Calhoun's nullification was intended to preserve both the integrity of the Union and the integrity of the South; Henry Grady's New South was formulated in terms which made it hard to tell whether the Sons of Confederate Veterans would infiltrate the Chamber of Commerce or the Chamber of Commerce would infiltrate the Sons of Confederate Veterans; Booker T. Washington's "separate but equal" doctrine was welcomed because it seemed to offer a way to achieve both hierarchy and equality, both discrimination and opportunity, both static caste and dynamic progress. I do not mean to offer any solutions of my own in the course of this review, but one of the truly diagnostic, perennial features in the life of the South has been the obsessive impulse of its people to be, as

J. D. B. De Bow and Richard Harwell would have them somehow contrive to be, at the same time Southerners and *Americans,* as well as MEN. Charles Sellers perceived this dualism of identity in *The Southerner as American,* but then, as it seems to me, he blunted his own insight by insisting that the identity which he approved of was real, while the one that he disapproved of was unreal—"a false image." There is abundant evidence that both images have been real.

If the conclusion is that we still have no definitive formulation of the essence of Southern identity, this is, of course, what everyone expected at the outset. Nothing would do more to paralyze the further development of the field of Southern history than the universal adoption of an agreed upon formula. It would be as bad as if all theologians had agreed upon the nature of the Trinity. And indeed, it is a little like the problem of the nature of the Trinity in that it is a somewhat metaphysical question. To historians with a more practical turn of mind, the problem of the identity of the South will seem less important than the problem of the destiny of the South. The identity of a region is not like the identity of a person: extinction does not follow when it is lost. If, as Ashmore predicted, Dixie should disappear as Dixie (Simkins makes the demise look far more distant), the people of the region would remain; the region itself would remain; there would still be social developments; and there would still be business for the historians to attend to.

Walter Prescott Webb, whose paper was delivered at the Rice symposium after his death, had this fact centrally in mind, and he refused to be drawn into speculations about either the race issue or the question of Southern identity. As to segregation, he had been disappointed in a previous conference on Southern industrialization where "the whole pack" of conferees "took off on the racial question," and his advice

to Southerners—more easily stated than put into execution—
is to "seek to bypass the racial issue and get on with the
main business." The main business, as Professor Webb saw
it, was that the South has gradually overcome its economic
handicaps, and has at last pushed through to a point where
it may become the dominant region in the American economy, so that "the next century may well belong to the
South." Although Webb spoke with evangelical fervor, his
gospel did not rely on faith alone. He made a brief but immensely cogent statement of the assets which could carry
the South to a condition of economic primacy: it is the
only region of the United States that fronts the sea on two
sides, and it has 2,700 miles of coast line to the North's 800
and the West's 1,300; it has two thirds of all the land with
forty inches of rainfall—"an asset too great to be measured";
it produces 45 per cent of the nation's oil and contains
"enormous deposits of coal and iron"; it has a long growing
season and is "the richest region in renewable resources";
and most notably, at a time when water supplies are becoming
economically crucial, it has "the greatest supply of fresh
water in the nation, if we exclude the Great Lakes."

When historians and social critics have exhausted their
resources in a vain attempt to find a thread of consistency
in a body of data, they invariably take refuge in the discovery
of paradox. More often than historians in general, historians
of the South have been obliged to resort to this recourse.
Today, the vein of Southernism may or may not be growing
thin, but the vein of paradox is certainly not growing thin.
More homogeneous with the rest of the nation than at any
time in the past, the South is seemingly more at odds with the
dominant trends of the nation than at any time since Appomattox, if not before. Wedded to the Democratic Party for
a century because of preoccupation with the racial issue, it
now seems likely to leave the party because of the same issue.

On the eve, if we can believe Professor Webb, of economic ascendancy in the nation, it seems to stand at the nadir of political impotence in the nation. And as it faces the disappearance of its historic identity, again if we can believe Professor Webb, it may be on the threshold of attaining its greatest fulfillment. The quest for a central theme, therefore, is likely to continue. For the South remains as challenging as it is baffling, which is about as challenging as a subject can be.

The Historian's Use of Nationalism and Vice Versa

In the secular world of the twentieth century, nationalism and liberalism are the faiths which have replaced the religions of an earlier age. This fact is widely recognized and the statement is something of a truism. But it is not so widely recognized that historians are caught in the ideology of these new faiths, and that a historian may have as much difficulty in treating nationalism with detachment as a devout Calvinist would have in viewing Presbyterianism clinically. Here I have made an attempt to regard nationalism as one of a variety of group loyalties, psychologically similar to religious affiliation, and to explore how the institutionalization of political loyalties in the nation-state could produce conditions violative of individual political impulses, just as the institutionalization of spiritual loyalties in the ecclesiastical system could produce conditions violative of individual spiritual impulses. Although I try to present this question as a general problem, the dual loyalties of the South during the sectional crisis furnish the context for my analysis.

*I*T IS ONE of the basic characteristics of history that the historian is concerned with human beings but that he does not deal with them primarily as individuals, as does the psychologist or the biographer or the novelist. Instead he deals with them in groups—in religious groups, as when he is concerned with the wars of the sixteenth century; in cultural groups, as when he is treating the broad history of civilizations; in ideological groups, as in the conflict between pragmatists and idealists; in interest groups, such as the landed interest or the moneyed interest; in occupational groups, such as the farmers and the ranchers; or in social groups, such as the gentry and the yeomanry. But most often the historian deals with people in national groups. These national groups usually coincide with a political state; but it would be too restrictive to say that the national group is simply a political group, for very often the historian is not concerned with the political aspects of the history of the group. As a social historian, for instance, he may be interested in the social development of the American people or the English people, and may be quite indifferent to the history of the United States or of Britain as a political entity. Similarly, if he is an intellectual historian, his field of inquiry may be the history of American thought or of British thought—again without any concern for governmental aspects.

Just as the rise of nationalism has been the major political development of modern times, so attention to the national group, rather than to these other groupings, has correspondingly become perhaps the major focus of modern historians. Accordingly, the identity of people in terms of their nationality has grown to transcend all other identities, so that we speak and think constantly in terms of the American people, the Japanese people, the Russian people, and so on. Our attribution of distinctive traits and attitudes, reactions and values, to these groups shows that we do not conceive of them merely in political terms as bodies who happen to be subject to a common political jurisdiction, but rather as aggregations whose common nationality imparts or reflects an integral identity. The idea that the people of the world fall naturally into a series of national groups is one of the dominating presuppositions of our time. For the historian it takes the form of a basic, almost an indispensable, generalization, so that even historians who recognize that exaggerated nationalism is one of the greatest evils of the modern world still are very prone to conceive of the structure of the world in terms of national units.

Because of the constant, pervasive use of this criterion of nationality as the basis for classifying the two and a half billion members of the world's population, the concept of nationality has become a crucial one in modern historical thought, with many far-reaching implications. It is the purpose of this essay, therefore, to explore some of the implications which reside in the historian's concept of nationalism, some of the unrecognized side effects which the concept, with its attendant ideas, has had, and something of the way in which it has affected the treatment of history.

Perhaps the most crucial fact in shaping the historian's use of the idea of nationalism is that he employs it in two quite distinct ways for two different purposes. On the one hand, he uses it in answering a question as to the degree of cohesiveness or group unity which has developed in a given aggregate of people. Here the question is primarily descriptive or observational, and it can be answered in qualified or relative terms, or in terms of degree, with fine distinctions and gradations. Such a question may concern the psychological attitudes of the group, and in fact the prevailing theory of nationalism today emphasizes its psychological character. Thus, for example, Hans Kohn affirms that "nationalism is first and foremost a state of mind, an act of consciousness," and, though he points out that one must also explain the surrounding conditions which produce the state of mind, he accepts as valid, though limited, the statement that a nation is "a group of individuals that feels itself one [and] is ready within limits to sacrifice the individual for the group advantage." [1] Proponents of this psychological view recognize, of course, that a subjective group-feeling is a phenomenon not likely to develop unless there are objective conditions which

[1] Hans Kohn, *The Idea of Nationalism: A Study of Its Origins and Background* (New York, 1944), 10–20, especially 10, 12.

give rise to it. Conceivably in theory, a group of people might form a nation simply by believing passionately enough that they shared qualities in common, even if this belief were an illusion. But this is only in theory, and in fact nearly all authorities on nationalism have given a great deal of emphasis to the objective or substantive conditions from which the sense of common identity is derived. Such conditions include the sharing of a common language, the occupation of a territorial area which constitutes a natural unit (an island, a river valley, or mountain-girt basin), the adherence to a common religion, and a heritage of common mores and traditions. But these factors in themselves are not regarded as components of nationality. They are rather prerequisites or raw materials, conducive to the development of the psychological manifestation.

The psychological character of this approach to nationalism deserves emphasis because it carries with it certain important corollaries. It would follow, to begin with, that since nationalism is a form of group loyalty, it is not generically different from other forms of group loyalty. From this it would follow further that nationality is not an absolute condition, but a relative one, for loyalty evolves gradually by imperceptible degrees, both in the individual and in the group; it ebbs and flows; and it is modified by contingencies. If nationalism is a relative manifestation, this fact would also imply that various national groups must vary in the degree of completeness or intensity of their nationality, and further that various elements of the population within the nationality group must vary in the extent to which they share the sense of group identity and the commitment to the group purpose. This, in turn, would mean that loyalty to the nation must exist in the individual not as a unique or exclusive allegiance, but as an attachment concurrent with other forms of group loyalty—to family, to church, to school, and to the individual's native region. Since it exists concurrently, it must also, as has been suggested, partake of the nature of these other forms of loyalty.

All of these corollaries are accepted, explicitly or implicitly, by most writers on nationalism. They are consonant with the theory which writers have found most tenable, and when historians are directly engaged in the specific study of the growth of nationalism, their analysis usually gives due weight to the variable, impalpable, evolutionary, and sometimes partially developed nature of the manifestations of nationalism. In such a context, the historian seldom loses sight of the fact that nationalism is a tendency, an impulse, an attitude of mind rather than an objective, determinate thing.

If the historian had only to deal with the question of the extent to which a group has become national, he would probably never treat it in other terms than these, which are so consistent with his theory and with his general disposition to take a functional rather than a formalistic view of historical phenomena.

But in another—a second—aspect, the historian uses the concept of nationalism in answering a second question which frequently arises in history, as to the validity of a given group's exercising autonomous powers. In human affairs, society has long since agreed to the proposition that when a multiplicity of individuals stand in a certain relation to one another— or to put it more concretely, when they form a community— they incur certain obligations toward one another which they would not have if they were not a community, and that the community has a "right," or enjoys a sanction, to enforce these obligations and to defend itself as a community, if necessary by the use of coercion and violence—which would otherwise be taboo. But the sanction to exercise these powers and the determination of whom they can rightfully be exercised upon—individuals or minority groups—depend entirely upon whether the body seeking to exercise them and the individuals upon whom they are to be exercised form a true community. Thus, the nature of the relation between the individuals involved, rather than the ethical character of the acts performed, actually becomes the standard for judging the rightfulness of the acts. Here the nation occupies a particularly crucial role, for of all human communities it is the one to which this power of regulation, control, coercion, punitive action, and so on, is especially assigned. Therefore in any given case where a body of people contests the exercise of authority by another body over it (and history is full of such cases), the crucial question is fundamentally whether the two are parts of a single community, or, more specifically, a single nation, in which case the exercise is valid; or whether they belong to separate communities, or nations, in which case it is not valid. In such a case, the determination of nationalism ceases to be a merely descriptive matter; it becomes an evaluative matter, for the attribution of nationality sanctions the acts of the group claiming autonomous powers. Further, this determination cannot be made by psychological analysis, which offers only relativistic, qualified, balanced terms, and does not yield yes-or-no, all-or-nothing answers. Such analysis can tell what measure of nationality a group has attained, for that is a question of degree; but it cannot determine whether the group has attained the measure of nationality appropriate to the exercise of national powers, for that is a categorical or classificatory question. The categorical nature of the problem he is dealing with, therefore, tends to draw the historian unconsciously away from his theory. Where his theory tells him that nationalism is a relative thing, existing in partial form, his practice may impel him to treat it as an absolute thing, existing in full or not at all. (For instance, national loyalty may vary enormously, or in subtle degrees, but national citizenship does not vary at all—a man is a citizen or he is an alien.) Where his theory emphasizes the view that national loyalty is a form of group loyalty, and generically similar to other forms of group loyalty, his practice impels him to treat it as a unique form of devotion, potentially antithetical to other forms of loyalty such as regional loyalty. (He even uses a different word for this loyalty—the word "allegiance"). Where his theory recognizes that nationalism is a form of emotion, and that, like other forms of emotion, it will attain varying degrees of intensity in varying segments of the population, his practice is to treat it as a matter of standard, fixed specifications (the citizen is either "loyal" or "disloyal").

Thus, the shift from a descriptive to a classificatory approach is also a shift from a psychological (or functional) approach to an institutional (or formalistic) approach. It is a deceptively easy and, at times, almost imperceptible shift to make, because the nation is, of course, in an extremely real and important sense, an institutional thing. The impulse of nationalism fulfills itself in the formation of the national institutions, and while a nation is truly a body of people who feel themselves to be one, it is also, quite as truly, the organized body of people who share this feeling, together with the organization which the feeling prompts them to set up.

But though these two concepts flow rather naturally into one another, they are in many ways inconsistent with and even antithetical to one another. One treats the nation as an abstraction having no physical reality (only on a political map, which is itself an abstraction, is it possible to see where one nation ends and another begins). But institutionally, the nation assumes all the concreteness which a census of population, an inventory of resources, an army and navy, and all the apparatus of public authority can give to it. In psychological terms, a nation exists only subjectively, as a convergence of men's loyalties; without this convergence there would be no nation. But once the nation has been institutionalized, men tend to regard the institution itself as transcendent—a thing on which the loyalties of men ought to converge simply because it does exist. Again, in theory, the nation survives as a unit because people continue to feel a psychological unity. But in operative terms, its survival may depend upon the power of the state to override divisive impulses and to control an aggregation of people as if they were one, even despite a significant degree of reluctance on the part of some of those who are being thus united.

In short, the institutional view does violence to the historian's theory, for it pulls him in the direction of treating nationality as objective rather than subjective, absolute rather than relative, and total rather than partial. It also impels him to isolate it from and place it in antithesis to other forms of group loyalty, instead of keeping in view the fact that the psychological ingredients of nationalism are the same as for other forms of human identification with large groups. Finally, and most important, it leads him to give a valuative rather than a purely descriptive property to his attribution of nationality.

The political state as we know it today possesses tremendously powerful devices for making the institutional aspects of nationality seem more real than the psychological aspects. With the paraphernalia of symbols (the flag, the crown, the national anthem, the constitution) it evokes the emotional responses of patriotism. By such means as citizenship, territorial boundaries, and sovereignty *vis-à-vis* other political states, it sets up demarcations which separate and even differentiate human beings on one side of an imaginary geographical line from human beings on the other side of this line. Even though it should be situated upon a terrain which lacks any natural geographical unity, it can employ the concept of a "common territory" so persuasively as to create the illusion of commonality for geographically diverse areas, whereas, in the absence of common political jurisdiction, real features of geographical unity will not be recognized as the basis for a commonality. As Karl Deutsch has suggested, there is no reasoning more circular than the argument that Detroit and San Francisco, for instance, are "united" by lying within a "common territory," while Detroit and Toronto are "separated" by not lying in a common territory.[2]

In the same way, although a state may have a population which is varied and lacking in homogeneity, it can bring the concept of a "common citizenship" to bear. By this concept it can create the illusion of an affinity between individuals whose interests may be in conflict, whose cultures may be diverse, and whose values may be antagonistic, while it inhibits the full recognition of features of commonality between individuals who do not share the same citizenship.

To say this is, of course, not to deny that most political states are based upon very real factors of nationality which make for their separateness and identity. The congruence of the nation and the political state is, indeed, very complete in many cases, for political nationality tends to follow cultural boundaries when it is forming and to reinforce the cultural separateness of a national population after it has formed. But the operative importance of formalistic features such as citizenship, jurisdiction, territoriality, and so on, tends to convey an image of nationality which is far more institutional than psychological. And this concept is, of course, far more categorical, more absolute, more unitary in its implications: the individual either is or is not a citizen; the public authority either does or does not have jurisdiction; the disputed area lies either inside or outside of the national boundary. None of

[2] Karl W. Deutsch, *Nationalism and Social Communication: An Inquiry into the Foundations of Nationality* (New York and London, 1953), 4.

these matters is partial, any more than sovereignty itself is partial—and sovereignty, it used to be said, is like virginity in that it cannot be surrendered in part.

The sheer weight and momentum of modern institutional nationalism makes it difficult for the historian to resist the institutional concept, especially when this concept is, in certain respects, entirely valid and realistic. He is himself, after all, not only an historian but also a "national" of one or another nation; he is the creature of an age which tends to reify the nation, the inhabitant of a globe which is commonly believed to be composed of one hundred and three "nations" more or less—each with one vote in the U.N., and therefore each, as a nation, interchangeable with each other nation. In theory, he knows that there is a great difference between the nation and the political state, but in a world where all the states claim to be nations and all the nations try to be states, it is difficult for him to remember that they are two things. When he is offered a complete set of "nations" neat in order, precise in outline, manageable in number, and all alphabetically arranged in the *World Almanac*, it requires a real effort of imagination and even of will on his part to think of the world as composed of inchoate, amorphous congeries of human beings, confused in their groupings, indeterminate in their alignments, and overwhelming in their number.

Nevertheless, historians are now to some extent on guard against mistaking the nation as a people for the nation as a state. Certainly most treatises on nationalism warn them against confusing nationality itself with the forms which the nationalistic impulse has projected.[3] But they are often not on guard against the subtle shift from describing the nationalistic impulse as a socio-psychological phenomenon to using the attribution of nationalism as a valuative device. For

[3] Kohn, *The Idea of Nationalism*, 18–20; Carlton J. Hayes, *Essays on Nationalism* (New York, 1928), 4–5.

it is a paradox not generally recognized that the historian cannot make a simple descriptive observation about the degree of group cohesion among an aggregate of people without inadvertently registering a valuative judgment as to the validity of the powers which this aggregation may assert for itself. If he were applying a standard of ethics, it would be recognized at once as a valuative standard, but since he seemingly applies only a measure of relationships, it is easy to overlook the valuative implications. Yet the concept of the nature of the group may be more crucial than the concept of right and wrong in determining the validity of acts committed in the name of nationality. For even the Declaration of Independence did not proclaim the right of everyone to resist tyranny, but rather the right of "one people to dissolve the political bonds which have connected them with another." The separability of "one people" and "another" was a necessary prerequisite to the dissolution of the bonds. Conversely, a belief that bonds ought to be dissolved would make it necessary to believe also that the Americans were "one people" and the British "another."

Indeed modern democratic thought, by adopting the view that the ultimate authority lies in the people, has brought us to the point where the nature of the association which constitutes a people takes on almost as mystical a quality as once pertained to the nature of the anointment which a crowned king received from God. For the major premise of democracy, that the majority shall rule, is predicated upon the assumption that there is a body of people forming a single whole of such clearly determinate number that more than half of the number may be recognized as forming a majority. Unless the minority really is identified with and part of such a whole, the decisions of the majority lack any democratic sanction. The majority is arithmetical, but the whole—of which the majority is more than 50 percent—is mystical.

For instance, if the Magyars under Louis Kossuth were a "people," they were morally justified in their "revolution" against the old Austro-Hungarian Empire; they were "patriots"; and their uprising was a "war of independence." But if not, they were morally censurable for "rebelling"; they were "traitors"; and their uprising was an "insurrection." If the Croats who, in turn, fought against Kossuth's authority were a "people," then Kossuth was a "tyrant," and his measures against them were "acts of oppression"; but if not, he was merely a resolute leader defending his "nation" against "disruptive elements" that sought to "subvert" it. There is hardly any historical situation for which semantics are more crucial: Indeed, where the concept of nationality is involved, the virtue or the evil of a man's act may not be determined by the character of the act itself, nor even by the motives for which it is executed, but entirely by the status of the group in whose behalf it is undertaken.

In sum, when the historian attributes nationality to any group, he establishes a presumption in favor of any acts involving an exercise of autonomy which the group may commit; when he denies nationality, he establishes a presumption against any exercise of autonomy. The attribution of nationality therefore involves a sanction—a sanction for the exercise of autonomy or self-determination.[4]

Of all the consequences of the shift toward an institutional concept, this insertion of the valuative or sanctioning implication has had, perhaps, the most sweeping consequences. Indeed, the element of sanction is almost the essence of this concept. It carries with it some far-reaching implications, and these implications have had such pervasive effects upon

[4] Rupert Emerson, in *From Empire to Nation: The Rise to Self-Assertion of Asian and African Peoples* (Cambridge, Mass., 1960), 134, speaks of the nation as "the community which legitimizes the state."

the interpretation of history that it becomes important to examine and recognize them.

To begin with, it is fundamental that once nationality is conceived to imply rights or powers for the national group, and not merely to describe the degree of cohesiveness within that group, the historian will begin to be influenced in his reasoning not only by his observations about the degree of cohesion, but also by his beliefs about the justice or the merits of the group's claim to autonomy. Instead of arguing forward, therefore, from the observation that the evidence indicates a high degree of psychological coherence (nationality), and that consequently the group was justified in acting as a nation, he may be tempted to argue backward, from the conviction that since the group was, in his opinion, justified in exercising national powers, it must have had, psychologically, a high degree of cohesiveness. What appears on its face to be a mere observational or descriptive statement about psychological attitudes may be in fact an indirect form of argumentation about the validity of a set of political claims.

In other words, the writer who is trying to rationalize a position need no longer do so with legal or ethical arguments, which are the normal medium of rationalization. Instead, he is likely to rationalize it in terms of cultural and psychological analysis, applying a criterion of relationship rather than a criterion of ethics or of formal sanctions.

On the surface, it often appears today that the nineteenth-century writer on nations who used to argue freely in abstract and formalistic terms—about "compact," "sovereignty," and the like—has been replaced in the twentieth century by a writer who takes a functional approach, tracing the gradual cultural development by which a "people" becomes self-consciously united, and measuring the extent of governmental power in terms of the degree of social need. But to an astonishing degree, the old formalism and the new functionalism come to the same thing. In the past, the ultimate sanction for a government was the possession of sovereignty; today its ultimate sanction is that it acts for a population which constitute a "people" in the special sense which entitles them to self-determination. But the effect, in either case, is to ascribe indirectly a right to the exercise of autonomy.

A second implication of the valuative aspect of nationalism is that it inhibits the historian's recognition of the generic similarity between national loyalty and other forms of group loyalty. It does this because national loyalty, in its valuative sense, must be singular, if not indeed unique. This inhibition cuts off a number of useful insights. It prevents the historian from seeing that in situations where nationalism and sectionalism are both at work they are not necessarily polar or antithetical forces, even though circumstances may cause them to work in opposition to one another. Nationalism, in fact, may be the terminal result of a full development of strong sectional forces, while sectionalism may be an emergent nationalism which has not yet matured.

At a deeper level, this inhibition may blind the historian to the fact that national loyalty, far from being opposed to other loyalties, is in fact strengthened by incorporating them. Harold Guetzkow, in discussing the creation of international loyalties, makes this point clearly: "The behaviorist leads us to believe that strong family, local and national loyalties are helpful in building international loyalties. The analyst assures us that loyalty is attachable to various objects—an international object as well as a national object. If loyalty is a generalized way of responding, the stronger the loyalty pattern in a given individual—no matter what its object—the easier it will be to build loyalties." Guetzkow also quotes the blunter statement of A. M. Rose that "people can have loyalty to two [or more] groups or two sets of values, even when these groups or values are in conflict." [5]

Going a step beyond Guetzkow, Morton Grodzins argues, in *The Loyal and the Disloyal*, that other loyalties not only are conducive to strong national loyalty, but are even indispensable to it. "Other loyalties," he says "are . . . the most important foundation of democratic national loyalty. . . . The welter of non-national loyalties makes a direct national loyalty a misnomer. It does not exist. Loyalties are to specific groups, specific goals, specific programs of action. Populations are loyal to the nation as a by-product of satisfactions achieved within non-national groups, because the nation is believed to symbolize and sustain these groups. From this point of view, one is loyal not to nation but to family, business, religion, friends. One fights for the joys of his pinochle club when he is said to fight for his country." [6]

Historians frequently write about national loyalty as if it were exclusive, and inconsistent with other loyalties, which are described as "competing" or "divided" and which are viewed as detracting from the primary loyalty to the nation. Yet it is self-evident that national loyalty flourishes not by challenging and overpowering all other loyalties, but by subsuming them all in a mutually supportive relation to one another. The strength of the whole is not enhanced by destroying the parts, but is made up of the sum of the parts. The only citizens who are capable of strong national loyalty are those who are capable of strong group

[5] Harold Guetzkow, *Multiple Loyalties* (Princeton, 1955), 37, 39. Also, Merle Curti, in *The Roots of American Loyalty* (New York, 1948), 47, says, "Local and regional loyalties did not necessarily conflict with loyalty to the nation."

[6] Morton Grodzins, *The Loyal and the Disloyal: Social Boundaries of Patriotism and Treason* (Chicago, 1956), 29. See also Morton Grodzins, "The Basis of National Loyalty," *Bulletin of the Atomic Scientists*, VII (December, 1951), 356–62.

loyalty, and such persons are likely to express this capacity in their devotion to their religion, their community, and their families, as well as in their love of country. The nationalism which will utilize this capacity most effectively, therefore, is not the one which overrides and destroys all other objects of loyalty, but the one which draws them all into one transcendent focus. A well-known phrase runs, "for God, for Country, and for Yale"—not "for God, or Country, or for Yale."

A third implication of the evaluative aspect of nationalism is that it sometimes impels the historian to deny nationality to groups of whom he morally disapproves, even though the group may in every sense fulfill his theoretical criteria of nationality. For instance, if a fascist group should claim a separate nationality, the historian, in theory, need only ask whether the members of the group do in fact feel themselves to be one and whether the regime which they are setting up is established "with the consent of the governed." But in fact he can scarcely accord nationality to a group without also seeming to accord some degree of sanction to the cause for which the group stands—namely the cause of fascism. Since he is reluctant to do this, he tends, as a lawyer would say, to "distinguish" the case and to rationalize a basis for denying the nationalism of the group in question. Most historians, if confronted with the abstract proposition that people who practice wrong cannot be united by deep cultural commonalities, would dismiss it as absurd. Yet the functional implications of the concept of nationalism are such that historians in fact are frequently unwilling to recognize cultural commonalities of this kind in the case of groups whose values they reject.

A fourth warping result of the same evaluative tendency is the belief that nationality must be based upon peculiarly deep-seated cultural affinities among a people, since only such fundamental ties would justify the kind of power and unique autonomy which is ascribed to the national group. No trivial or unworthy grounds for association could justify a group in claiming the kind of immunity from external control, and the power to abuse internal minorities, which are accorded to a nation. Therefore, when the historian is faced with manifestations of nationalism, he will, almost by reflex, begin his analysis of these manifestations by searching for profound common elements in the culture of the group involved. Indeed, there is a standard formula, accepted by all the authorities on the subject, which enjoins him to give his attention to "certain objective bonds [which] delimit a social group, [such as] common descent, language, territory, political entity, customs and tradition, and religion." [7] Accordingly, students of nationalism have emphasized the growth of the vernacular languages in Western Europe; they have ransacked folklore and the popular culture for any features which illustrate a common tradition among the people. Also they have often treated the territorial area which finally eventuated, no matter how fortuitously, from any nationalist movement as the logical fulfillment of a mystic impulse among the folk to unite a "common territory." The true believer who found it an evidence of divine providence that all our seaports have harbors evinced no greater faith than the historian who defines all the land within a given national jurisdiction as a "common territory" and then uses the assumption that it is a common territory to prove the validity of the national jurisdiction.

This does not mean, of course, that the common cultural

---

[7] Kohn, *The Idea of Nationalism*, 6–10, 13–14. These criteria, so clearly stated by Kohn, are not distinctively his, but are standard criteria among students of nationalism. For a critique of the "illusions concerning the basis of nations and nationalism," however, see Boyd C. Shafer, *Nationalism: Myth and Reality* (New York, 1955), 13–56.

factors are not real or, in many cases, of immense importance. Indeed, some of the oldest and most famous nations—England, Japan, and France, among others—lend support to the contention that a population isolated by physical or linguistic or other barriers may develop an extremely clear-cut cultural identity, which may prove by far the most enduring and most cohesive basis of nationality.

But the very preoccupation of historians with classic examples such as these has perhaps led them to overemphasize the cultural component of nationality,[8] and to assume too simple an equation between nationality and culture. There is, of course, no doubt that commonalities in culture have a primary role in generating the spirit of nationalism, but secondarily there is also the reverse effect that movements for political statehood, which are commonly regarded as nationalist movements, tend to claim commonalities of culture as a sanction for their objectives; and if these cultural elements do not exist in reality, the nationalist movement may fabricate them. It is notorious, for instance, that Gaelic was culturally a dying speech in Ireland, and Welsh a dying speech in Wales, and that both have received a somewhat artificial rejuvenation because of the zeal of Irish and Welsh nationalists.[9]

In this instance, we are confronted by common cultural factors that are attenuated, yet still very real. But it has seemed increasingly evident in the last quarter of a century

[8] Emerson (*From Empire to Nation*, 103) comments that "theoretical approaches to the concepts of nation and nationalism have been dominated by the European experience, even though this European-derived framework fitted the facts in much of the rest of the world in only indifferent fashion at the best."

[9] Shafer (*Nationalism*, 189) remarks that "within groups not yet nations, linguistic studies were the first signs of a rising national consciousness. They were also consciously made to stimulate it." On the Welsh language, artificially sustained, see Sir Reginald Coupland, *Welsh and Scottish Nationalism: A Study* (London, 1954), 357–66.

that many "nationalist" movements have a minimum of common cultural content and that the impulse which moves them is primarily a negative political reaction against an existing regime (especially a colonial regime). For instance, some of the new nations of Africa appear to consist of territories which, instead of coinciding with any unified culture areas of their own, correspond to the administrative divisions laid down for purposes of bureaucratic convenience by their former colonial masters. It is perhaps the final irony of European colonialism that it is likely to fix the patterns and alignment of the nationalism which replaces it and utterly repudiates it.[10] When a new "nation" is being formed in such circumstances, it will behoove the leaders to claim for their country all the attributes which have been regarded as giving a sanction to the older and more organic nations. If the highest of all sanctions—a national culture—is lacking, the spokesmen of the "nationalism" in question will be impelled to fabricate or simulate the cultural factors which are needed as

[10] Emerson (*From Empire to Nation*, 60) observes: "Indeed, the creation of nations themselves is in some instances, as in the Philippines and Ghana, to be attributed primarily to the bringing together of diverse stocks under a single imperial roof. . . . Uncertain as the precise meaning of the term 'national character' may be, it is beyond doubt that the character of the nations now coming into the world has been greatly influenced by the type of colonial regime to which they have been subjected." The heavily negative character of nationalism in modern Africa is suggested by Thomas Hodgkin, in *Nationalism in Colonial Africa* (New York, 1956), 21–23, when he asks, "At what stage is it reasonable to describe a movement of colonial protest or opposition to European authority as 'nationalist' in respect of its aims and character?" and answers, "My own inclination is to use the term nationalist in a broad sense to describe any organization or group that explicitly asserts the rights, claims, and aspirations of a given African society (from the level of the language group to that of Pan-Africa) in opposition to European authority, whatever its institutional form and objectives."

proofs of the validity of their nation. Such simulation will, indeed, not be anything new, for the spokesmen of nationalism have always exaggerated the degree of separateness and coherence of the national group, even in the oldest and most fully defined nations, and these nations have always relied upon a certain amount of carefully cultivated mythology to reinforce the unity of their people. Their success in fostering a belief in a common identity has often been an essential part of the process of forging the identity itself; the belief has operated as a kind of self-fulfilling prophecy. If the members of a population are sufficiently persuaded that they have cause to be a unified group, the conviction itself may unify them, and thus may produce the nationalism which it appears to reflect.

But while it is to be expected that nationalist leaders will if necessary contrive a synthetic culture for a particular state, it is all the more vital that the historian should be forever alert to distinguish between a genuine culture generating a genuine nationalism, and a trumped-up nationalism generating the pretense or illusion of a culture. Yet there are certain prevailing traits among historians which limit their capacity to maintain this distinction. For one thing, the historian's conviction that he has a professional duty to ransack all the sources for every scrap of evidence means that he will usually find some data, no matter how tenuous, which can be construed to "prove" the existence of the pretended culture. Further, the historian is not only a historian; he is also a man and a citizen, and his national loyalties as a citizen may sometimes neutralize his impartiality as a historian; it is well known that history has often been a handmaiden of patriotism. Finally, the examples of nationalism which have dominated the historical imagination are deeply rooted, clearly defined, long-sustained nations, and this very preoccupation prompts the historian to think of nationalism as the outgrowth of a cultural group identity of unique depth and pervasiveness— in short, to regard nationalism simply as an aspect of culture. This impulse accords well with his deep-seated moral feeling that no entity ought to enjoy the sanctions which pertain to nationality unless it is based upon a deeply rooted culture.

To repeat, then, the historian has an extremely strong predisposition to equate nationality and culture. This predisposition is so strong that if other important sources of nationalism should exist, recognition of them would be inhibited under our present rationale of nationalism. A question arises, therefore, whether other important sources of nationalism do exist, and, if so, what their nature may be.

There is certainly at least one other important factor besides common culture which may bind an aggregate of individuals together, and this is community of interest, not in the narrow sense of economic advantage only, but in the broad sense of welfare and security through membership in society. It is axiomatic that people tend to give their loyalty to institutions which "protect" them—that is, safeguard their interests—and political allegiance throughout history has been regarded as something given reciprocally in return for protection. Historians have clearly recognized this relationship, and one may add that historians of nationalism have often called attention to it. Thus, when modern nationalism was in its infancy, Voltaire defined the word *patrie* in terms of community of interest. Among modern historians, Hans Kohn affirms that a nationality derives part of its strength from being regarded as "a source of economic well being"; Karl Deutsch states that when he and his collaborators were "studying cases of successful amalgamation" of diverse groups into a single nation, "they found that it was apparently important for each of the participating territories or populations to gain some valued services or opportunities"; Boyd Shafer is particularly explicit in pointing out that for many nationalists "devotion to the national welfare . . . after all was but devotion to their own welfare," that monarch and middle classes at the inception of modern nationalism "found mutual benefit in the joint extension of their mutual interests, which they also could conceive of as *the* national interests," and that these parties were like "stockholders with voting rights in the common enterprise, the nation." One of the clearest affirmations of this idea was made by Harry M. Schulman in a statement to Louis L. Snyder, quoted in Snyder's *The Meaning of Nationalism.* Nationalism, said Schulman, is not a *we*-sentiment, but "a form of homeostasis, the equilibration of opposed vested interests within a series of specialized interdependent functional systems." [11]

But despite the presence of theoretical statements such as these, when historians turn to the examination of nationalism in specific cases, they often seem to neglect the factor of common interest, and to focus their attention very heavily upon common cultural factors. This neglect—curious in any case—has been all the more strange in view of the fact that an emphasis upon the importance of self-interest would fit in well with certain points which the historians customarily stress. One of these is the idea that modern na-

[11] "Quand ceux qui possèdent, comme moi, des champs et des maisons, s'assemblent pour leurs intérêts communs, j'ai ma voix dans cette assemblée; je suis une partie du tout, une partie de la communauté, une partie de la souveraineté, voilà ma patrie." Voltaire, *Dictionnaire Philosophique,* under the entry, "Patrie"; Kohn, *The Idea of Nationalism,* 17; Karl W. Deutsch and others, *Political Community and the North Atlantic Area* (Princeton, 1957), 55; Shafer, *Nationalism,* 100–105, 115; Louis L. Snyder, *The Meaning of Nationalism* (New Brunswick, N. J., 1954), 83. See also Curti, *The Roots of American Loyalty,* Chap. 4, "The Economics of Loyalty," 92–121, 161

tionalism has risen concurrently with modern democracy. Hans Kohn, for instance, regards this correlation as so close that he denies the existence of any fully developed national-ism prior to the French Revolution.[12] In this connection it is clear that the rise of democracy represents an admission of the masses to certain civic privileges and expectations of property ownership—that is, to a stake in society. The nation state, of course, served as the instrument for the protection of this stake, and the people's spirit of loyalty to the nation was partly their response to that which protected their in-terests. Until democracy gave them an interest to protect, they were incapable of this response—incapable of nationalism. Hector St. Jean de Crèvecoeur recognized this factor of self-interest very clearly in 1782, when he explained why Euro-pean immigrants to America proved so quick to develop a loyalty to their new country: "What attachment can a poor European emigrant have for a country where he had nothing? The knowledge of a language, the love of a few kindred as poor as himself, were the only cords that tied him: his coun-try is now that which gives him land, bread, protection, and consequence. *Ubi panis, ibi patria* is the motto of all emi-grants." [13]

Another well-recognized aspect of nationalism, into which the factor of self-interest again fits clearly, is the invigorating effect which war has had upon national spirit. Heinrich von Treitschke reduced this to a simple and oft-repeated formula: "Again and again, it has been proved that it is war which turns a people into a nation." Frederick Hertz, who deplored the fact as much as Treitschke rejoiced in it, agreed: "War could be called the greatest instrument of national unification,

[12] Kohn, *The Idea of Nationalism*, 3, 10.
[13] Hector St. Jean de Crèvecoeur, *Letters from an American Farmer* (London, 1782, in Everyman's Library, New York, 1912), 41–44.

but for the fact that it also fosters the growth of forces which often imply a new menace to national unity." [14]

How does war produce this effect? No doubt it does so in a variety of ways and by appealing to a variety of impulses, some of which are irrational. But certainly one of the effects of war is to reorient the pattern of conflicts of interest within any national population. In times of peace, the diversity of interests of various kinds tends to divide the people into antagonistic groups—what James Madison called factions and what we now call pressure groups—and these groups compete for control of public policy. Their relation to one another is primarily one of rivalry. Even in wartime these rivalries will continue; but they tend to become secondary, for war subjects all interests to a common danger and to more vital danger than they ever incur from one another. In the presence of such danger, all interests tend to work together. In this way, war harnesses the motives of self-interest, which ordinarily pull in various directions, and causes them all to pull in the same direction and thus to reinforce the spirit of nationalism.

Despite the importance of democracy as a means of enlarging the community of interest, despite the importance of war as a means of drawing interests which would otherwise be divisive into conjunction, and despite the close correlations which historians have drawn between nationalism on the one hand and democracy and war on the other, these same historians have, for the most part, still failed to follow the logic of their own arguments, and have continued to explain specific nationalistic movements in terms of culture. One has only to read Louis L. Snyder's exhaustive book-length review of the treatments of nationalism by historians,

[14] Frederick Hertz, *Nationality in History and Politics* (New York, 1944), 37, 218–19. Treitschke is quoted in Shafer, *Nationalism*, 45.

political scientists, economists, social psychologists, psycho-analysts, and psychiatrists to perceive how constantly social scientists of all kinds have relied either upon cultural factors or upon social behavior that results from cultural factors as the master key to nationalism.

This commitment extends far. It controls the thinking of many historians so completely that whenever a population manifests nationalistic tendencies, the historian, by reflex, reaches for evidence of the growth of cultural bonds as the only conceivable means of explanation. Conversely, when-ever deep cleavages appear in a previously nationalized group he hypothesizes the evolution of a separate, new culture as the basis of a new nationalism, and husbands every scrap of evidence, however tenuous, which lends itself to his hypoth-esis. Although he perhaps recognizes the importance of in-terests in the abstract, he almost never focuses upon them when analyzing a specific national movement.

To argue that the factor of common interests is an im-portant and somewhat neglected element in nationalism, and that it ought to receive substantial attention, does not mean at all that the concept of interest should replace the concept of culture. The point is rather that nationalism rests on two psychological bases rather than one—feeling of common culture on the one hand and feeling of common interests on the other. It is questionable whether either basis can support a superstructure of nationality without the other. If the historian will recognize this dualism, he will not only possess an effective working concept, but will also free him-self from his present compulsion to prove a growth of cultural unity every time he observes an intensification of nationalism and to prove the emergence of a new culture every time a dissident group proclaims its solidarity in nationalistic terms.

Here, then, are a number of propositions about the historian's treatment of nationalism: that he conceives of it abstractly, in sound theoretical terms, regarding it as a form of group loyalty, psychologically similar to other forms of group loyalty, and having the subjective, relativistic, developmental qualities which other forms of group loyalty possess; that the close relation between nationalism and the political state warps the historian's view and causes him to treat it functionally as a monolithic form of loyalty, in antithesis to other forms of group loyalty, instead of recognizing that it is associated with and even derived from those other loyalties; that his use of the concept as a sanction to validate the demands of some groups for autonomy, while denying the similar demands of other groups, leads him into a fallacious correlation between the ethical rightness of a group's policies and the objective separateness of the group's identity; that this valuative use of the concept also impels him to explain the origins of nationalism in terms of deep-seated, long-enduring natural affinities among a people, or in other words to rely too heavily upon cultural factors in his explanation, even where they are tenuous; that this cultural emphasis has, in turn, caused him frequently to overlook factors of self-interest, which have been vital in many historic situations in the integration or in the disintegration of national loyalties.

If these general propositions have any validity, it should be possible to test them by applying them to specific historical situations. Any reader of this paper will perhaps test them in terms of the historical treatment of the nationality or national movement with which he himself is most familiar. For myself, they can most readily be applied in the field of American history. The rest of this paper, therefore, is devoted to a consideration of their applicability at that point in American history where the question of nationalism is most critical and most complex—namely in the crisis leading to the Civil War.

It is a truism that because of the vast extent of the United States and its great physiographic variety, major areas within the Union have often found their interests in conflict, and the alignment on public issues has followed geographical lines far more often than would occur in a smaller or more homogeneous country. These geographically aligned differentials have, in fact, been a pervasive factor and have presented themselves in many different forms. At times, such as the period of Jacksonian democracy or the Populist revolt, the divisions between East and West have seemed more fundamental than those between North and South, and careful analysis has always shown that these regional differentiations extended beyond a mere dualism. The West, with its frontier attributes, played a distinctive role even during the period when North-South antagonisms were most acute, and indeed the struggle which came to a crisis in 1861 has been seen by Frederick Jackson Turner to consist of a rivalry between the North and the South to draw the West into their respective orbits. Even while North and South were approaching the climactic rivalry of the Civil War, internal conflicts also made themselves felt at a different level, as issues arose between industrial and agricultural areas within the North, or between plantation belts and backwoods districts within the South.

Historians speak of these areas in which distinctive groups are localized or concentrated as sections, and they recognize sectionalism (the tension between such areas) as one of the major themes of American history. In most cases of sectional rivalry, the question of nationalism has not been involved, for the people of one sectional area have not called into question the Union which they share with the rival section, and the loyalties which they give to their own area have not impinged directly upon their national loyalty to the Union. Even when sectional bitterness reached the emotional pitch which it developed in 1896 the rivals sought only to impose their policies upon one another within the Union, not to sever their ties with one another by disrupting the Union.

In the era between 1848 and 1861, however, America's geographically aligned rivalries were drawn into a pattern of intense conflict between the North and the South, and the group loyalties of the people in the South were focused upon a Southern republic in a way which undercut the American nationalism that had previously focused upon the Union. In this case, then, Southernism, instead of working sectionally within a framework of nationalism, tended to take on the character of nationalism itself and to break down the existing pattern of nationalism. Since the Southern movement began as a sectional reaction against this existing pattern, historians frequently evaluate the conflict which developed in terms of sectionalism versus nationalism.

In strict logic the antithesis of sectionalism versus nationalism would not necessarily link one region (the South) with sectionalism, or the other region (the North) with nationalism. On the contrary, it might be argued that nationalistic forces in both the North and the South which placed the welfare of the Union above all regional values were pitted against sectional forces in both regions which gave primary values to regional objectives—such as, for the South, the protection of slavery in the territories or, for the North, the exclusion of slavery from the territories. Viewed in this way, the conflict might be said to involve the triumph of sectionalism over American nationalism within both regions and an ensuing conflict between Northern sectionalism and Southern sectionalism. Alternatively, it might also be argued that Northern group loyalty of the most fundamental kind found a focus in the Union formed in 1787, while Southern group loyalty, also of the deepest sort, found a new focus in a separate Southern republic. Regarded in this way, the conflict might be construed as, in fact, many historians do construe it—as a conflict between Northern (Union) nationalism and Southern (Confederate) nationalism.

Either of these formulations has a certain tenability in theory. In operative terms, however, the forces which saved the American Union were of course centered in the North and those which sought to disrupt it were centered in the South. Consequently it seemed natural afterward, in light of the Union's survival, to link each of the forces at work with one of the rival regions and to speak of nationalism as Northern and sectionalism as Southern.

This attribution, however, at once has the effect of bringing the valuative aspect of the concept of nationalism into play. It clearly implies a sanction for the Northern position —the sanction that the "people" involved in the crisis were the American people, both North and South, since the Union was the nation, whereas those in the South who "felt themselves to be one" were not one in the ultimate sense, since the impulse which prompted their unity was sectional rather than national. Of course, insofar as hindsight furnishes a legitimate criterion, the conclusion, if not the reason, was valid, for what the North defended has found fulfillment as a nation and what the South defended has not. But the questionable feature of this reasoning is that it moves completely away from the psychological or functional aspects of nationalism toward an analysis that is almost entirely institutional. It has the effect of prejudging the question which is purportedly under examination, settling by ascription a point which ought to be settled by the evaluation of evidence. Instead of testing the validity of Union and Confederacy as nations by examining the character of the group loyalties attached to them, it bases a judgment of those group loyalties upon a prior assumption concerning the character, respectively, of the Union and the Confederacy. By a trick of semantics it makes the question of group loyalties irrelevant, the assumption being that no matter what degree of cohesion or intensity these loyalties may have attained, they are not "national" unless they attach to a national institution. But the national institution is the result simply of success in fulfilling national impulses, and to say that the Southern impulse was not nationalism because it did not in the long run maintain its attempted institutional form (the Southern Confederacy) is simply to say that it was not nationalism because it was not successful. Here one is reminded of the old riddle, Why is treason never successful? Answer: Because if it is successful it is not treason. In fact, the answer has a kind of truth, for treason, as a legal offense, has to be institutionally defined. But nationalism should not be treated in such institutional terms.

I have already suggested that the element of sanction in the institutional concept sometimes makes it difficult for the historian to attribute nationality to movements of which he morally disapproves, since the attribution itself would imply that the movement has a kind of validity. This factor has certainly influenced the treatment of the question whether the Southern Confederacy was a nation, for the issue between the Union and the Confederacy also became an issue between freedom and slavery. To ascribe nationality to the South is to validate the right of a proslavery movement to autonomy and self-determination. Since few historians in the twentieth century have been willing to do this, their moral position has sometimes run counter to their theory of nationality and has impelled them to shirk the consequences of their own belief that group identity is the basis for autonomy.

In other words, once the ethical question of the character of Southern institutions becomes linked with the factual question of the nature of the group loyalties in the South, it becomes very difficult for the historian to deal with the factual question purely on its own merits. If the finding that a majority of Southern citizens wanted a nation of their own is inseparable from the conclusion that the institution of slavery enjoyed a democratic sanction, it is always possible to reverse the reasoning and to argue that since slavery could not have enjoyed a democratic sanction, therefore the Southern people must not have been a "people" in the sense that would entitle them to want a nation of their own.

The position of the strongly antislavery historian on the question of Southern nationality tends to be particularly ironic, for he usually emphasizes more than do most writers the depth of the division between the North and the South. No one stresses more than he the profound authoritarian implications of slavery for the entire intellectual and social life of the South, and the sharpness of the contrast between this society, with its system of legalized caste status, and the free, democratic society of the North. Yet, after making this case, the antislavery historian often takes the view that the Southern assertion of nationality was not justified. Of course, he might simply follow the logic of his moral position and argue that war is justified if waged by one nation to compel another nation to give up slavery. But since he also attaches moral value to the right of self-determination, the recognition of Southern nationality would place him in a moral dilemma. The only way he can have his crusade against slavery and his right of self-determination too is to deny that the principle of self-determination is involved in the case of the crusade against slavery, or in short to deny that the slaveholding belligerent was endowed with such nationality as his own analysis has pretty well demonstrated.

This statement, it might be added, is not intended to deny
or question the primacy of moral considerations. It may well
be that the abolition of slavery is worth more to mankind
than the right of self-determination of peoples, especially
since slavery itself denies this right to the slaves. Even if
coercion is an evil, it may not be the worst of evils, and a
war of subjugation may well be justified by the emancipation
of 3,950,000 slaves. It may also be, as Lincoln apparently
believed, that the preservation, even by force, of the union
which had been formalized by the Constitution of 1787
has a higher value than the purely voluntary self-determination of peoples. All I mean to argue is that a historian should
not assert that he regards the right of self-determination as
an absolute and then argue that it is not involved in cases
where he is unwilling to apply it, or where he thinks some
other value has a higher priority.

The equation of Northernism with nationalism and Southernism with sectionalism not only denies by prejudgment, and
without actual analysis of group feelings, that the Southern
movement could have been national; it also leads to an
easy assumption that all Northern support for federal authority must have been nationalistic rather than sectional. But
this view tends to obscure the fact that in the North as well
as in the South there were deep sectional impulses, and
support or nonsupport of the Union was sometimes a matter
of sectional tactics rather than of national loyalty. For instance, Northern support for a sectional tariff or for sectional
internal improvements, adopted by sectional majorities in the
national government, was no less sectional than Southern
opposition to them. Northern efforts to put the terminus
of a Pacific railroad at Chicago were no less sectional than
Southern efforts to put it at New Orleans. Northern determination to keep Negroes (rather than just slaves) out of the
territories was no less sectional than Southern determination

to carry them there. Even Northern support for Lincoln, who did not so much as run in most of the slave states in 1860, was perhaps just as sectional as Southern support for Breckenridge or for Bell, who did not carry a single free state.

But in the North, sectional forces tended to support a strong Union because it was evident that this Union was becoming one in which the sectional forces of the North would be dominant. Thus the national Union could be made the instrument of these sectional interests. The South, on the other hand, finding itself in a minority position, could not hope to secure national support for sectional objectives, nor even to keep sectional and national interests in coordination with one another, and therefore it was forced to choose between section and nation. If the proslavery elements seemed less nationalistic than the antislavery elements, it was not because one more than the other put peace or national harmony above the question of slavery—for neither of them did—but because the antislavery elements could expect, with their majority status, to employ the national authority for their purposes, while the proslavery forces could not. A Northerner could, and many Northerners did, support the Union for sectional reasons;[15] no Southerner was likely to support it for any other than national reasons.

The historian certainly should make some distinction between the nationalistic motive to support the Union as the embodiment of the "people" as a whole, and the tactical motive to use the authority of the Union for the promotion of sectional interests; but very often both of these impulses are called by the same name, i.e. nationalism.

If the antithesis of Northern nationalism and Southern

[15] Curti (*The Roots of American Loyalty*, 111) says, "Webster cleverly associated national interest with all the policies which his opponents declared to be sectional in character—tariffs, internal improvements . . . and restriction of the disposal of public lands in the West."

sectionalism conceals the sectional motivation of much that was done through national means in the North, it also obscures another important reality: namely that a mixture of regional and national loyalties prevailed on both sides. These mixed loyalties did not seem ambiguous or inconsistent in the North because they were not in conflict there, whereas in the South they did conflict and, because they did, were made to seem evidence of what amounted to duplicity—as if devotion to the section in itself demonstrated alienation from the nation and as if nationalism could flourish only as regional loyalties withered away. But in fact, this view is mistaken. To take one concrete example, there was no equivocation on the part of Josiah Quincy of Massachusetts when he declared in 1811 that "the first public love of my heart is the Commonwealth of Massachusetts . . . the love of this Union grows out of this attachment to my native soil." Nor was there ambiguity in Sam Houston of Texas when he asserted that he was a Southerner and a Unionist too, with "a Southern heart, large enough, I trust, to embrace the whole Union if not the whole world"; nor in J. B. D. De Bow when he appealed to his fellow citizens, "as Southerners, as *Americans*, as MEN"; nor in Alexander H. Stephens of Georgia when he said, "I have a patriotism that embraces, I trust, all parts of the Union, . . . yet I must confess my feelings of attachment are most ardent toward that with which all my interests and associations are identified. . . . The South is my home, my fatherland." [16]

[16] Josiah Quincy, in *Annals of Congress*, 11th Cong., 3rd Sess., col. 542 (Jan. 14, 1811); Sam Houston, in *Congressional Globe*, 31st Cong., 1st Sess., Appendix, 102 (Feb. 8, 1850); J. D. B. De Bow in *De Bow's Review*, III (May, 1847), 421, quoted in Robert F. Durden, "J. D. B. De Bow: Convolutions of a Slavery Expansionist," *Journal of Southern History*, XVII (November, 1951), 445; Alexander H. Stephens, in *Congressional Globe*, 28th Cong., 2nd Sess., Appendix, 313–14 (Jan. 25, 1845).

If the point here were only that the people of the South became trapped in a conflict of loyalties, it would hardly be worth stating; historians have known it as a truism for a long time. The point is rather that the Northerners and the Southerners were not distinguished from one another by a singularity of loyalty on one side and a multiplicity of loyalties on the other, as though one had been monogamous and the other polygamous. In fact, they both had multiple loyalties, and what distinguished them was that one, being in a majority, was able to keep all its loyalties coordinated, and therefore undivided, while the other, being in a minority, was not able to keep them coordinated, with the result that they did become divided. Multiple loyalties do not inherently produce conflict, and the question whether conflict will develop is entirely separate from the question whether loyalties are multiple.

It would be misleading in the extreme, however, to suggest that the valuative implication of the concept of nationalism has warped only the views of writers whose sympathies lie with the Union. For if it has led some of them to deny that the South was entitled to the sanction of nationality, and to make this denial with little or no reference to psychological realities, it has also led some writers whose sympathies lie with the South to assert that the Southern claim to nationhood was validated by a complete cultural separateness, and to make this assertion with equally small reference to the cultural realities.

This is not to deny that there was distinctiveness in the Southern culture. Southern conservatism, Southern hierarchy, the cult of chivalry, the unmachined civilization, the folk society, the rural character of the life, the clan values rather than the commercial values—all had a deeply significant distinctiveness. But this is not quite the same as *separateness*, and the efforts of historians to buttress their claim that the

South had a wholly separate culture, self-consciously asserting itself as a cultural counterpart of political nationalism, have led, on the whole, to paltry results. Southern writers, like the nationalistic fabricators of culture mentioned above, issued periodic manifestoes proclaiming that the South should have its own literature, but their efforts failed for lack of support from Southern readers. Southern educators likewise deplored the infiltration of Yankee ideas in the schools, and when the crisis was most acute, Southern students departed with great fanfare from Northern colleges. But Southern education continued to be American education. In the economic area, a few Southern fire-eaters made a conspicuous point of the fact that they were wearing homespun, proclaiming the need for a Southern economic self-sufficiency which was never realized. But it is crucial that the advocates of a Southern culture spent much of their time complaining that the South would not accept their cultural program. Evidence of this kind is a tenuous basis indeed for arguing that Southern nationalism sprang from a full-bodied Southern culture.[17] If historians had not been captives to the idea that nationality

[17] Important studies of cultural aspects of Southern nationalism are: Jay Hubbell, "Literary Nationalism in the Old South," in *American Studies in Honor of William K. Boyd*, ed. David Kelly Jackson (Durham, N. C., 1940), 175–220. John S. Ezell, "A Southern Education for Southrons," *Journal of Southern History*, XVII (August, 1951), 303–27; Merle Curti, *The Growth of American Thought* (New York, 1943), Chap. 17; Curtis Carroll Davis, *Chronicler of the Cavaliers: A Life of the Virginia Novelist, Dr. William A. Caruthers* (Richmond, 1953); Rollin G. Osterweis, *Romanticism and Nationalism in the Old South* (New Haven, 1949); Avery O. Craven, *The Growth of Southern Nationalism, 1848–1861* (Baton Rouge, 1953). Despite voluminous data, however, these studies lend themselves to the argument that a great effort was being made to create a sense of cultural separateness by self-conscious means, where it scarcely existed objectively. An unpublished paper by Stanley Bailis, written in my graduate seminar at Yale in 1958–59, develops this point very forcibly and effectively.

equates with culture, and that where there is separate nationalism there must be culture of equivalent separateness, they
would probably have been far quicker to recognize how very
thin the historical evidences of a separate Southern culture
really are. They would also have been disposed to give more
emphasis to the many important cultural features which
Southerners shared with other nineteenth-century Americans:
the common language which was a transatlantic modification
of English, much the same in both the North and the South;
the common religion of a people who were overwhelmingly
evangelical and Protestant as well as Christian; the common
political commitment to democratic institutions; the common
system of values which exalted progress, material success,
individual self-reliance, and distrust of authority; and the
bumptious Americanism which scorned the "decadent mon-
archies" of the Old World.[18]

But some historians have been compulsively impelled to
minimize these factors and to assert the existence of a separate Southern culture, just as others have been compulsively
impelled to deny that the Southern movement represented
a full nationalism. Just as the antislavery sympathizer finds
that his view of the degree of Southern nationalism cannot
be formed on the merits of the question without reference
to his conviction that the South had no right to thwart the
forces working toward emancipation, so the Southern sympathizer finds that his view of the separateness of Southern
culture cannot be formed on the merits of the question
without reference to his conviction that the South enjoyed
a full national identity, which finds its ultimate sanction in

[18] Hans Kohn, *American Nationalism: An Interpretative Essay*
(New York, 1957), 106–21, demonstrates far better than most historians of the South the ambivalence in both the cultural affiliations
and the loyalties of the people of the South on the eve of the Civil
War.

the possession of a full-fledged culture. The attribution of culture is evaluative for the question of nationality, just as the question of nationality, in turn, is evaluative for the justification of the acts of a group claiming a right to exercise autonomy.

To appreciate one important reason for the emphasis of modern historians upon the separateness of the Southern culture, it is necessary only to look at the difference in the way in which the defense of the South has been argued in the more remote and in the more recent past. From the Civil War until 1900, it was notorious that no Southerner seemed capable of writing on any aspect of the Civil War without including a lengthy disquisition on the legal and constitutional right of secession, with copious attention to the exact contractual understandings reached in 1787. But no historian has elaborated such arguments now for more than a generation. Why? Certainly not because the South no longer has defenders. The answer, I think, is that nowadays we do not couch our historical defenses in formalistic or legalistic terms. The sanction for what the South did in 1861 is no longer believed to be what it had agreed to in 1787. The sanction depends rather upon what the Southerners were in 1861—whether they constituted a people in the sense which entitled them to exercise what we now call autonomy or self-determination, rather than what we used to call sovereignty. But insofar as the same conclusion is reached as to whether the South was justified, and insofar as the reasons ostensibly leading to the conclusion may be in fact derived from the conclusion instead of the conclusion being derived from them, the great transformation since the nineteenth century from formalism to functionalism has perhaps not increased the realism of our thinking as much as we sometimes fondly imagine.

The significance of this subtle relation between descriptive observations and their valuative implications is not that it results in specious reasoning, from conclusion to premise instead of from premise to conclusion. It is rather that it tends to reduce the whole analysis to a set of oversimplified antitheses or polarities whose greatest fault is not that they are partisan, but simply that they do not explain anything.

If North and South fought; if one was a "nation" and one was not; if the people of one were "loyal" and those of the other were "disloyal"; or, on the other hand, if they constituted two diverse civilizations, then the investigator is under strong compulsion to reduce the complex forces of the 1850's to simplicity and to come up with antitheses which will fit these dualisms. Hence, we have had a series of sweeping and dramatic contrasts which present North and South in polar terms. Indeed the historiography of the subject is largely a record of how one pair of alternatives has been set up, only to be knocked down and replaced by another.

Thus we were once told that the South was a land of cavaliers, the North, an abode of Puritans; or that the South stood for states' rights, while the North stood for the federal supremacy. Later historians rejected these formulae as fallacious or superficial,[19] but the old yearning for a sharp, clear-cut antithesis still shaped historical thought, and two other, more formidable dualisms were advanced. One of these was primarily an economic argument, brilliantly set forth by Charles A. Beard, that Southern agrarianism and Northern industrialism must necessarily clash because of their dissimilarity. The other was the more broadly social view that North and South were, in

[19] The "Puritan versus cavalier" thesis began to fade in 1910, when Thomas J. Wertenbaker published *Patrician and Plebeian in Virginia* (Charlottesville, Va., 1910); the formalistic weakness of the concept of states' rights versus nationalism was demonstrated by Arthur M. Schlesinger in "The State Rights Fetish," *New Viewpoints in American History* (New York, 1922), 220–44.

fact, "diverse civilizations," and, as such, incapable of maintaining a union with one another.[20]

The quest for an unqualified antithesis still continues. Interpretations now current have turned back to an emphasis, formerly popular in the nineteenth century, upon the basic incompatibility between a slaveholding and a nonslaveholding regime, with all the far-reaching differences in social values and in mode of life which such systems must entail.[21]

These antitheses are in a sense caricatures, perhaps accurate in singling out some distinctive feature, but grossly distorted in the emphasis which they give to it. Because of their vulnerability, revisionist critics have been able to direct damaging criticism at every one of them. The fervently evangelical South, with a large infusion of frontier primitivism and equalitarianism, was by no means cavalier, while the Puritanism which may have dominated New England but had certainly never dominated the North as a whole was already beginning to be diluted by immigration and urbanization at least two decades before the Civil War. Moreover, there were no fully articulated "planter" and "industrial" civilizations, standing in juxtaposition to one another, for the common conditions of life of plain farmers throughout an overwhelmingly rural republic

[20] Charles A. and Mary R. Beard, *The Rise of American Civilization* (2 vols.; New York, 1927). One of the authoritative spokesmen of the idea of diverse civilizations was Edward Channing, in his *History of the United States* (6 vols.; New York, 1905–25), VI, 3–4.

[21] Arthur Schlesinger, Jr., in "The Causes of the Civil War: A Note on Historical Sentimentalism," *Partisan Review*, XVI (October, 1949), 469–81; and Harry V. Jaffa, in *Crisis of the House Divided: An Interpretation of the Issues in the Lincoln-Douglas Debates* (New York, 1959), have done much to reinstate the idea that the conflict was a struggle between freedom and slavery, but Leon F. Litwack, in *North of Slavery: The Negro in the Free States, 1790–1860* (Chicago, 1961), shows that even a genuine sectional division on the slavery question did not necessarily mean any great sectional discrepancy in attitudes toward the Negro. Racism was nationwide.

completely transcended these distinctions. Dirt farmers, South and North, were the backbone of both sections, planter aristocrats and rising industrialists notwithstanding.[22]

Similarly, the political and economic antitheses contain fallacies. Shrewd observers have always perceived the states' rights doctrine to be less a philosophical position than a tactical device, attractive to any minority regardless of latitude, and the doctrine of national supremacy to be one exalted by those who possessed power and wanted to take advantage of it. Scratch a spokesman of state sovereignty and you find, not necessarily a Southerner, but almost invariably a man who sees that he is outnumbered; look beneath the rhetoric which exalts federal supremacy and you discover a motive on the part of a majority group to remove some irksome restriction upon the use of power.

The once-regnant theory that the Civil War was a "clash of economic sections," and that agriculture and industry must inevitably conflict, was hardly less than an assumption that where economies are diversified, they must invariably be antagonistic. There were, in fact, serious antagonisms between the cotton economy and the manufacturing interest, but the trouble with making a theory of them is that it will lead logically to the conclusion that no country can ever achieve real integration economically: although a country without economic diversity would find its integrity as a nation threatened because it is not self-sufficient, if it were to attain economic diversity, it would theoretically find its integrity as a nation threatened because diverse interests had led to internal dissensions. The assumption in the first instance is that diverse inter-

[22] James G. Randall, in "The Civil War Restudied," *Journal of Southern History*, VI (November, 1940), 439–57, exposed some of the fallacies in the views that agrarian and industrial societies were certain to clash, and that North and South formed diametrically opposed civilizations.

ests will be complementary; in the second instance, that they will be incompatible. Both are merely assumptions, valid or not according to the individual circumstances; there are many situations in which agricultural areas and industrial areas serve each other as sources of supplies and as markets. Such complementary situations show the fallacy in the a priori supposition that points of dissimilarity are equivalent to points of dissension.

Compared to these other dualisms, the antithesis between slaveholding and nonslaveholding states is at least valid in that there were in fact two groups of states sharply differentiated in the legal status they gave to slavery. This distinction was clear-cut and incontrovertible, as was not the case with the other dualisms that have been mentioned. But even here, the antithesis is less deep than might be supposed, for the distinction was not between one society which accorded equality to the Negro and another which denied it; in fact racism was nationwide, and neither Abraham Lincoln nor any other major leader proposed to place the Negro on the same basis with other citizens. The issue as it stood at that time, unfortunately, was less a question whether the Negro should have status as an equal than a dispute over what his form his inferior status should take. For the Negro in America, chattel servitude was sectional but caste inferiority was still national, and thus the slavery issue also failed to present a complete contrast.

Even the seemingly manifest difference between the loyalties of a nationalistic North and a sectionalistic South becomes tenuous when it is examined closely. For copious evidence shows that national as well as local loyalties prevailed in both the North and the South. The North's so-called "nationalism," consisted, as I have already pointed out, partly in its control over federal policy, and in the ability to keep it in alignment with sectional interests, while the South's "sectionalism" was, at least initially, an expression of the lack of such a capacity.

The problem presented by such antitheses as these in the interpretation of history, however, arises not from their over-simplifications or their exaggeration of differences, but from their mistaken attribution of mutual exclusiveness to phenomena which naturally coexist and overlap as national identity and regional identity do. It is false to assume that nationalism is a matter of homogeneity and therefore to conclude that regional diversity—at least when it appears on a North-South axis—is inconsistent with national unity. Once the mistaken assumption of mutual exclusiveness is accepted, the false conclusion follows that sectional distinctiveness can serve as an index of deviation, and by the same token that loyalty to the section can become an index of disloyalty to the Union. Besides mistaking dissimilarity for antagonism, this kind of interpretation has the tendency, where friction exists, to shift attention away from specific disputes between parties and to emphasize their mere lack of resemblance to one another.

The habit of equating diversity with dissension, and of using the word "difference" to mean both at the same time, has taken such deep root in the historiography of the Civil War that it becomes difficult to dissociate the two; nevertheless, history abounds in instances where diversity does not lead to antagonism, where regional identity does not detract from national integrity, and where no one expects them to do so. Outside the United States, for instance, the French, Catholic, peasant culture of the Quebec province presents sharper contrasts to the English, Protestant, pioneer culture of Ontario than North and South ever presented, and strong elements of antagonism have been involved historically; yet there was no "irrepressible conflict" in Canada, and today the diversity is hardly regarded as a serious problem. Within the United States, New Englanders, with their Puritan heritage and their

Yankee ways, have kept their distinctiveness, along with a strong affection for their "stern and rockbound coast"; yet these qualities are regarded as reinforcing rather than diminishing the Yankee's Americanism. Even where the South itself is involved, historical interpretation of sectional differences has been too inconsistent to bear scrutiny. From the ratification of the Constitution until the high noon of the New Deal, and to some extent even down to the present, the South has been set apart by its rural society, its staple-crop economy, its tradition of leadership or control by the landowning interest, its large proportion of Negro population, and its formalized system of caste in race relations. In 1787 these differences were perhaps more pronounced than during the crisis which led to the Civil War, yet historians who assume that such regional dissimilarities made a continuation of peaceful union impossible after 1850 seem completely untroubled by the fact that the very same diversities did not at all prevent the formation of at least a loose union in 1787–88, or the rapid and triumphant growth of American nationalism for nearly forty years thereafter. Since the Civil War, the one-party system of the "solid" South, and the relative poverty of the region, as well as the heritage of bitterness from Civil War and Reconstruction, have made the sectional contrasts in some respects sharper than they were during the antebellum period. Yet these strong sectional factors proved not inconsistent with the swift restoration of American nationalism in the South, which increased steadily at least until 1954.[23] The sectional differences were still there, but in this new context, since they did not lead to war,

[23] Paul H. Buck, *The Road to Reunion, 1865–1900* (Boston, 1937), traces a swift and easy restoration of harmony between North and South within thirty-five years of Appomattox, which could not possibly have occurred if Southern nationalism had been so deep-seated as, for instance, Polish nationalism was.

no one supposed any longer that they must be inherently disruptive. In fact, the readiness with which the South returned to the Union will defy explanation unless it is recognized that Southern loyalties to the Union were never really obliterated but rather were eclipsed by other loyalties with which, for a time, they conflicted. It was a dim awareness of this among the participants in the Civil War which gave the conflict its peculiarly tragic tone—its pathos as a "brothers' war."

The historian may feel acutely the need for an explanation of the deep alienation which developed between North and South in the middle of the nineteenth century, but he ought not to allow the urgency of this need to blind him to the fact that he also needs an explanation for the growth of American nationalism between 1800 and 1846 and for the smoothness of the "road to reunion" between 1865 and 1900. No explanation of the sectional strife is really much good if it makes these phenomena of harmony and reconciliation appear impossible. Yet the historian's reliance upon the sharpest conceivable antitheses has led him to explain the schism in terms so deep and total that the subsequent readiness of Southern men, in 1898 and 1917, to enlist in the United States Army and to fight under the American flag would seem quite incredible.

To explain an antagonism which sprang up suddenly, and died down suddenly, the historian does not need to discover, and cannot effectively use, a factor which has been constant over a long period, as the cultural difference between the North and the South has been. He needs to identify a factor which can cause bitter disagreement even among a people who have much basic homogeneity. No factor, I would suggest, will meet this need better than the feeling, widespread in the 1850's in the South, that the South's vital interests were being jeopardized, and that the region was being exposed to the dangers of a slave insurrection, as a result of the hostility of antislavery men in the North. Applied to the sectional crisis, such a view of the sources of friction would make possible the explanation of the Civil War, without making impossible the explanation of the rapid return to union after the war. No cultural explanation will do this.

The cultural factor and the factor of self-interest are, of course, not wholly unrelated, for essential interests are determined partly by cultural values and vice versa. But the fact remains that within an integrated culture acute conflicts of interest may be generated, and between diverse cultures strong community of interests may develop. A body of citizens may exalt the national state as the instrument that unites them with those with whom they have an affinity, but they may also exalt it as the guardian of certain essential interests and social values which they do not necessarily share with the overall society. Despite the emphasis in historical literature upon cultural homogeneity, history itself offers extensive evidence that if a state protects the interests—either real or fancied—of culturally disparate groups in its population, it can command the nationalistic loyalty of such groups without reducing them to a homogeneous body of citizens, and that if it systematically disregards the interests of a group it alienates the group and makes cultural affinities with the majority seem irrelevant.[24] The state, of course, frequently adopts measures adverse to the specific advantage of a given

[24] Grodzins (*The Loyal and the Disloyal*, ii) quotes George Washington: "Men . . . may talk of patriotism . . . but whoever builds upon it as the basis for conducting a long and bloody war will find themselves deceived in the end. We must take the passions of men as nature has given them, and those principles as a guide which are generally the rule of Action. I do not mean to exclude altogether the Idea of Patriotism. I know it exists, and I know it has done much in the present Contest. But I will venture to assert, that a great and lasting war can never be supported on this principle alone. It must be aided by a prospect of Interest or some reward."

group without seriously endangering the basis of their loyalty, but when it acts against what the group conceives to be its fundamental welfare, there is a question whether loyalty can survive. In fact the members of a group may become alienated even more readily when they feel that they have been victimized by their own kindred rather than by strangers. In this sense, community of interest may sometimes be a more important condition for nationalism than cultural homogeneity, and conflict of interest may be a greater danger to national union than cultural diversity.

Without laboring this point, it may be worth noting that in situations where conflict occurs, cultural diversity is never the direct cause. This diversity will generate friction only when it has been translated into opposing policies for dealing with a particular question. Therefore even the historian who relies entirely upon cultural explanations to account for a given conflict must reckon with the fact that the disruptive potentials inherent in cultural diversity remain latent until conflicts of interest bring them into play.

Insofar as it is sound to regard the equilibration of interests as a condition necessary to nationalism, it follows that the American Civil War must be interpreted less in terms of antitheses and dissimilarities between North and South, and more in terms of the prolonged sequence of interest conflicts which crystallized along sectional lines. Southerners became progressively more alienated as they became more convinced, first, that the Union was sacrificing their economic welfare by its tariff policy; later, that it was denying them parity in the process of national expansion; and finally, that it was condoning the activities of men who would loose a slave insurrection upon them and expose them to possible butchery.

This does not mean, of course, that anyone need turn to a simple economic interpretation of history, but rather that we should recognize that cultural similarities alone will not provide a basis of affinity between groups who regard each other's policies as endangering their own security. The danger of these conflicts to national unity was fully recognized as early as 1797 and was a major theme in Washington's Farewell Address. Later, control of the national political system became itself a weapon in the warfare between opposing interests, and as it did so, the central government lost much of its potency as a symbol evocative of national loyalties.

Whether slavery did or did not constitute a vital interest for the South is too large a question to be explored here, but there is no doubt that the South believed it did. Also there is no doubt that the emancipation of the slaves was the largest expropriation of property that has ever occurred in the United States—the heaviest blow that any large interest group has ever sustained. The slavery question was a thoroughly tangible matter, and far more than a symbol in a conflict of cultures, but many historians prefer to treat it as if it were no such thing. Southern writers have never wished to believe that the South fought for slavery, while Northern writers have preferred to think in terms of the fulfillment of an ideal of freedom rather than the overthrow of a vast property interest.

By focusing upon conflict of interest as a basic factor it is possible to explain the otherwise stubborn anomaly that the sectional crisis grew in intensity even as the republic grew in homogeneity. Originally, cultural unity was not deemed necessary to the welfare of the Union under the Constitution, and both the Northern and the Southern states fully intended to preserve their respective sectional peculiarities, of which they were acutely aware when they ratified the Constitution. Indeed, they did not ratify it until shrewd calculation had assured each section either that it might hope to gain preponderant weight, or at least that it would be strong enough to maintain the sectional equilibrium in the new system. If the republic had remained static, with the area and population of 1790 more or less permanent, an equilibrium might have been maintained, and the Union might have enjoyed harmony, even without homogeneity. The "house divided," which had in fact been divided from the beginning, might have continued to stand as it had stood for seventy years.

But when growth ensued—with uneven rates of advance for the two sections—the equilibrium was upset. The minority section lost its ability to exercise a joint control in the federal government, and with this control went the power of coordinating national with sectional objectives and thus of maintaining the image of the federal government as the guardian of the essential interests of values of Southern society. The South, therefore, was forced more and more to regard national objectives on the one hand and sectional objectives on the other as the alternatives of a painful choice. Meanwhile, the North did not have to choose between national and sectional objectives because by use of its power it could incorporate sectional goals into the national program. What was good for the North was good for the country, and thus no problem of priority need arise. The potential dilemma of Josiah Quincy's loyalties, which he had stated so clearly, remained a latent dilemma, never developed beyond the verbal level. But Sam Houston and Alexander Stephens lived to see a situation where bigness of heart was not enough and where the Union was so divided that patriotism could no longer embrace it.

If the adjustment of conflicting interests rather than the elimination of cultural differences is in this instance the key to the perpetuation of national unity, and if an equilibrium of power is the condition most favorable to the adjustment of conflicting interests, then the historian has an explanation for the seeming paradox that the crisis of American nationalism came not when regional diversity was greatest, but after many common denominators between the sections had developed and had substantially increased the measure of cultural uniformity. He has also a key to the anomalous fact that from 1787 to 1861 national growth always seemed to endanger national unity: it upset the equation between North and South by introducing new factors of power which potentially jeopardized sectional interests that had previously seemed to be in balance.

If the pattern of loyalties in America between 1820 and 1860 was more intricate than the stark antithesis of nationalism and sectionalism would imply, and if the ultimate conflict between North and South was in part the consequence of the failure of the Union to solve the problems of chronic conflict of interest, even after it had successfully begun to transcend the presumably more difficult obstacles of cultural dissimilarity, the implication is not that a new single-factor analysis should be applied, developing a view which presents the Civil War in the exclusive terms of a conflict between culturally similar groups which both spelled their version of nationalism with the alphabet of self-interest. It is rather to suggest that the valuative elements in the concept of nationalism have influenced too many of the findings of the historian, that the concept has warped his analysis as much as it has assisted it, and that the historical process is far too intricate to be handled in terms of the simple dualisms of culture versus culture, nation versus section, interest versus interest, or Americanism versus Southernism.

Part 2

THREE HISTORIOGRAPHICAL FORAYS

CHAPTER IV

The Literature on the Background
of the Civil War

A word may be needed about what this essay is and what it is not. In 1957 Richard L. Watson asked me to write a paper for publication in a collection, primarily for teachers, describing what had happened to the treatment of various aspects of American history in the preceding twenty years. My essay would discuss the background of the Civil War. It was not expected to be wholly historiographical nor wholly bibliographical, but a little of both. I accepted the assignment, and the paper was written and published as noted in the preface.

Eight years later, when I dusted off the essay with the idea of including it here, I found that historical literature on the background of the Civil War had developed far in directions which left my discussion dated. I began to insert material here and there, and ended by extensive rewriting; so that, in effect, I regard this as almost a new essay.

The first section, "The Causes of the Civil War," is primarily historiographical. Readers may note that I have not shrunk from the tendentious word "causes." I agree with J. H. Hexter's comment, in his Reappraisals in History, *that although it is fashionable now to avoid the word, we really cannot write history without reference to how one thing leads to another, and that we have therefore only been driven to look for another, more refined equivalent, such as the word "determinants." This first section deals with overall considerations. The second section, "Factors Contributing to the Crisis of the Union," deals primarily with the South and the sequence of specific events preceding the war; it is heavily bibliographical.*

The omissions in the bibliographical side of the essay, which are inevitable given its scale, distress me, especially when I compare the material here with the admirable bibliography in J. G. Randall and David Donald, The Civil War and Reconstruction *(1961), and with the excellent chapters on the Southern economy by J. C. Bonner, on slavery by Bennett H. Wall, on the mind of the antebellum South by Herbert J. Doherty, Jr., and on the coming of the war by the late Charles Cauthen and Lewis P. Jones, in Arthur S. Link and Rembert W. Patrick, edi-*

87

tors, Writing Southern History (1965). *Neither of these treat-*
ments is as brief as mine, and neither minimizes the material
before 1940 as I do. But I console myself with the belief that the
focus of my piece is not the same as that of these others, and
also that with luck my essay may, for a limited time, claim the
adventitious and transitory merit of being the most recent piece
on the subject.

INTRODUCTION

*T*HE PERIOD from 1830 to 1861 in American history may
conceivably have an integral, free-standing significance
of its own, apart from the Civil War which followed, but
historians have rarely been able to treat this era in any way
except as a prelude to the war. Some writers have made half-
hearted efforts to read the record of the decades in question
without reference to the ensuing crisis, and, accordingly, have
pointed out the importance of such developments as the
growth of railroads, the rise of industry, the great waves of
immigration, the thrust into the Trans-Mississippi region, the
technological revolution, and the like, which engaged the
attentions and energies of men, sometimes to the exclusion
of the slavery controversy. But even the very historians who
call attention to these factors usually go on to a treatment
which reverts to the growing antagonism between the sections
as the central topic of the whole period. The implicit acceptance of this emphasis shows in the fact that no one
questioned the aptness of the title *Ordeal of the Union* for
a work, by Allan Nevins, which treated American history for
the decade 1850–60 comprehensively in four volumes without
any visible ordeal materializing, until it came as a climax in
Volume V. It is singular that in our historical literature, the
decades 1763–73 and 1850–60 are almost invariably treated

simply as preludes to war, while the years before 1917 and
1941 are seldom treated in this way.

Because of the intensity of this focus, a high proportion of
the literature on the period from about 1830 to 1861 deals
either (a) directly with the question of the causes of the Civil
War or (b) with topics which bear indirectly upon the schism
between North and South, such as the development of sectionalism in its economic and cultural phases, the institution
of slavery, the humanitarian movement in its antislavery
aspect, the nature of Southern society, both as to social structure and as to intellectual climate, and the specific steps, such
as the Compromise of 1850, the Dred Scott decision, and so
forth, which led toward a final crisis.

This essay attempts to summarize the developments of the
historical literature since 1940 as it relates to these two areas.

THE CAUSES OF THE CIVIL WAR

The last three decades have witnessed considerable advances
in the historical understanding of many of the developments
which preceded the Civil War, but it can hardly be said that
they have brought us visibly closer to the point at which a
jury of historians seems likely to arrive at a verdict which will
settle the controversy as to causes. Indeed some of the most
fundamental issues in the controversy, namely those turning
upon the significance of the slavery question, have been re-
activated and seem now to have given new dimensions to the
whole dispute.

By 1940, the literature on the Civil War had already been
accumulating for eighty years.[1] During these eight decades,

[1] Efforts to explain the war in historical terms began as early as
1861–62, with interpretations by John L. Motley, George Bancroft,
Francis Parkman, and Edward A. Pollard. For general discussion of

interpretation of the war had passed through three major phases. First, during the immediate postwar era, there had been a literature by participants and partisans, designed to justify their own course of conduct and therefore striving either to vindicate or indict. Both sides had appealed to absolute values: if they were partisans of the Union, they had explained the war in terms of slavery and disunion, appealing to the moral absolutes of human freedom and national unity; if they were partisans of the South, they had explained it in terms of the secession issue, appealing to the legal absolute inherent in the theory of state sovereignty and to the moral absolute of the right of self-government.

Second, in the period after the wounds of war began to heal, there had been a nationalistic interpretation, well exemplified in the seven-volume history by James Ford Rhodes (1893–1906), which avoided the attribution of blame and emphasized the sincerity and high motive of both the Blue and the Gray.[2] Rhodes himself argued unequivocally that slavery was the cause of the war, but he held the nation rather than the South responsible for slavery, and if he blamed the South for secession, he blamed the North for Reconstruction. In such an interpretation the concept of an inevitable or "irrepressible" conflict fitted well, for if the war could not possibly have been prevented, then no one could be blamed for failing to prevent it, and thus no one was guilty. Charles Francis Adams pushed this view to its logical limit in 1902

---

the historiography of the war, including these writers, see Thomas J. Pressly, *Americans Interpret Their Civil War* (Princeton, 1954), and Howard K. Beale, "What Historians Have Said About the Causes of the Civil War," in *Theory and Practice in Historical Study*, Social Science Research Council Bulletin 54 (New York, 1946).

[2] *History of the United States from the Compromise of 1850 to the Final Restoration of Home Rule in the South in 1877* (New York, 1893–1906).

by declaring that "Everybody, in short, was right; no one wrong." [3]

Third, in the 1920's, after ideas of economic determinism began to prevail widely in American intellectual circles, Charles and Mary Beard had published an immensely influential interpretation of the war in their *The Rise of American Civilization* (1927). Seeing the great contests of history as struggles for power, rather than for principle, and regarding moral and legal arguments as mere rationalizations, the Beards had denied that the South really cared about states' rights or the North about slavery. The South had simply used states' rights as a tactical device in defending a minority position. The Republicans had simply used the slavery issue to turn public opinion against the South, but in fact the Republicans had not been abolitionists and had done nothing to help the slaves, but had sought only to "contain" the power of the slaveholders by excluding them from the new territories. The war, therefore, had not been a contest over principles but a struggle for power—a clash of economic sections in which freedom did not necessarily combat slavery but industrialism most assuredly combated the planter interests.

These three were, in brief, the major interpretations which had held sway up to 1940. Since 1940, the major tendencies have been: (1) the development of a so-called "revisionist" interpretation which minimized the importance of slavery or any other fundamental factor as a cause of the war and also argued that the war could have been and should have been averted; (2) a counterattack upon the revisionists by writers who reassert the causative importance of the slavery question; and (3) a shifting of the question away from a sharp focus

[3] "The Ethics of Secession," an address delivered in 1902 and printed in *Studies Military and Diplomatic, 1775–1865* (New York, 1911), 208.

upon the "causes" of the hostilities as such, together with a more generalized concern with the relation between the war and the pattern of race relations in the United States.

The Revisionists

Although sometimes mentioned as if they were a "school," the so-called revisionists have in fact been a number of distinctively independent scholars, working separately, disagreeing on occasion, and united only by their skepticism about the role of slavery as the heart of the sectional issue and by their doubt that the conflict was irrepressible.

These doubts are as old as the war itself, but modern revisionism possibly begins with Albert J. Beveridge, Republican Senator from Indiana and biographer of John Marshall. About 1920, Beveridge set out to write a biography of Lincoln. He approached this undertaking with the traditional Republican reverence for an almost superhuman being—the inevitable protagonist of the antislavery drama in which there had to be an antagonist or villain, and in which Stephen A. Douglas was inevitably stereotyped for the latter role. But when Beveridge began his research, he found the facts far more complex than the tradition, and when he came to the Lincoln-Douglas debates, he concluded that Douglas had acted with integrity and had represented a very respectable point of view —namely that the question of slavery in the territories was a fictitious issue, not worth a crisis which would endanger the nation. Because the abolitionists had "agitated" this issue in such a way as to precipitate the crisis, Beveridge formed an unfavorable opinion of them and began to think that, without them, there might have been no war—indeed that slavery might in time have disappeared peaceably under the pressure of economic forces.[4]

[4] Claude G. Bowers, *Beveridge and the Progressive Era* (Boston, 1932), 561–79.

In 1927, Beveridge died. His life of Lincoln, published in the following year,[5] had been completed only to the year 1858, and we can never know what broad, overall interpretation he would have advanced. But certain of the ideas which he had foreshadowed continued to develop in the decade of the thirties. In 1933, Gilbert H. Barnes published an account of the early abolitionist movement (*The Anti-Slavery Impulse, 1830–1844*) in which he emphasized the neglected figure of Theodore Dwight Weld, and de-emphasized the importance of William Lloyd Garrison, at the same time condemning the fanaticism of the abolitionists in general. During the same year, Gerald W. Johnson of the Baltimore *Sun* published a small interpretive volume on *The Secession of the Southern States*, which stated brilliantly the argument that dogmatic, rigid adherence to "principle" on the part of both antislavery zealots like Charles Sumner of Massachusetts and doctrinaire legalists like John C. Calhoun of South Carolina had caused an unnecessary war in which "everybody was wrong and no one was right." Johnson's little book has been neglected,[6] perhaps because he was not a professional historian, but it remains to this day one of the most vigorous and effective statements of a major thesis of revisionism. In 1934, George Fort Milton, editor of the Chattanooga *News*, brought out a full-scale biography of Douglas, based on extensive new manuscripts and bearing the significant title *The Eve of Conflict: Stephen A. Douglas and the Needless War*. Like Beveridge, Milton considered Douglas statesmanlike in his effort to play down the territorial issue, and believed that unwise political leadership was responsible for the war.

After these preliminaries, the full tide of the revisionist

[5] *Abraham Lincoln, 1809–1858* (2 vols.; Boston, 1928).

[6] It is not mentioned at all in Pressly, *Americans Interpret Their Civil War*, a book-length historiographical survey which deals at length with a number of less important items.

reaction struck in the late thirties and early forties, primarily as the result of the work of two men—James G. Randall and Avery O. Craven—advancing independently along somewhat parallel lines.

Craven first enunciated his views clearly in an article, "Coming of the War Between the States: An Interpretation," in 1936.[7] He followed this with a brief interpretive volume, *The Repressible Conflict*, in 1939, and with a full-scale history of the years from 1830 to 1861 in *The Coming of the Civil War* in 1942. Since then he has continued to develop and to modify his ideas in a number of writings, including notably a volume in the History of the South series, *The Growth of Southern Nationalism*, 1848–1861 (1953), a set of interpretive lectures, *Civil War in the Making*, 1815–1860 (1959), and a volume of essays, *An Historian and the Civil War* (1964).

Perhaps the crucial feature of Craven's interpretation is his belief that the basic and essential differences between North and South were not great enough to make war necessary. The dissimilarities between the agrarian society of the South and the industrial society of the Northeast were, to be sure, a fertile seedbed for friction and for misunderstandings, but these misunderstandings were not, on the whole, realistic. The great difference traditionally emphasized is that of slavery, but Craven argued that the economic condition of the Negro as an unskilled laborer engaged in the cotton culture was much more important in controlling the conditions of his life than his legal status as a chattel. Because of these economic factors the condition of the Negro after emancipation changed very little until the cotton economy itself changed in the 1930's. Craven also emphasized the fact that three-quarters of the Southern whites were not slaveholders and were not directly involved in the slavery complex. North and South did not, in fact, present polar extremes.

[7] *Journal of Southern History*, II (August 1936), 303–22.

But if sectional antagonisms did not arise out of fundamental differences, what did they arise from? Craven believed that they resulted from the creation of false images of each section by the other, and from the charging of these images with a high, unreasoning emotional content. He believed that these stereotypes were to some extent manufactured by irresponsible political agitators, both North and South—that is by the "fire-eating" secessionists and by the abolitionists. In other words, the explanation lies more in psychological attitudes than in objective conditions. From this conclusion, it follows that we should beware of any arbitrary assumption that the conflict was irrepressible (though Craven later concluded that the opposite assumption should also be avoided, since the question really cannot be determined). It follows, too, that slavery should be played down: Craven suggested "the possibility that behind the determination to put slavery on the road to ultimate extinction there may have lain drives that had little to do with Negro slavery or the American South, as well as others that were the direct product of slavery itself and of the so-called 'Slave Power.' " Since, in his opinion, "the great body of Americans were moderate and conservative in their attitudes [and] . . . came to the brink of Civil War reluctantly," [8] a heavy burden of what may really be called war guilt rests with the political leaders ("extremists") like Charles Sumner and Barnwell Rhett who played upon public emotions until they brought about a conflict which the circumstances did not require and which neither the Northern nor the Southern majority wanted.

While Craven was developing these themes at the University of Chicago, James G. Randall at the University of Illinois was concurrently working out an interpretation to which he himself applied the term "revisionist." His first clear-cut statement of this interpretation appeared, but was

[8] *Civil War in the Making, 1815–1860*, vi–vii.

not heavily emphasized, in his *The Civil War and Reconstruction* in 1937. It was more fully elaborated in three important articles, "The Blundering Generation," "The Civil War Restudied," and "When War Came in 1861," all published in 1940.[9] Finally, in *Lincoln, the President: Springfield to Gettysberg* (1945), he set forth his views in their fully matured form.

Critics sometimes discuss Craven and Randall as if their views were identical. It is easy to see why this happens, for both men held a number of major ideas in common: that sectional differences were not great enough to necessitate a war; that the crisis resulted more from the whipping-up of emotions than from the impact of realistic issues; that extremists on both sides were responsible for this emotional jag, but that the responsibility of the extremists of the North (i.e., the abolitionists), which had been disregarded by many historians, needed to be emphasized rather more than the responsibility of the extremists of the South (i.e., the fire-eating secessionists), whom historians had blamed excessively; and above all, that the war was both avoidable and unnecessary and that it occurred as the result of a failure of leadership. But within this broad framework of agreement, Craven and Randall each developed distinctive points of emphasis. Where Craven argued that the Civil War in particular ought not to have occurred, Randall showed greater concern with the problem of war as such, and writing at a time when the world was rapidly losing the international peace which World War I and the League of Nations were supposed to have won, he argued that war as such should be prevented, that it is a "fallacy" to believe that "fundamental motives produce

[9] These articles appeared, respectively, in *Mississippi Valley Historical Review*, XXVII (June, 1940), 3–28; *Journal of Southern History*, VI (November, 1940), 439–57; and *Abraham Lincoln Quarterly*, I (March, 1940), 3–42. The first and third of these essays were republished with some revision in James G. Randall, *Lincoln, the Liberal Statesman* (New York, 1947).

war." [10] Indeed, he contended that analysis of the causes of war must fail unless it takes into consideration psychopathic factors.

Because of his greater concern with the general problem of the causation of war, Randall was also more concerned than was Craven to refute the idea of economic determinism, in the Beardian sense, as an explanation of war. In some of his best analysis, Randall pointed out that economic determinists have a kind of "heads, I win—tails, you lose" formula. If a people who lack economic diversity make war, their belligerence can be explained in terms of the need for economic self-sufficiency. But if a people with diversity have an internal war, their conflict can be explained in terms of the clash of diverse interests. In either case, the explanation for war stands ready-made. As Randall argued, features of diversity may lead to mutual interdependence rather than to war, and the existence of economic differences creates no presumption that antagonism need follow. Where antagonism exists, it must be explained on specific grounds. [11]

A second respect in which Randall's emphasis differed from Craven's is that where Craven discounted the significance of slavery as an institution, Randall minimized its significance as an issue. One of his most effective arguments was his contention that, while the broad issue of freedom versus slavery may be worth a war, the issue as defined by the opposing forces in 1861 was not that broad, and was not worth a war in the form in which they defined it. For the Republicans in 1861 did not propose to emancipate the slaves; they even agreed in 1861 to guarantee slavery in the existing slave states and to return fugitives to slavery. The one point on which they stuck was that they would not sanction slavery in any of the new territories. But since the climate and the economy of these

[10] Randall, *Lincoln, the Liberal Statesman*, 88.
[11] *Ibid.*, 88.

new regions made them inhospitable to slavery anyway, the territorial question could be viewed as an abstraction—a contest over "an imaginary Negro in an impossible place," and a very inadequate cause for a war. The idea that the territorial issue was a fictitious one was not new—it had been vigorously expressed by James K. Polk—but Randall gave it a new application in his treatment of the causes of the War.

A third major expression of revisionism appeared in 1948, when Roy F. Nichols of the University of Pennsylvania published his *The Disruption of American Democracy*. Unlike Craven and Randall, Nichols did not undertake a general interpretation of the sectional crisis as a whole. Instead he set himself to the more specialized study of the impact of sectional antagonisms in shattering a national political party— the Democratic Party. His work, which won the Pulitzer Prize, was, therefore, an institutional study of the impact of sectional pressures upon American political machinery. But the findings fitted well with the revisionist thesis, for Nichols showed how the defects of the political system (excessive localism, the need for agitation in order to stimulate voters in the frequent elections, etc.) contributed to the breakdown of a national political organization under the weight of sectional pressures. Moreover, Nichols asserted in clear-cut terms his belief that the "hyperemotionalism" of the times made it possible for "irresponsible and blind operators of local political machinery" to exploit the inflammable issues which led to war.

Toward the end of the forties, revisionism had very largely swept the field of Civil War literature. With the partial exception of Allan Nevins' *Ordeal of the Union* (1947), all the major works on the Civil War for a decade had reflected a revisionist view. Revisionism had made its way into the textbooks and had been taken up by popular writers. It is perhaps symptomatic that, in 1951, William E. Woodward's posthumous history of the war, tentatively entitled *The Civil War:*

A *National Blunder,* was finally issued under the title *Years of Madness.*[12]

The Counterattack on Revisionism

About nine years after Craven and Randall had sounded the first trumpets of a broad revisionism, Arthur Schlesinger, Jr., in his *The Age of Jackson* (1945) entered a dissenting opinion. In a brief discussion, made in passing, Schlesinger affirmed his belief that "the emotion which moved the North finally to battlefield and bloodshed was moral disgust with slavery." He also denied the Beardian thesis that slavery was resisted because it constituted an obstacle to industrial capitalism; on the contrary, he said, "the aspirations which were first felt to be menaced by the slave power were in actuality democratic aspirations." [13] Four years later, in an article on Randall's contention, he returned to the subject for a more extended treatment.[14] Attacking the revisionists for using the claim of objectivity and the concept of automatic progress as devices for avoiding consideration of the moral issue of slavery, Schlesinger argued that the focus of the slavery contest had fallen on the territories, not because industrialists on-the-make were covetous of power in new regions and indifferent to slave hardships in old ones, but because Americans found their moral scruples about slavery in conflict with their civic scruples to obey the Constitution, which protected slavery in the slave states.[15] Therefore, their powerful impulse against human bondage was deflected from its natural target, slavery in the

[12] These titles are mentioned in Pressly, *Americans Interpret Their Civil War,* 285.

[13] Schlesinger, *The Age of Jackson,* 432–33.

[14] Arthur Schesinger, Jr., "The Causes of the Civil War: A Note on Historical Sentimentalism," *Partisan Review,* XVI (1949), 469–81.

[15] The same point of view was also put forward in the same year by David M. Potter, in David M. Potter and Thomas G. Manning, *Nationalism and Sectionalism in America, 1775–1877: Select Problems in Historical Interpretation* (New York, 1949), 215–16.

states, and was sublimated, as it were, into an attack on the peripheral question of slavery in the territories. But despite this displacement of the objective, Schlesinger felt no doubt that the moral question of slavery was basic in precipitating conflict between the sections.

During the same year when Schlesinger published this latter article, Pieter Geyl, an eminent Dutch historian of major stature, also published, in Dutch, a critique of Randall's idea that the war could have been avoided. (A part of this was published in English translation in 1951).[16] Geyl focused his attention especially on Randall's contention that because the majority did not want conflict, war should have been avoidable. He argued that the historical process is not as rational as Randall assumed, and that the issues of sectional disagreement could not be neatly separated from the emotions which they generated, and which ultimately got out of control. His criticism must rank with Schlesinger's as one of the two major rebuttals to the revisionist argument, but other voices have been raised as well. Bernard De Voto assailed the revisionists in two influential articles in *Harper's* which were notable for their early date (1946) as well as for their vigorous, hard-hitting tone.[17] In 1950, Oscar Handlin, in a review of Nevins, deplored the practice of equating the abolitionists and the secessionists because both groups were fanatics: "There is surely a difference," he said, "between being a fanatic for freedom and being a fanatic for slavery." [18]

[16] Pieter Geyl, *De Amerikaanse Burgeroorlog en het Probleem der Onvermijdelijkheid* (Amsterdam, 1949), 295–340. A translation of part of this appeared as "The American Civil War and the Problem of Inevitability," *New England Quarterly*, XXIV (June, 1951), 147–68. Reprinted in Geyl, *Debates with Historians* (Groningen, 1955), 216–35.

[17] Bernard De Voto, "The Easy Chair," *Harper's*, CXCII (February, 1946), 123–26. *Ibid.* (March, 1946), 234–37.

[18] Oscar Handlin, Review of Nevins, *The Emergence of Lincoln,* in *Nation*, CLXXI (December 2, 1950), 512–13.

Harry V. Jaffa has provided an important full-scale criticism of much of the revisionist position.[19] Jaffa denied that slavery had reached the geographical limits of its expansion and that the political restriction was redundant. He denied also that Douglas' popular sovereignty and Lincoln's restrictionism would both have come to the same thing, that is, freedom in the territories, and that the two men's views did not conflict in any basic way. Instead he argued, Douglas was willing to sacrifice the principles of freedom and equality to the principle of majority rule, while Lincoln, though not a doctrinaire equalitarian, wanted "the highest degree of equality for which general [majority] consent could be obtained." Emphasizing this distinction as he did, he dismissed the idea that emotions of the crisis period were "whipped up" or unrealistic.

By the time Jaffa published his refutation, revisionism had reached the end of its active phase. James G. Randall's voice had been stilled by death in 1953, and Avery Craven had greatly modified his earlier arguments as to the irrepressibility of the conflict.[20] In certain respects, revisionism, like many other historical correctives, had served its purpose—not by winning adoption of its own doctrinal views, but by forcing a correction of previous stereotypes and oversimplifications. Never again could well-trained historians explain the Civil War purely in terms of economic determinism or as a moral crusade against slavery. Nor could they dismiss questions of responsibility and the failure of leadership with an unsupported assertion that the conflict was irrepressible.

But much of the revisionist position remained under attack. One of the most protracted and intensive controversies that

[19] Harry V. Jaffa, *Crisis of the House Divided: An Interpretation of the Issues in the Lincoln-Douglas Debates* (New York, 1959).

[20] For a more detailed analysis of Craven's position and of the changes in it, see my review of his *An Historian and the Civil War*, in *Journal of Southern History*, XXXI (1965), 207–10. The review is published as an appendix to this chapter.

had ever occurred among American historians had not terminated in agreement. This was true despite the fact that revisionism was woven into such major historical studies as those of Randall, Craven, and Nichols, while most of the critics of revisionism had been essayists making their forays from other fields: Jaffa from political science, Geyl from Dutch history, and Schlesinger from the New Deals of Andrew Jackson and Franklin Roosevelt. Perhaps the dispute remained unresolved because, although it purported to be disagreement of an analytical sort about the nature of historical forces, it was also, in cryptic and indirect form, a disagreement of a philosophical sort about the relative importance of three moral objectives: the avoidance of war, the abolition of slavery, and the preservation of the American union. In each case there was an issue not only as to the relative moral priority of the objective (e.g., Was it more important to avoid war than to free slaves?), but also as to whether there were acceptable alternative ways of attaining the objectives (e.g., Could the slaves have been freed without waging a war? Could the Union have been preserved without sacrificing the objectives of ultimate emancipation? Could war have been averted without destroying the Union or leaving the blacks permanently enslaved?). The shifting emphases on first one moral objective and then another, without a corresponding shift in attitudes toward the contingent alternatives, had resulted in constant alterations of the questions which historians were trying to answer. For instance, Randall was so deeply preoccupied with the evil of war that he concentrated primarily on why it was not avoided, without giving full consideration to the evil of slavery, even as a secondary thought. Schlesinger and Kenneth Stampp have given primacy to the evil of slavery and have at least implied that while war is, in most situations, worse than the alternatives, there are cases such as that of Hitlerite Germany where war is preferable, and that the confrontation with slavery was such a case. In the historical writing of today, the Union is usually taken for granted, and historians no longer ask to what extent union has enough intrinsic worth to justify either a resort to the evil of war or a compromise with the evil of slavery. But in the 1860's, this was the crucial question for many. Paul C. Nagel's *One Nation Indivisible: The Union in American Thought, 1776–1861* furnishes striking evidence of the intensity with which the union was regarded, in the mid-nineteenth century, as an absolute value.

In short, while the revisionists and their critics systematically conducted their discourse in the terminology of causation, they were usually bent upon defending the moral priority of one objective over another. Insofar as this was true, they were engaged more in justification than in explanation. Disputes on points of moral justification cannot be settled by objective means. That is one reason why the results of the great revisionist controversy remained inconclusive despite the vast barrage of factual data that was thrown into the campaign by both the revisionists and their critics.

Redefining the Question:
The Problem of Race Adjustment

While much of the literature of revisionism and of the counterattack upon it was almost ostentatiously focused upon what purported to be systematic analysis, the shifting fortunes of the revisionist view were illuminated in an especially revealing way in a major work which scarcely attempted such analytical interpretation at all, but which undertook instead to provide the first modern, full-scale narrative of the period from 1850 to 1861. This was the work of Allan Nevins. Many years ago, Nevins began a study of the vast array of source materials that had accumulated in repositories throughout the country, and he set himself to write such a comprehensive and at the same time detailed history as no one had even attempted since James Ford Rhodes. The triumphant results of this enterprise began to appear in 1947 when Nevins published two volumes, *Ordeal of the Union*, covering the period 1850–57. Two more in 1950, *The Emergence of Lincoln*, carried the narrative to 1860, and a fifth and sixth, *The War for the Union*, in 1959 and 1960, have covered the outbreak of war and major aspects of the war itself.

The primary importance of Nevins' work, as I have tried to emphasize, is that it stands today as the only great overall narrative based upon modern research. But for the examination of historiographical trends, it is pertinent here to concentrate upon the rather brief and infrequent passages in which Nevins offers observations on the causative aspects of his theme. At times, especially in the earlier volumes, he seemed to some extent to share the ideas of the revisionists. He spoke of "the unrealities of passion" and of "the failure of American leadership" and he even stated a conviction that "the war should have been avoidable." It is worth noting, however, that this is by no means the same thing as saying that it could have been avoided. But in *The Emergence of Lincoln*, he struck at the chief weakness of revisionism by observing that "while hysteria was important, we have always to ask what basic reasons made possible the propaganda which aroused it." Also in 1950, he rejected the older simplistic idea that slavery in the strict sense of the chattel servitude of Negroes, was the crux of the controversy, and he offered instead the hypothesis that "the main root of the conflict (and there were minor roots) was the problem of slavery *with its complementary problem of race-adjustment. . . .* It was a war over slavery *and* the future position of the Negro race in North America." [21]

[21] Quotations are from *Ordeal of the Union*, I, viii–ix, and *The Emergence of Lincoln*, II, 463, 468–71.

Nevins' striking observation is valid or not, according to the level of meaning at which one reads it. If it is read to mean that the men who fought each other did so because they held opposing views about the future position of the Negro race in America, it is not tenable, for the evidence is abundant that North and South, in 1860, both regarded the subordination of the Negro as axiomatic. In this sense, it may be argued that although the war perhaps ought to have been about the future position of the Negro, in fact that is not what it was about, since American whites did not recognize that question as an issue. Just as Randall sought to refute the assertion that slavery was the cause of the war by showing that the Republicans, during the slavery controversy, disavowed any purpose to tamper with slavery, and declared their intention only to monopolize the territories for white settlers, so a critic of Nevins might even more persuasively refute the assertion that the future position of the Negro race was the main root of the conflict by showing that hardly anyone at that time contemplated raising the Negro from his position of inferiority, much less fighting a war for such a purpose. From this view, the tragedy of the war is that Americans sacrificed so much without tackling or even perceiving the ultimate question—without even recognizing what was really at stake.

But it is by no means certain historically that the participants in a war necessarily understand why they fight, nor that the conscious objectives of belligerents are an adequate measure of the historical meaning of a war. If Nevins' statement is read to mean that in the crisis leading to the Civil War the blind forces of history were working toward a long-protracted and agonizing readjustment of the future position of the Negro, it is entirely tenable, and may also be regarded as having a broad significance which previous explanations had lacked. In fact, coming as it did, four years before *Brown* vs. *the Board of Education,* and five years before Martin Luther

King's Montgomery Improvement Association, Nevins' statement was historiographically prophetic in foreseeing the viewpoints of historians for at least the next two decades.

Even if historians between 1950 and 1968 had not been plying their trade in a society whose foremost development was the Negro Revolution, probably they would have corrected some of the excesses of the revisionist position simply because the revisionists had carried some of their claims to an extreme. For instance, from the time of Albert J. Beveridge through that of J. G. Randall, the prevailing treatment of Lincoln had insisted that his only greatness appeared after he became President, that there was little to choose between him and Stephen A. Douglas (except that Douglas was more straightforward), and that morally, Lincoln was an opportunist who skillfully contrived to win the votes of both antislavery men and Negrophobes.

The first serious refutation of this view in almost a generation appeared in Don E. Fehrenbacher's *Prelude to Greatness: Lincoln in the 1850's* (1962). Fehrenbacher shunned all the legendary melodrama which pictured Lincoln as a foreordained Emancipator, but he showed very accurately and specifically that Lincoln's position was fundamentally incompatible with that of Douglas, and that he was eager to emphasize the divergence. Fehrenbacher's Lincoln was politically ambitious, but not opportunistic, and his ambition "was leavened by moral conviction."

This emphasis upon Lincoln's moral stature and responsibility was a reaffirmation, at a more subtle and more scholarly level, of a view that had prevailed widely before the revisionist onslaught. But when the focus shifted from Lincoln to the abolitionists, there was very little in the way of accepted legend to build upon. Ever since the Civil War, every historian who sympathized with the South or gave a priority to peace or to Union over emancipation held the abolitionists answerable for driving the South into secession, and thus responsible for both disunion and war. Partly in consequence of these reactions and also perhaps because they did manifest more than the average amount of self-righteousness and moral absolutism, the abolitionists were customarily portrayed as "fanatics" or "extremists." But by 1960, a widespread sense of guilt about American racial attitudes had reached such a degree of intensity that many people, both inside and outside of the historical profession, had lost all interest in the complexities of the relationship between the slavery issue and the war, and had come to regard emancipation and equality for the Negro as the only meaningful aspects of the conflict. In short, the problem of justification had replaced the closely related problem of explanation. As it did so, there was a compulsion to understand the war once more not as a clash of interests but as a crusade against slavery. The shift is well indicated by the titles of the two principal books in the last thirty years which have covered the whole period from the Mexican War through the Civil War. The first of these, by Roy F. Nichols, published in 1961, was entitled *The Stakes of Power, 1845–1877*; the second, by Elbert B. Smith, published in 1967 was *The Death of Slavery, 1837–1865*.

To validate the crusade against slavery, it was, of course necessary to legitimize the crusaders (just as it had been necessary, in discrediting the crusade, to disparage the crusaders). David Donald discovered this historical correlation in 1960 when he published the first volume of his biography of the foremost political adversary of slavery, *Charles Sumner and the Coming of the Civil War*. Donald had researched his subject superbly, and in many respects it seems that he appreciated Sumner's qualities of conviction and devotion to all worthy causes. But he portrayed quite explicitly Sumner's rigid self-righteousness, his arrogance and tendency to quarrel even with his close friends, and his humorless egoism. Although he won a Pulitzer prize for his work, Donald was assailed in at least three articles or lengthy reviews for dealing so harshly with an antislavery leader. He had unwittingly violated an axiom which has served many writers, not all of them outside the historical profession: a man's character is to be inferred from the cause with which he is or was identified and not from the evidence of his personal behavior. Although the slavery question was certainly an ethical one, it does not follow that the vice or virtue of any given individual is a direct coefficient of his position on that question. But nonetheless, true believers will never doubt that if Sumner was sound on slavery, he was one of the good guys, and therefore must, by definition, have had a sense of humor.

This comment should not be read as a covert attack on the abolitionists. They may well have been maligned more indiscriminately in the past than they were lauded indiscriminately in the 1960's. But it is unfortunate that one school, which admires "moderation," tends to denounce the abolitionists as unmitigated bigots, while another school, which admires morality, cannot admit that moral absolutism leads to excessive self-righteousness. All parties tend to avoid facing the fact that every value has its cost. The cost of deep commitment is a certain measure, more or less, of intolerance, and the cost of tolerance is a certain measure, more or less, of moral apathy.

In a larger sense, the vital question concerning the abolitionists is not whether they were "fanatics," but first whether they were humanitarians in a broad sense—that is whether the dynamic of their antislavery was an outgoing concern for the welfare of others or a neurotic impulse to find outlets for psychological problems of their own—and second, whether they really perceived the problem of race adjustment in America, to which Nevins alludes, and which was the essence of the problem of slavery.

The literature of antislavery began to treat its theme somewhat more broadly beginning about 1930. Perhaps the first scholarly modern treatment appeared in 1933 when Gilbert H. Barnes published *The Anti-Slavery Impulse, 1830–1844*. This work broke the monopolistic focus upon William Lloyd Garrison as the one standard symbol of abolitionism by showing the great importance of Theodore Dwight Weld and others. At the same time, it shifted attention from New England to the Middle West. It also began to link antislavery with other forces by demonstrating the integral relationship of abolitionism with the fervent evangelical religion of which Weld was apostle. With the Garrisonian mold thus broken, other writers did much more to explore the social and intellectual origins and relationships of the antislavery movement. Illustrative of this tendency are: Alice Felt Tyler, *Freedom's Ferment* (1944), which deals comprehensively with the many-faceted movement of humanitarian reform, within the context of which the antislavery movement developed; Thomas E. Drake, *Quakers and Slavery in America* (1950), which focused attention again on some of the less sensational, less militant aspects of the resistance to slavery; Samuel Flagg Bemis, *John Quincy Adams and the Union* (1956), which told the story of Adams' career as an antislavery leader in Congress, and thus showed how broad the antislavery movement was in comparison with the abolitionists' campaign for immediate emancipation; and Philip S. Foner, *The Life and Writings of Frederick Douglass* (1950–55), which emphasized the role of free Negroes in the abolition movement.

Identification of the antislavery movement with the humanitarian movement usually implies a measure of approbation for the abolitionists. But, while this approval has certainly been prominent in part of the literature, there also remained a marked tendency to question the basic motivation of abolitionists, sometimes in modern psychological terms. The abolitionists have, of course, always been condemned by writers who attribute the disruption of the Union to the fanaticism of the antislavery crusade. But some of the recent criticism, coming from quite an opposite direction, reflects a belief that the abolitionists were motivated less by a concern for Negro welfare than by other objectives and even by a drive to fulfill certain peculiar psychological needs of their own.

This theme was implied in 1949, in Russell B. Nye's *Fettered Freedom* which argued that the slave system, both in itself and in its zealous defensiveness, constituted a threat to civil liberties and thus provoked the opposition of men who opposed the slave power without necessarily caring about the slave. At almost the same time, Richard Hofstadter, in his *The American Political Tradition*, described Lincoln as one who owed his success to his skill in finding a way "to win the support of both Negrophobes and antislavery men." Hofstadter did not picture the antislavery men as being Negrophobes themselves, but Joseph C. Furnas has actually carried the argument to this position in *Goodbye to Uncle Tom* (1956). Furnas castigates the abolitionists for paving the way to the later system of segregation by their acceptance of the idea of the inferiority of the Negro, and he shows very clearly that many abolitionists, although rejecting slavery, nevertheless did "type" the Negro as an inferior. Since his book appeared, Robert F. Durden's *James Shepherd Pike* (1957) has shown how the strands of antislavery and Negrophobia were strikingly united in the person of one of the editors of the New York *Tribune*, the most important journalistic organ of the antislavery cause.

More recently, biographies of Cassius M. Clay by David Smiley (1962), of George W. Julian by Patrick Riddleberger (1966), and of Hinton R. Helper by Hugh C. Bailey (1965) have illustrated other striking cases of men who hated slavery but had no love for the Negro.

Meanwhile, David Donald has advanced some generalizations about the abolitionists, based upon a study of the backgrounds of 106 prominent antislavery men. He found them, in general, conservative, indifferent to the exploitation of industrial labor, and hostile to Jacksonian democracy. He also suggested that many of them were descendants of New England clerical families who found their leadership challenged by the new industrialism and who turned to reform as a medium through which "their own class" could reassert "its former social dominance . . . an attack upon slavery was their best, if quite unconscious, attack upon the new industrial system." [22]

In short, Donald applied to the abolitionists the same concept of status anxiety and status politics which Richard Hofstadter and the authors of *The New American Right* (1955) were applying, at about the same time, to the Progressives and to the McCarthy Era—and with the same disparaging results.

The treatment of individual abolitionists was usually more favorable than in the generalized accounts. This is true, for instance, of biographies of Gerrit Smith, by Ralph V. Harlow (1939), Harriet Beecher Stowe, by Forrest Wilson (1941), William Lloyd Garrison and Wendell Phillips, by Ralph Korngold (1950), Theodore Weld by Benjamin P. Thomas (1950), William Lloyd Garrison, by Russel B. Nye (1955), James G. Birney by Betty Fladeland (1955), and Wendell Phillips, by Oscar Sherwin (1958).

But the real watershed in antislavery histories came with the publication of Louis Filler's *The Crusade Against Slavery, 1830–1860* and Clifford S. Griffin's *Their Brothers Keeper's: Moral Stewardship in the United States, 1800–1865,* both in

[22] David Donald, "Toward a Reconsideration of Abolitionists," in *Lincoln Reconsidered* (New York, 1956), 19–36. But see also Robert A. Skotheim, "A Note on Historical Method: David Donald's 'Toward a Reconsideration of Abolitionists,'" *Journal of Southern History,* XXV (August, 1959), 356–65.

1960, and Dwight L. Dumond's *Antislavery*, in 1961. Filler provided the first modern, general, scholarly account of the antislavery movement and one sympathetic to the cause whose history it recorded. Griffin identified antislavery with a reform tradition that was somewhat self-righteous, paternalistic, and given to the use of compulsory methods, but which was nevertheless high-minded, public-spirited, and civicly responsible. Dumond, who approached his subject with immense erudition (only partly reflected in his editing of the Weld and Grimke papers [2 vols., 1934] and the Birney Papers [2 vols., 1938]), launched the most learned, most extensive, and most uncritical history of antislavery since Pillsbury Parker had published *The Acts of the Antislavery Apostles* in 1883. This work, a kind of fifth gospel according to Dumond, asserted that the antislavery movement was "the greatest concentration of moral and intellectual power ever assembled in support of any cause before or since."

Dumond's hyperbole was such as to make his book, with all its learning, something of a curiosity,[23] but any reader who compared his panegyric with previous acerbic treatments of the abolitionists could easily tell that "the times they are a-changing." Four years later, Martin Duberman, as editor of a collection of essays by various hands, *The Antislavery Vanguard*, made the same point with vastly more restraint and with strong effect. Duberman specifically rejected the stereotype of the abolitionist as a crank and a fanatic, and claimed for the antislavery movement an immense constructive value. No longer were abolitionists the irresponsible and bigoted men who brought disunion and civil war upon the country. Rather they were the defenders of freedom when none else would defend it.

This account of the literature of antislavery might be ex-

[23] See the important review of this book by C. Vann Woodward in *The American Scholar*, XXXI (1962), 318–36.

tended to include a discussion of biographies of Wendell Phillips by Irving H. Bartlett (1961—the best treatment), of Elijah P. Lovejoy by Merton L. Dillon (1961), of Thomas Wentworth Higginson by Mary Ann Wells (1963), of Lydia Maria Child by Helene G. Baer (1964—with some shortcomings), of John P. Hale by Richard H. Sewell (1965), of James Russell Lowell by Martin Duberman (1966), of Benjamin Lundy by Merton L. Dillon (1966), of Owen Lovejoy by Edward Magdol (1967), of Sarah and Angelina Grimke by Gerda Lerner (1967), and two 1963 biographies of William Lloyd Garrison, one by John L. Thomas, the other by Walter M. Merrill. Larry Gara's history of the fact and legend of the Underground Railroad, *The Liberty Line* (1961), should also be mentioned. Finally, it is important to note James M. MacPherson's *The Struggle for Equality* (1964), for Mac-Pherson followed the careers of the antislavery men into the era of Reconstruction and argued with considerable force that many of the leading abolitionists were not racists, did not hold the unrealistic view that all the slaves needed was to be set legally free, did not abandon the freedman to his fate, and were motivated by concern for the welfare of the blacks and not by neurotic anxiety concerning their own status.

Since MacPherson's book deals with Reconstruction, it may seem completely misguided of me to include it in a discussion of the literature concerning the background of the Civil War. But it is pertinent because MacPherson is one of the first writers who applied Nevins' idea that the main root of the conflict—whether the participants knew it or not—was the problem of "slavery *and* of the future position of the Negro race in North America." For almost a century, the histories of slavery had treated it as something unique, and either did not consider its relation to the broader practice of the subordination of the blacks, or even treated the subordination as one result of the stigma of slavery. So long as slavery was conceived to be central, the two main questions were: what did slavery have to do with causing the Civil War and how necessary was the war to the ending of slavery. But by the 1960's, it was beginning to be recognized that slavery was only a special form of racial subordination, and not everyone would even agree that it was the severest of all forms, though it was certainly one of the most complete. But if racial subordination was the essence, and slavery was only an overt form, then the question had to be restated: what did racial subordination have to do with causing the Civil War and how did the war impinge on racial subordination? Unless the war played a vital part in these connections, perhaps it was really not as important as people had imagined, and not worth all the controversy that had raged for a century.

To express this in another way, the war was certainly vital in the history of slavery, but it was not necessarily significant in the history of racism, except insofar as the end of slavery transformed the real social position of the blacks, which clearly it did not do. Perhaps as a result, the focus on the war began to be diffused. In a somewhat anomalous way, a more pervasive influence was attributed to slavery as social subordination, while at the same time it was recognized that, as chattel bondage, it constituted only one dimension of the more enduring problem of racial caste.

Thus, Thomas Jefferson came under fire. Jefferson had always been the South's symbol of its own intrinsic liberalism, and in the eyes of Southern liberals, Calhoun had only been an unfortunate aberration. But Leonard Levy in 1963, in a study of *Jefferson and Civil Liberties: The Darker Side*, pictured the great Democrat as repressive and illiberal in many important respects. A year later, Robert McColley, in *Slavery in Jeffersonian Virginia*, made the most sustained assault ever launched upon the long-standing legend that Jefferson and Virginia would have abolished slavery if they had only gotten around to it. Similarly, for a century, the nullification crisis was believed to have turned upon the tariff issue, but in 1966, William W. Freehling approached the question in a new way. In *Prelude to Civil War: The Nullification Controversy in South Carolina, 1816–1936* he advanced the theory that slavery underlay nullification.

Slavery is now being emphasized more than ever before, to the exclusion of economic and other sectional factors which once received major stress. However, it is not slavery as chattel servitude, but slavery as racial subordination. Leon Litwack's *North of Slavery: The Negro in the Free States, 1790–1860* (1964) showed conclusively that complete segregation, formalized discrimination, and belief in Negro inferiority prevailed throughout the states that fought for the Union in the Civil War. How could the Union victory mean a defeat for racism, when both of the antagonists were racists? William Stanton, *The Leopard's Spots: Scientific Attitudes Toward Race in America*, shows how ideas of Negro biological inferiority were supported by a widely accepted doctrine that the races of men were actually distinct species. Philip J. Stadenraus, *The African Colonization Movement, 1816–1865* (1961), showed to what a great extent the idea of sending freed slaves to Liberia meant in fact deporting Negroes to Africa.[24] Eugene F. Berwanger's *The Frontier Against Slavery: Western Anti-Negro Prejudice and the Slavery Extension Controversy* (1967) documented the antipathy toward Negroes which made so many Northern whites eager to keep them out of the territories. Finally, and perhaps most significant of all, David Brion Davis' ground-breaking *The Problem of Slavery in Western Culture* (1967) has shown the depth of the roots of ideological belief in slavery, and Winthrop Jordan's massive study, *White over Black: American Attitudes*

---

[24] Also see the essay by Frederic Bancroft on Lincoln's plans for colonization, in Jacob E. Cooke, *Frederic Bancroft, Historian* (1957).

Toward the Negro, 1550–1812 (1968), has noted the protracted duration and the pervasiveness of the rejection of the
Negro by American whites. On this long road, the Civil War
scarcely seemed more than a jog.

Increasingly in recent years, the period preceding the Civil
War has been discussed in terms of racism and the subordination of the Negro, rather than in terms of slavery alone, or
of the territorial issue. Ironically, this emphasis leaves the
explanation of the war even more remote than ever before.
The work of men like Litwack, Stanton, Stadenraus, Berwanger, and Jordan shows that the dominant forces in both
sections spurned and oppressed the Negro. Since this was true,
it is difficult to understand why the particular form which this
oppression took in the South should have caused acute tension, as it did, between the sections. Was it because Northerners hated and envied the aristocratic pretensions of the
slaveholders, but at the same time stood aloof from the slaves?
Was the South needlessly frightened into breaking up the
Union, and was the issue of union really much more vital
than we are now psychologically prepared to believe?

The overwhelming preoccupation with racial questions during the 1960's has to some extent diverted attention from
analytical explanations of the war. Despite this general shift
in focus away from what was for a time *the* central question
in American historiography, a few genuinely analytical approaches are still being taken. Two especially may be mentioned here. First, Barrington Moore's chapter "The American Civil War: the Last Capitalist Revolution" in his *Social
Origins of Dictatorship and Democracy* (1966), has been
written with remarkable cogency and decisiveness. Moore
argues that "the strictly economic issues were very probably
negotiable"; he also accepts the view that the Northern public did not care enough about slavery to fight for its overthrow.
As to conflict of interests, he regards the "tugging and haul-

ing and quarreling and grabbing" by diverse interest groups as chronic in any society, and therefore useless for diagnostic purposes in explaining a civil war. Generally, slavery was a form of capitalism, not inherently incompatible with industrial capitalism: "There is no abstract general reason why the North and South had to fight. Special historical circumstances, in other words, had to be present." The special historical circumstance which brought on a war, as Moore sees it, was the fact that the slave system was an obstacle "to a *particular kind* of capitalism at a specific historical stage." The South wanted a capitalism with fixed hierarchical status; the North wanted "a competitive democratic capitalism" and "was still committed to notions of equal opportunity," deriving from "the Puritan, American, and French Revolutions." It was impossible "to establish political and social institutions that would satisfy both" North and South. The Civil War was the last of several major nineteenth-century conflicts waged by the bourgeois against the landed classes.

In Moore, old ideas are echoed in a new, somewhat Marxian context. A second important interpretation, also Marxist, but not at all literal-minded in its Marxism, has appeared in Eugene D. Genovese, "Marxian Interpretations of the Slave South," in *Towards a New Past: Dissenting Essays in American History* (Barton J. Bernstein, editor, 1968). The heart of Genovese's argument is to be found in his critique of Moore. The fallacy in Moore, he contends, is the view that since both slavery and industry were forms of capitalism, there was therefore no necessary ground for conflict between them, in general terms, and that specific circumstances had to be invoked. But, says Genovese, while slavery may have partaken of the nature of capital, it "simultaneously extruded a ruling class with strong prebourgeois qualities and economic interests." In short, if industrialists and slaveholders were both capitalists, the resemblance was purely semantic and at an abstract level.

Concretely, they clashed partly because one group was bourgeois while the other, although not feudal (the distinction is brilliantly made), was prebourgeois.

Today, historians seem to have agreed on a good many points: that the North did not hate slavery enough to go to war about it; that slavery was too close to capitalism to justify the old antithesis of industrialism versus agrarianism; that the conflict of economic interests was negotiable and the conflict of civilizations was, to some extent, trumped up; that the power of the planters was real; that slavery was not a dying institution; and that the South was not a land primarily of Jeffersonian yeomen. Thus the "causes of the Civil War" remain moot.

Nevertheless, in every aspect, slavery was important. Economically, it was an immensely powerful property interest, somewhat inimical to the interests of free farming, because the independent farmer could not compete with the slave. Socially, it was the keystone of a static society of social hierarchy which challenged the dynamic, mobile, and equalitarian modes of life and labor that prevailed in the free states. Ideologically, it was a negation of the basic American principles of freedom and equality. It is futile to draw analytical distinctions between the slavery issue and (a) economic conflict of interest, (b) cultural incompatibilities, and (c) ideals as a social force. For the slavery issue was not, for explanatory purposes, an alternative to any of the others. It was part of the essence of all of them.[25]

[25] In this section, I have not discussed, but would like to call attention to, two articles which approach the question from the standpoint of the philosophy of history, focusing more on the theoretical concept of causation than on the historical explanation of "why the Civil War." One of these is Lee Benson and Cushing Strout, "Causation and the American Civil War: Two Appraisals," in *History and Theory*, I (1961), 163–85; the other, William Dray, "Some Causal Accounts of the American Civil War," with Comments by Newton Garver, in *Daedalus* (Summer, 1962), 578–98. Also, see Kenneth

FACTORS CONTRIBUTING TO THE CRISIS OF THE UNION

While general treatments of the coming of the war have formed the main focus of historical interpretation, there has also appeared, during the last thirty years, a remarkably extensive literature on all aspects of the sectional divergencies and sectional antagonisms which came to a crisis in 1860. The emphasis in this literature has shifted from a heavy stress upon the political and economic aspects to a broader treatment which continues to develop further analytical insights into political and economic themes, but which has also ranged out to a more comprehensive consideration of the nature of sectionalism and of the social, cultural, and ideological factors in the sectional cleavage.

In reviewing this specialized literature, I would like to note, first, that, because of the vast extent of it, I have felt constrained to omit (a) almost all periodical articles despite the importance of some of them, (b) unpublished dissertations, and (c) books which deal with the antebellum period but which do not deal specifically with the background of the Civil War. My discussion will divide the literature into two categories, treating (1) sectionalism and the South as a section and (2) specific episodes or developments in the mounting sectional crisis from 1820 to 1861.

Sectionalism and the South as a Section

Sectionalism involves the interplay of more or less opposing human groups, geographically set apart but operating within

Stampp's introduction to his collection of sources, *The Causes of the Civil War* (Englewood Cliffs, N.J., 1959); Thomas N. Bonner, "Civil War Historians and the Needless War Doctrine," *Journal of the History of Ideas*, XVII (1956), 193–216; and Edwin Rozwenc, "The Present Crisis in the Historical Explanation of the American Civil War," *The Causes of the American Civil War* (Boston: D. C. Heath, 1961), 225–30.

a common political organization. The understanding of sectionalism, therefore, involves an understanding of the forces involved in this adverse relationship. These forces, in the United States between 1830 and 1860, were, on the one hand, the development of "the South" as a distinctive, self-conscious entity, to some degree separable from the rest of the Union, and the development outside the South of an opposition to what the South conceived to be its interests, especially insofar as these interests were identified with the institution of slavery. Historians dispute whether the South was a conscious minority defending itself, or an aggressive slavocracy seeking to dominate the Union. They also disagree as to whether Northern opposition to the South sprang from an idealistic rejection of slavery as such, or from more subtle incompatibilities and more sordid motives of sectional advantage. But no matter how these questions are resolved, an understanding of sectionalism must depend upon an understanding first of what was intrinsic in the identity of the South, and how this intrinsic identity was brought into an adverse relationship with the region outside the South, a region which is less readily recognized as a section because it constituted a majority whose interests could therefore be made to coincide with the national interest.[26]

The importance of sectionalism has been recognized for a long time and some of its aspects were worked out many years ago in studies which still remain standard. For instance, on the institution of slavery, important studies which have not yet become dated were made for Missouri, North Carolina, Georgia, Mississippi, Alabama, Louisiana, and Ken-

[26] Merrill Jensen (ed.), *Regionalism in America* (Madison, Wis., 1951) contains essays by Fulmer Mood and Vernon Carstensen (5–98, 99–118) on the development of sectional-regional concepts, and an essay by Francis B. Simkins on "The South" (147–72).

tucky.[27] Similarly, on secession, Dwight L. Dumond's general treatment in 1931[28] and a number of state studies of long standing still remain unsuperseded: South Carolina, Missouri, Alabama, Virginia, Mississippi, Louisiana, and North Carolina.[29] Some of the major themes of Southern history were fully developed by William E. Dodd, who did all his significant work before 1920, and by Ulrich B. Phillips, who died in 1934. Phillips' views on slavery have been sharply challenged by Kenneth M. Stampp, but even Stampp does not question the fundamental importance of Phillips' *American Negro Slavery* (1918) and his studies of the antebellum economy and society (1929).[30] Lewis C. Gray's classic two-volume *History of Agriculture in the Southern United States to 1860* (1933) has never been approached as a final and comprehensive treatment of the pre-Civil War agricultural economy.

[27] Harrison A. Trexler, *Slavery in Missouri, 1804–1865* (Baltimore, 1914): Rosser H. Taylor, *Slaveholding in North Carolina: An Economic View* (Chapel Hill, 1926); Ralph B. Flanders, *Plantation Slavery in Georgia* (Chapel Hill, 1933); Charles S. Sydnor, *Slavery in Mississippi* (New York, 1933); Charles S. Davis, *The Cotton Kingdom in Alabama* (Montgomery, 1939); Roger W. Shugg, *Origins of Class Struggle in Louisiana* (Baton Rouge, 1939), Chaps. 1–5; John Winston Coleman, *Slavery Times in Kentucky* (Chapel Hill, 1940).

[28] *The Secession Movement, 1860–1861* (New York).

[29] Philip M. Hamer, *The Secession Movement in South Carolina, 1847–1852* (Allentown, Pa., 1918); Chauncey S. Boucher, *The Secession and Cooperation Movements in South Carolina, 1848–1852* (St. Louis, 1918); Walter H. Ryle, *Missouri: Union or Secession* (Nashville, 1931), Clarence P. Denman, *The Secession Movement in Alabama* (Montgomery, 1933); Henry T. Shanks, *The Secession Movement in Virginia, 1847–1861* (Richmond, 1934); Percy L. Rainwater, *Mississippi, Storm Center of Secession, 1856–1861* (Baton Rouge, 1938); Willie Malvin Caskey, *Secession and Restoration of Louisiana* (Baton Rouge, 1938); Joseph Carlyle Sitterson, *The Secession Movement in North Carolina* (Chapel Hill, 1939). Also, for Georgia, see Horace Montgomery, *Cracker Parties* (Baton Rouge, 1950).

[30] *Life and Labor in the Old South* (Boston) and numerous articles.

But without discounting the continuing importance of basic earlier works and interpretations, one can still note vast advances in the past three decades. Nothing illustrates this development more forcibly than the fact that nine volumes of a projected ten-volume History of the South have appeared since 1947. This important enterprise, edited by Wendell H. Stephenson and E. Merton Coulter, has included *The South in the Revolution, 1763–1789* (1957), by John R. Alden; *The Development of Southern Sectionalism, 1819–1848* (1948), by the late Charles S. Sydnor; and *The Growth of Southern Nationalism, 1848–1861* (1953), by Avery O. Craven. These volumes have done much to throw new light upon the nature of sectionalism. Alden's volume shows the emergence of conflict between North and South at a time when it has been assumed that the only significant sectional cleavage was on an East-West axis between coastal areas and frontier districts. To Alden it seemed justifiable to say that "by the end of the Revolutionary epoch . . . the South had emerged as a section and the Southerners as a people different from Northerners." [31] But these early sectional demarcations tended to disappear during the ascendancy of the Jeffersonian party, and Sydnor regarded the sectional factor as almost negligible as late as 1819. At that time, he wrote, the South still remained an "unawakened" area, where "regional differences had not borne the evil fruit of sectional bitterness" and where "perhaps it is anachronistic to speak of Southerners." [32] Sydnor then proceeded to trace the development of a really deep-seated sectionalism which grew up between the Missouri Controversy and the end of the Mexican War. His way of treating his theme was important in two ways especially. One

[31] Alden, *The South in the Revolution*, 2. See also Alden, *The First South* (Baton Rouge, 1961), which is perhaps the best account of early evidences of southern sectionalism.
[32] Sydnor, *The Development of Southern Sectionalism*, 32.

of these was his emphasis upon the idea that the South was not a region ruled by a high-handed planter aristocracy, but one in which democratic political and social forces were steadily increasing their dominance. The political aspects of this democracy have also been developed by Fletcher M. Green, both before and since Sydnor's contribution,[33] and the theme of social democracy has been intensively stressed through a series of census analyses by the late Frank L. Owsley, his wife, and his students, designed to show that plain nonslaveholding farmers occupied an important and respected place in the Southern social structure. These studies, begun before 1940, reached their fullest exposition in Owsley's *Plain Folk of the Old South*,[34] but the length to which he carried the argument had already provoked an adverse critique, closely and lengthily argued, by Fabian Linden in the *Journal of Negro History* in 1946.[35] It is ironical that, after a vast amount of intensive study by many scholars, the essential structure of society in the antebellum South still remains in dispute.

[33] Fletcher M. Green, *Constitutional Development in the South Atlantic States, 1776–1860* (Chapel Hill, 1930); "Democracy in the Old South," *Journal of Southern History*, XII (February, 1946), 3–23.

[34] Frank L. and Harriet C. Owsley, "The Economic Basis of Society in the Late Ante-Bellum South," *Journal of Southern History*, VII (February, 1940), 24–45; and "The Economic Structure of Rural Tennessee, 1850–1860," *ibid.*, VIII (May, 1942), 161–82. Blanche H. Clark, *The Tennessee Yeoman, 1840–1860* (Nashville, 1942). Harry L. Coles, Jr., "Some Notes on Slaveownership and Landownership in Louisiana, 1850–1860," *Journal of Southern History*, IX (August, 1943), 381–94. Herbert Weaver, *Mississippi Farmers, 1850–1860* (Nashville, 1945). Frank L. Owsley, *Plain Folk of the Old South* (Baton Rouge, 1949).

[35] Fabian Linden, "Economic Democracy in the Slave South: An Appraisal of Some Recent Views," *Journal of Negro History*, XXXI (April, 1949), 140–89. James C. Bonner, "Profile of a Late Ante-Bellum Community," *American Historical Review*, XLIX (July, 1944), 663–80. Both of these articles present data which indicate an undemocratic social structure.

The second important feature of Sydnor's work was its tracing of the rise of sectionalism in terms of cultural self-consciousness and psychological feelings of separateness. This concept was, of course, not original with him, but he developed and applied the idea with unusual effectiveness. Avery Craven, in the volume following Sydnor's, also traced the course of sectionalism in terms of psychological reactions to crucial events, such as the Kansas-Nebraska Act, which was used to arouse the North, although Southern opinion seemed relatively indifferent toward it, and John Brown's raid, which was crucial in the polarization of Southern feeling.

Along with emphasis upon psychological factors, there has also been a growing attention to the aspects of sectionalism which can be developed through the study of intellectual history. This is one of the phases of Southern history which has advanced most rapidly. As recently as 1940, probably the best treatments were a section in Parrington's *Main Currents of American Thought*, three chapters in Dodd's *Cotton Kingdom*, and one rather lonely monograph by William S. Jenkins, *Pro-Slavery Thought in the Old South*.[36] In 1940, however, Clement Eaton published his *Freedom of Thought in the Old South*, which traced the transition in the South from the liberalism of the Jeffersonian era to the conservatism of the time of Calhoun. Eaton found Southern defensiveness on the slavery question at the root of this conservative reaction, and he showed this same defensiveness leading to the imposition of an "intellectual blockade" to keep out all liberal or modern ideas. Only a year after Eaton, Joseph C. Robert's *The Road from Monticello* developed another aspect of this conservative theme by tracing the decline of the antislavery

[36] Vernon Louis Parrington, *Main Currents in American Thought* (3 vols.; New York, 1927–30), II, 1–179; William E. Dodd, *The Cotton Kingdom* (New Haven, 1919), 48–117; William S. Jenkins, *Pro-Slavery Thought in the Old South* (Chapel Hill, 1935).

movement in Virginia.[37] More recently, John Hope Franklin's *The Militant Smith*, 1800–1861 (1956) has shown still another phase of Southern defensiveness—the pugnacious temper of the antebellum South.

Study of the social philosophy of the South has centered upon two figures—George Fitzhugh and John C. Calhoun. Fitzhugh adopted the prevailing Southern argument that chattel slavery was less exploitative than "wage slavery," and carried this claim to its logical conclusion by contending that slavery was preferable for white as well as Negro workers.[38] His ideas never won any appreciable acceptance, but they have some significance in showing the implications of the ideal of a status society. This ideal found its leading champion in Calhoun, who was long regarded as a hair-splitting constitutional theoretician, but who has been appraised more recently as an important social thinker. A significant essay by Richard Hofstadter and an important three-volume biography by Charles M. Wiltse have served particularly to show Calhoun as a defender of the idea of an organic society with a fixed social order.[39]

[37] This study showed that the abolitionist attack on slavery was less instrumental than is commonly supposed in causing the South to swing to the defense of slavery.

[38] Harvey Wish, *George Fitzhugh: Propagandist of the Old South* (Baton Rouge, 1943); Louis Hartz, *The Liberal Tradition in America* (New York, 1955), Part IV, "The Feudal Dream of the South"; Arnaud B. Leavelle and Thomas I. Cook, "George Fitzhugh and the Theory of American Conservatism," *Journal of Politics*, VII (May, 1945), 145–68.

[39] John C. Calhoun, the Marx of the Master Class" in Richard Hofstadter, *The American Political Tradition and the Men Who Made It* (New York, 1948). Charles M. Wiltse, *John C. Calhoun* (3 vols.; Indianapolis, 1944–51). Margaret L. Coit, *John C. Calhoun, American Portrait* (Boston, 1950). Ralph H. Gabriel, *The Course of American Democratic Thought* (New York, 1940), 103–10. Louis Hartz, "South Carolina vs. the United States," in Daniel Aaron (ed.), *America in Crisis* (New York, 1952), 73–90. August O. Spain, *The Political*

While these writers have emphasized the conservative factor in Southern thought, others have stressed the importance
of romanticism in shaping the Southern mind. Wilbur J. Cash
in 1941 wrote a brilliant synthesis which was especially effective in showing how frontier strains of romanticism merged
with upper-class chivalric strains in forming a Southern romantic image of life.[40] In 1949, Rollin G. Osterweis published a study showing some of the ways in which the
romantic strain entered into the Southern nationalism of
the decade before secession.[41] Other studies, in the field of
literature, have also pointed up the importance of cultural
nationalism as a phase of Southern nationalism. Perhaps the
most important of these are Jay B. Hubbell's monumental
literary history of the South, a long essay by him on cultural
nationalism in the South, and a biography of William A.
Caruthers, by Curtis Carroll Davis, in which Davis shows how
the novels of Caruthers contributed to the South's image of
itself as the stronghold of the cavalier tradition.[42]

In the broad treatment of Southern thought and culture,

Theory of John C. Calhoun (New York, 1951). A new edition of
The Papers of John C. Calhoun has been launched and the first
volume, edited by the late Robert Lee Meriwether, appeared in 1959
(Columbia, S. C.). Two subsequent volumes have been edited by
W. Edwin Hemphill. Gerald M. Capers, John C. Calhoun—Oppor-
tunist (Lexington, Ky., 1960). Richard N. Current, John C. Calhoun
(New York, 1966). Current minimizes Calhoun's importance as a
political thinker—in this he reflects contemporary appraisals.

[40] The Mind of the South (New York).

[41] Romanticism and Nationalism in the Old South (New Haven).

[42] Jay B. Hubbell, The South in American Literature, 1607–1900
(Durham, 1954); Jay B. Hubbell, "Literary Nationalism in the Old
South" in David K. Jackson (ed.), American Studies in Honor of
William Kenneth Boyd (Durham, 1940); Curtis Carroll Davis,
Chronicler of the Cavaliers: A Life of the Virginia Novelist, Dr.
William A. Caruthers (Richmond, 1953). Also important in the
cultural history of the South is Mary C. Simms Oliphant, Alfred T.
Odell, and T. C. Duncan Eaves (eds.), The Letters of William
Gilmore Simms (5 vols.; Columbia, S.C., 1952–56).

the more recent notable works include those of Richard Beale Davis, *Intellectual Life in Jefferson's Virginia, 1790–1830* (1964), and Melvin M. Leiman, *Jacob N. Cardozo: Economic Thought in the Antebellum Years* (1966), which, as the title implies, is one of the few treatments of economic ideas in the Old South. William R. Taylor's *Cavalier and Yankee: The Old South and American National Character* (New York, 1961) has caught some of the most subtle psychological aspects of Southern sectional attitudes, and occupies a niche which no other item in the literature has quite claimed. Meanwhile, Clement Eaton retains his position as the foremost student of antebellum cultural and intellectual history. His books, *The Growth of Southern Civilization, 1790–1860* (1961) and *The Mind of the Old South* (1964)— the latter a series of sketches on the social thought of diverse Southern men of prominence—have filled out a dimension not covered by any other writers.

Although there has been more significant work on these new social and cultural themes than on slavery, secession, politics, and similar favored topics of earlier writers, these traditional areas of study continue to attract a share of able interpreters. The older state monographs on secession have been supplemented by two excellent studies of South Carolina: Harold S. Schultz, *Nationalism and Sectionalism in South Carolina, 1852–1860* (1950), and Charles E. Cauthen, *South Carolina Goes to War, 1860–1865* (1950). Schultz and Cauthen both argue that unionism and disunionism in this strategic Southern state were not coefficients of love or lack of love for the Union, but that they varied in direct proportion to Southern fears that antislavery would dominate the North. That is, unionism was a contingent value, relative to slavery, not an absolute value, reflecting only the intensity of patriotic feeling.

Also the older literature on the economy of the South has been enriched by the addition of important new studies on the staple crops, plantation agriculture, and the economics of slavery.[43] As for the institution of slavery, there have been four more full-scale monographs on slavery in the states of Alabama, Tennessee, Louisiana, and Arkansas,[44] and one of these, Chase C. Mooney's *Slavery in Tennessee*, has broken new ground by its intensive study of how slaveholding was related, statistically, to land tenure and to agricultural production. Also, John Hope Franklin has provided the first

[43] Joseph C. Robert, *The Tobacco Kingdom: Plantation, Market, and Factory in Virginia, 1800–1860* (Durham, 1938); J. H. Easterby (ed.), *The South Carolina Rice Plantation as Revealed in the Letters of Robert F. W. Allston* (Chicago, 1945); Albert V. House (ed.), *Plantation Management and Capitalism in Ante-Bellum Georgia: The Journal of Hugh Fraser Grant, Rice-grower* (New York, 1954); J. Carlyle Sitterson, *Sugar Country: The Cane Sugar Industry in the South, 1753–1950* (Lexington, Ky., 1953); Harold D. Woodman, *King Cotton and His Retainers* (Lexington, Ky., 1968); Cornelius O. Cathey, *Agricultural Developments in North Carolina* (Chapel Hill, 1956); Alfred G. Smith, Jr., *Economic Readjustment in an Old Cotton State: South Carolina, 1820–1860* (Columbia, S.C., 1958); John Hebron Moore, *Agriculture in Ante-Bellum Mississippi* (New York, 1958); James C. Bonner, *A History of Georgia Agriculture, 1732–1866* (Athens, Ga., 1964); William Kauffman Scarborough, *The Overseer: Plantation Management in the Old South* (Baton Rouge, 1966); Alfred H. Conrad and John R. Meyer, *The Economics of Slavery and Other Studies in Econometric History* (Chicago, 1964); Harold D. Woodman, *Slavery and the Southern Economy: Sources and Readings* (New York, 1966); Robert W. Vogel and Stanley L. Engerman (eds.), *The Reinterpretation of American Economic History*, Pt. 7, "The Economics of Slavery" (New York, 1968); Lewis E. Atherton, *The Southern Country Store, 1800–1860* (Baton Rouge, 1949).

[44] James B. Sellers, *Slavery in Alabama* (University, Ala., 1950); Chase C. Mooney, *Slavery in Tennessee* (Bloomington, 1957); Orville W. Taylor, *Negro Slavery in Arkansas* (Durham, 1958) Joe Gray Taylor, *Negro Slavery in Louisiana* (Baton Rouge, 1963). Also, at a more general level, see Rosser H. Taylor, *Ante-Bellum South Carolina* (Chapel Hill, 1942), and F. Garvan Davenport, *Ante-Bellum Kentucky* (Oxford, Ohio, 1943).

satisfactory general history of the Negro in America.[45] But the first major development in the historiography of slavery since Ulrich B. Phillips was Kenneth M. Stampp's *The Peculiar Institution,* an overall account, with its focus on the question: What was it like to be a slave? Stampp sees the harsh factors looming very large; he also believes that slavery was more profitable than is usually supposed, and that there was no chance that it would have fallen of its own weight, as some Southern historians have claimed.[46]

Since Stampp's treatment, the pace of historiography has quickened. Four years later, Stanley Elkins' *Slavery: A Problem in American Institutional Life* appeared. Elkins shifted the focus upon slavery from a social question to a psychological question. Instead of arguing as did Stampp that Negroes and whites were culturally interchangeable ("Negroes are, after all, only white men with black skins"), Elkins contended that slavery had acculturated the Negro in a differential way—had infantilized him, made him psychologically dependent, impaired his personality, converted him into the very obsequious, irresponsible Sambo which the Southern patriarchal legend depicted. Elkins' thesis lent itself to critical analysis on a number of points, including especially the extent to which Negroes who appeared to be Samboes were actually engaged in role-playing, without any real impairment of personality.

[45] *From Slavery to Freedom: A History of American Negroes* (New York, 1947; Rev. ed., 1956). But see also August Meier and Elliot M. Rudwick, *From Plantation to Ghetto: an Interpretive History of American Negroes* (New York, 1966).

[46] Kenneth M. Stampp, *The Peculiar Institution: Slavery in the Ante-Bellum South* (New York, 1956). The discovery that slavery was reasonably profitable is not original with Stampp, nor does he claim it to be. Lewis C. Gray and others have recognized the fact since 1930, but Stampp developed the significance of the profitability of slavery in indicating that the institution could not have been left to extinguish itself.

But before the questions raised by Elkins were ever resolved, the focus shifted again, this time to Eugene D. Genovese's *The Political Economy of Slavery*, published five years
after Elkins, in 1965. In brief, Genovese put old wine into
new bottles. He pointed to the curious dualism by which
Southern historians had portrayed the South either as a land
of agrarian small farmers or of capitalist planters engaged in
the commercial production of staple crops. But, he insisted,
"the slave South was neither a strange form of capitalism nor
an indefinable agrarianism, but a special civilization built on
the relationship of master to slave." If this sounded like a
revival of Southern apologetics, the resemblance was quickly
dispelled by the clear indications that Genovese was a Marxist
of his own independent kind, that he rejected racist doctrines
totally, and that he recognized the terrors as well as the
redeeming features of the mastery and dependence, which
have existed in many employer-employee relations, though
usually in a concealed or indirect fashion, and not in the
naked, inescapable form which characterized the relation of
master to slave. More recently, Genovese has further under-
scored the independent nature of his position by asserting
that slaves in the Southern states were far less prone to rebellion than those in other parts of the Americas, and by giving
unorthodox explanations for this phenomenon.[47]

As one turns from the internal analysis of antebellum
Southern society to the study of aspects of sectional friction,
it appears that studies of state-by-state secession, or other
political accounts, are less prevalent than in the past. Nonetheless, the last decade has witnessed two very searching
studies of the impact of sectional strife in causing divisions

[47] For further comment on Genovese, see Chapter VI; also see two
articles by Genovese, "The Legacy of Slavery and the Roots of Black
Nationalism," in *Studies on the Left*, VI (1966), 3–26, and "Rebel-
liousness and Docility in the Negro Slave: A Critique of the Elkins
Thesis," in *Civil War History*, XIII (1967), 293–314.

within the churches. One of these is Ernest T. Thompson, *Presbyterians in the South*, I, 1607–1861 (1963); the other, Donald G. Mathews, *Slavery and Methodism: A Chapter in American Morality*, 1780–1845 (1965). Also, new techniques in political science have stimulated two studies of the relative cohesion of sections and of parties during the antebellum period. One of these is Joel H. Silbey, *The Shrine of Party: Congressional Voting Behavior*, 1841–1852 (1967); the other, Thomas B. Alexander's *Sectional Stress and Party Strength* (1968). Both of these works employ roll call analysis, and they undoubtedly give a precision to political history which it has hitherto lacked; both seem to show that party affiliations had a stronger cohesive effect than sectional ones—in other words, that sectionalism was not as dominant a force as some have supposed. But critics have expressed some cogent doubts about how far one can rely on this kind of data in evaluating the cohesive force of sectional loyalties.[48]

A century after the Civil War, the development of sectional forces has now been examined in immense detail. More than a generation ago, the conflict in the political and constitutional arena over specific sectional issues had already been worked out quite fully. More recently, the cultural and psychological aspects of Southernism have received greater attention. Thus, the most important recent advances have occurred in establishing the character of the section rather than in recounting its conflicts. With all the analysis that has gone into the interpretation of the cultural factors, however, great disagreement still exists as to the extent to which the Old South was democratic or aristocratic in its regime. Doubt also surrounds the question whether cultural affinity or common interests maintained in common defense against the North were primary in creating a sense of Southern unity. On

[48] See review by Charles G. Sellers in *American Historical Review*, LXXIII (1967), 231.

the one hand, there is no doubt that staple-crop agriculture, biracialism, and a status society shaped a distinctive way of life for the South, but, on the other, the so-called cultural nationalism of the South had a certain thinness about it which suggests that instead of a real Southern nationalism producing friction with the North, friction with the North may have produced the figment of nationalism. In this sense, it is perhaps unfortunate that the theme of conflict of interest tends to be neglected by cultural historians. Years ago studies of the commercial conventions which were held in the South, and of the economic aspects of sectionalism showed that the economic grievances of the South, and the growing economic disparities between it and the North, were accompanied by expressions of militant Southernism.[49] But, except for a study by Robert R. Russel of the sectional conflict over the building of a Pacific railroad,[50] there has been relatively little analysis of the economic aspects of sectionalism for many years. Far the most significant general economic study of the period of recent date is George R. Taylor's *The Transportation Revolution, 1815–1860* (1951). This volume does a masterly job of depicting the economic transformation which strengthened the links between the Northeast and the West at the expense of the South, and indeed it shows the

[49] The principal studies were Robert Royal Russel, *Economic Aspects of Southern Sectionalism, 1840–1861* (Urbana, Ill., 1924); John G. Van Deusen, *Economic Bases of Disunion in South Carolina* (New York, 1928); John G. Van Deusen, *The Ante-Bellum Southern Commercial Conventions* (Durham, 1926); Herbert Wender, *Southern Commercial Conventions, 1837–1859* (Baltimore, 1930).

[50] Expansion to the Pacific brought with it a prolonged rivalry, partly between sections, partly between commercial centers in the Mississippi Valley, for control of the eastern terminus of an overland route or railroad to the Pacific coast. This rivalry, an important phase of sectional and economic history, is fully analyzed in Robert R. Russel, *Improvement of Communication to the Pacific Coast as an Issue in American Politics, 1783–1864* (Cedar Rapids, 1948).

creation of the economic basis for a more consolidated Union. But it pays relatively little attention to the sectional reactions to these developments, or to the effects of differential rates of sectional growth in accentuating sectionalism. Without taking these factors into account, it is difficult to know whether Southernism was primarily generated from the inside by factors and feelings of cultural affinity or induced from the outside by economic rivalries and by Southern feelings of shared disadvantage and danger.

The Mounting Sectional Crisis

Along with a study of the opposing sectional forces, any study of the background of the Civil War must also take account of the long series of developments which marked the increase of sectional tension, mounting steadily until the bonds of union snapped in 1860–61. These developments include the Missouri Controversy of 1820, the Tariff and Nullification Controvery of 1832, the contest over the annexation of Texas between 1836 and 1844, the struggle over the status of slavery in the territory acquired from Mexico—beginning with the Wilmot Proviso in 1846 and ending with the Compromise of 1850—the resistance in the North to the Fugitive Slave Act, the repeal of the Missouri Compromise by the Kansas-Nebraska Act in 1854, the chronic violence which became known as Bleeding Kansas, the Dred Scott decision, the Lincoln-Douglas debates, John Brown's Raid at Harpers Ferry, the election of Lincoln, the secession of the Lower South, the formation of the Southern Confederacy, and the outbreak of hostilities at Fort Sumter.

All of these events have received intensive study. Some of them were investigated so thoroughly many years ago that little of significance has been added in the last score of years; for instance, this is largely true of John Brown's raid. But others have been the objects of new research—sometimes with results that have required drastic reinterpretation.

The Missouri Controversy, to begin with, has been re-examined by Glover Moore.[51] In addition to giving a fuller account than was previously available, Moore has shown that the majority of Southern congressmen did not vote for the line 36° 30' as a boundary to divide the Louisiana Purchase between freedom and slavery. Since there was no acceptance of the settlement by both contesting groups, there was no compromise in the true sense. Hence it was not entirely accurate to say that a "solemn compact" had been violated when the 36° 30' line was repealed thirty-four years later.

On the sectional rivalries for the period after the Missouri Compromise and before the Compromise of 1850, many of the most useful interpretive treatments have appeared in biographies. These include not only the definitive studies of Calhoun by Wiltse and of J. Q. Adams by Bemis, mentioned above, but also a life of Sam Houston which for the first time treats fully his career after the annexation of Texas, two full-scale studies of John Tyler, and thorough, scholarly accounts of Silas Wright, Millard Fillmore, and John Bell. Charles G. Sellers has now published the first two volumes of a life of James K. Polk, dealing with his career up to 1846. There have been two lives of Zachary Taylor, by Brainerd Dyer and by Holman Hamilton (the latter discussed below), and two of Thomas Hart Benton, by William N. Chambers and by Elbert B. Smith, of which the former is more broadly concerned with Benton's times while the latter is more a personal portrait. Biographies of Andrew Stevenson, George Bancroft, William L. Marcy, and John Bigelow are in many instances just as significant historically as the lives of the major figures. On Henry Clay and Daniel Webster, the earlier full-scale

[51] *The Missouri Controversy, 1819–1821* (Lexington, Ky., 1953).

biographies by Glyndon G. Van Deusen (1937) and by Claude Fuess (1930), respectively, remain the standard works, but Clement Eaton and Richard Current have written valuable brief, interpretive lives of these two men, and the University of Kentucky Press has begun publication of a definitive edition of the writings of Clay, under the editorship of James F. Hopkins and Mary Wilma Hargreaves. There has been no good overall biography of Van Buren, though Robert V. Remini has provided a thorough treatment of a crucial stage of his career between 1821 and 1828.[52] The most recent summing up of the period, and a notably judicious one, is Glyndon G. Van Deusen's *The Jacksonian Era, 1828–1848* (1959).

On the expansionist drive to make the United States a transcontinental republic—a drive which brought sectional rivalries into sharp focus—significant new contributions have been limited. One of the most important is Norman A.

[52] Llerena Friend, *Sam Houston, The Great Designer* (Austin, 1954); Oliver P. Chitwood, *John Tyler, Champion of the Old South* (New York, 1939); Robert Seager, *And Tyler Too: A Biography of John and Julia Gardiner Tyler* (New York, 1963); John A. Garraty, *Silas Wright* (New York, 1949); Robert J. Rayback, *Millard Fillmore: Biography of a President* (Buffalo, 1959); Joseph Parks, *John Bell of Tennessee* (Baton Rouge, 1950); Charles G. Sellers, *James K. Polk* (2 vols.; Princeton, 1957, 1966); Brainerd Dyer, *Zachary Taylor* (Baton Rouge, 1946); Holman Hamilton, *Zachary Taylor* (2 vols.; Indianapolis, 1941–51); William N. Chambers, *Old Bullion Benton, Senator from the New West: Thomas Hart Benton* (Boston, 1956); Elbert B. Smith, *Magnificent Missourian: The Life of Thomas Hart Benton* (Philadelphia, 1958); Francis F. Wayland, *Andrew Stevenson: Democrat and Diplomat, 1785–1857* (Philadelphia, 1949); Russell B. Nye, *George Bancroft, Brahmin Rebel* (New York, 1944); Ivor D. Spencer, *The Victor and the Spoils: A Life of William L. Marcy* (Providence, 1959); Margaret A. Clapp, *Forgotten First Citizen: John Bigelow* (Boston, 1947); Clement Eaton, *Henry Clay and the Art of American Politics* (Boston, 1957); Richard N. Current, *Daniel Webster and the Rise of National Conservatism* (Boston, 1955); Robert V. Remini, *Martin Van Buren and the Making of the Democratic Party* (New York, 1959).

Graebner's *Empire on the Pacific* (1955), which challenges the long-standing tradition of agrarian expansionism by arguing that the desire of Eastern commercial interests to control Pacific coastal ports was an important factor in Manifest Destiny. Next to this in importance, perhaps, is a study by James C. N. Paul of the effects of the expansion question in causing a split, which was later covered up but never healed, between the Polk and the Van Buren wings of the Democratic Party at the Baltimore Convention in 1844.[53] The ultimate result of this split was the Wilmot Proviso, which deadlocked the proslavery and antislavery parties and prevented the organization of the territories for four years. This episode has long called for effective monographic treatment, and has at last received able attention in Chaplain W. Morrison, *Democratic Politics and Sectionalism: The Wilmot Proviso Controversy* (1967).

The development of the Free Soil movement at this time was centered very much in Massachusetts, and the intricate developments in that state have been admirably recorded in four recent books: Donald's *Sumner*, mentioned above, Martin Duberman's *Charles Francis Adams* (1961), Frank Otto Gatell's *John Gorham Palfrey and the New England Conscience* (1963), and Kinley J. Brauer, *Cotton Versus Conscience: Massachusetts Whig Politics and Southwestern Expansion* (1963).

All the sectional friction of the 1840's came to a head in

[53] Paul, *Rift in the Democracy* (Philadelphia, 1951). Perhaps the severest critic of the expansionist politics of the Polk administration is Richard R. Stenberg. See, for instance, his "Intrigue for Annexation," *Southwest Review*, XXV (October, 1939), 58–69. A significant footnote to the election of 1844 is provided in Edwin Miles's " 'Fifty-Four Forty or Fight'—an American Political Legend," *Mississippi Valley Historical Review*, XLIV (September, 1957), 291–309. Miles shows that the slogan was not used in the campaign and actually "did not gain currency until approximately one year after Polk's inauguration."

the first session of Congress after Zachary Taylor's inauguration, when North and South fought over the question of
the status of slavery in the Mexican Cession, and emerged
with the compromise of 1850.[54] By 1940, the history of the
compromise had already been worked and reworked; historians
had recognized the importance of Stephen A. Douglas, rather
than Henry Clay, in getting the compromise adopted; and
an article by Herbert D. Foster had convinced most historians
that disunion was really imminent when the compromise was
enacted.[55] But the finality of these conclusions, like the finality
of the compromise itself, was advertised prematurely. Since
then, Holman Hamilton, in an important series of journal articles, later summarized in a book, and in his biography

[54] On the Mexican War itself, rather than its causes, four recent
treatments are Bernard De Voto, *The Year of Decision, 1846*
(Boston, 1943); Alfred Hoyt Bill, *Rehearsal for Conflict: The War
with Mexico, 1846–1848* (New York, 1947); Robert Selph Henry,
The Story of the Mexican War (Indianapolis, 1950), and Otis A.
Singletary, *The Mexican War* (Chicago, 1960). On the later stages
of filibustering and Southern expansionism during the Pierce administration, there have been no major contributions in the past
two decades, but the following have added important information
on this phase of Manifest Destiny: Ollinger Crenshaw, "The Knights
of the Golden Circle," *American Historical Review*, XLVII (October, 1941), 23–50; C. A. Bridges, "The Knights of the Golden
Circle: A Filibustering Fantasy," *Southwestern Historical Quarterly*, XLIV (January, 1941), 287–302; Robert F. Durden, "J. D. B.
De Bow: Convolutions of a Slavery Expansionist," *Journal of
Southern History*, XVII (November, 1951), 441–61; Basil Rauch,
American Interests in Cuba: 1848–1855 (New York, 1948); and a
series of articles in various periodicals by C. Stanley Urban on Southern attitudes and activities in connection with filibustering.

[55] George D. Harmon, "Douglas and the Compromise of 1850,"
Journal of the Illinois State Historical Society, XXI (January, 1929),
453–99. George Fort Milton, *The Eve of Conflict: Stephen A. Douglas and the Needless War* (Boston, 1934), 75–78. Frank H. Hodder,
"The Authorship of the Compromise of 1850," *Mississippi Valley Historical Review*, XXII (March, 1936), 525–36. Herbert D. Foster,
"Webster's Seventh of March Speech and the Secession Movement,
1850," *American Historical Review*, XXVII (January, 1922), 245–70.

of Zachary Taylor, has told the story of the Compromise anew.[56] His brilliant analysis proves two important facts: first, that there was not a majority supporting the compromise as such, but only a minority which secured adoption by garnering votes alternatively from Northern ranks or from Southern ranks for specific measures which, in composite, made up the compromise; and second, that the interests of the holders of Texas bonds were strategic in securing adoption. Hamilton also advanced an important argument: he contended that the South would not have seceded in 1850, and that Zachary Taylor's unyielding policy was better than compromise. If Hamilton's presentation does not prove this contention, it certainly reopens the question.

Less than four years after the Compromise, the Kansas-Nebraska Act released the sectional furies again. This episode, too, has caused floods of ink to be shed. By 1940, the historical tides in this perennial dispute were running in favor of Stephen A. Douglas. Defenders of Douglas denied that he had been motivated by Presidential ambition, and they stressed the importance of his purpose to open the West, as well as the truly democratic character of his proposal to use the principle of popular sovereignty in settling the status of slavery in the territories.[57] Since 1940, battle over Douglas

[56] "Democratic Senate Leadership and the Compromise of 1850," *Mississippi Valley Historical Review*, XLI (December, 1954), 403–18. "The 'Cave of the Winds' and the Compromise of 1850," *Journal of Southern History*, XXIII (August, 1957), 331–53. "Texas Bonds and Northern Profits: A Study in Compromise, Investment, and Lobby Influence," *Mississippi Valley Historical Review*, XLIII (March, 1957), 579–94; *Prologue to Conflict: the Crisis and Compromise of 1850* (Lexington, Ky., 1964). For a precise analysis of the provisions on slavery in the Compromise, which have been handled loosely by many historians, see Robert R. Russel, "What was the Compromise of 1850?" *Journal of Southern History*, XXII (August, 1956), 292–309.
[57] Frank H. Hodder, "The Railroad Background of the Kansas-Nebraska Act," *Mississippi Valley Historical Review*, XII (June, 1925),

has continued. Allan Nevins in *Ordeal of the Union* provided an excellent critique of previous interpretations of Douglas' motives. He himself interpreted Douglas in terms which emphasized his vigor and ability, but pictured him as insincere, coarse, and casuistical.[58] But this verdict gained no more universal acceptance than previous ones, and in 1959, Gerald M. Capers, in a new biography of Douglas, depicted the Little Giant as a true nationalist who has been the historical victim of personal slander at the hands of self-righteous leaders of the antislavery movement.[59] Meanwhile James C. Malin has advanced the hypothesis that, in a larger sense, Douglas, with his localistic principle of popular sovereignty, was fighting the centralizing forces of industrialization. Malin also contended that developments had made the issue of slavery on the Missouri frontier obsolete and that Douglas was striving to avoid it, but that sectionalists, eager for a fight, forced it into Douglas' bill.[60] A particularly able historiographical article by Roy F. Nichols has further demonstrated how completely Douglas was swept away from his original purpose.[61] Thus, by an irony, Douglas now appears as the key figure in the adoption of the Compromise of 1850, which was traditionally identified with Clay, and not as the real creator of the Kansas-Nebraska Act, with which his name has always been linked.

3–22. Beveridge, *Abraham Lincoln, 1809–1858* (4 vols.), III, 187. Milton, *The Eve of Conflict*, 114–54. Craven, *The Coming of the Civil War*, 328–32.

[58] *Ordeal of the Union*, II, 11, 101, 102–106, 143–44, 422–23.

[59] *Stephen A. Douglas, Defender of the Union* (Boston), 72–77, 231.

[60] Malin, *The Nebraska Question, 1852–1854* (Lawrence, Kan., 1953).

[61] "The Kansas-Nebraska Act: A Century of Historiography," *Mississippi Valley Historical Review*, XLIII (September, 1956), 187–212. Also, in *Blueprints for Leviathan* (New York, 1963) Nichols has given a full account of the parliamentary struggle over Kansas–Nebraska, especially in the House.

The strife in Kansas which followed the Kansas-Nebraska Act presents a confused and much controverted story. Recent scholarship suggests that much of the aggressive activity in the new territory resulted from competition for land, and that the settlers were not motivated solely by their opposing convictions on the subject of slavery—a subject which was extremely abstract for most of them.[62] In a literature which often reflects the confusion of the subject itself, two recent works are outstanding for their clarity. Samuel A. Johnson has written a history which for the first time arrives at the truth, lying between proslavery accusations and antislavery evasions, about the role of the New England Emigrant Aid Society in the Kansas crusade.[63] James C. Malin, in *John Brown and the Legend of Fifty-Six* (1942), has applied the rigorous pruning hook of historical method to the luxuriant growth of unsupported assertion about John Brown in Kansas. The residue of fact which remains presents such startling contrasts to the legend that Malin's study has value, apart from the Kansas question, as a case study in historical method.

Three years after the Kansas-Nebraska Act, the Supreme Court, in the Dred Scott case, declared that the Missouri Compromise had been null from the beginning. Since the justices held that Scott was not eligible to bring his plea to court in any case, there was no clear necessity for them to decide about the applicability of the Missouri Compromise to his case. Consequently, historians have wrestled ever since with the question why the justices went out of their way— if they did go out of their way—to rule on this explosive question. Antislavery tradition regarded their act simply as another illustration of the aggressiveness of the slavocracy. In

[62] See discussion in Craven, *The Coming of the Civil War*, 362–65, with citations to Paul Wallace Gates and James C. Malin.
[63] *The Battle Cry of Freedom: The New England Emigrant Aid Company in the Kansas Crusade* (Lawrence, Kan., 1954). Also see Alice Nichols, *Bleeding Kansas* (New York, 1954).

1933, however, F. H. Hodder advanced the argument, widely accepted since then, that two Northern justices, McLean and Curtis, forced the reluctant Southerners to a broad decision by writing dissenting opinions in which they asserted, at length, the constitutionality of the act of 1820.[64] But in 1950, Allan Nevins included a close analysis of the Dred Scott case in his *The Emergence of Lincoln*. In this critique, he advanced strong proof that the Southern justices were already prepared for a broad decision before McLean and Curtis took their positions. Nevins also showed that while there is no proof of collusion in the decision, as Republicans at the time asserted, there is evidence of marked impropriety in the communication between James Buchanan and the members of the Court before the decision was rendered.[65] Perhaps the fullest discussion of the Dred Scott decision is in Vincent C. Hopkins, *Dred Scott's Case* (1951).

For the period from the Dred Scott decision to the crisis at Fort Sumter, a number of excellent studies have filled out the historical picture without substantially modifying the prevalent interpretations. Paul M. Angle has published an edition of the complete text of the Lincoln-Douglas debates, with admirable editorial background.[66]

On John Brown's raid, no new insight into Brown himself has been as important as Avery Craven's demonstration of the psychological impact of the raid in precipitating Southern sectional feelings, which had never been as "solid" as Southern sectionalists wished and Northern sectionalists feared.[67]

[64] Frank H. Hodder, "Some Phases of the Dred Scott Case," *Mississippi Valley Historical Review*, XVI (June, 1929), 3–22.

[65] *The Emergence of Lincoln*, I, 90–118; II, 473–77.

[66] Angle (ed.), *Created Equal? The Complete Lincoln-Douglas Debates of 1858* (Chicago, 1958).

[67] Craven, *The Growth of Southern Nationalism*, 303–11. Joseph C. Furnas, *The Road to Harpers Ferry* (New York, 1959), is an account of the antislavery movement in general, with special attention to Brown. Also see Herbert Aptheker, *American Negro Slave Revolts* (New York, 1943).

On the election of Lincoln, Reinhard H. Luthin, *The First Lincoln Campaign* (1944), and Ollinger Crenshaw, *The Slave States in the Presidential Election of 1860* (1945), have superseded an older study by Emerson D. Fite.[68]

On the secession of the Lower South, most of the political record, at least, was worked out more than thirty years ago.[69] On the Northern reaction to secession, however, interest has been more active. Philip Foner's *Business and Slavery: The New York Merchants and the Irrepressible Conflict* (Chapel Hill, 1941) showed the strong support for compromise in the New York financial community. This showed an influential but limited segment of opinion, but Howard C. Perkins' two volumes of *Northern Editorials on Secession* (1942), revealed more clearly than ever before the full range and complexity of Northern responses to the issue of disunion. Perkins' materials have not yet been adequately used, and attention has focused on the policy of the Lincoln administration during the secession crisis. Did Lincoln want war with the South? Did he accept it as necessary? Or did he hope to avert it? All three views have been maintained. The first view was ably argued by Charles W. Ramsdell in 1937 and was overstated by a Montgomery attorney, John Shipley Tilley, in 1941, in a demonstrably fallacious way which may have caused a reaction against it.[70] The second was held by Kenneth M. Stampp in *And the War Came* in 1950. I argued the third in 1942 in a study which contended that Northern rejection of compromise resulted in part from an unrealistic belief that threats of seces-

[68] Fite, *The Presidential Campaign of 1860* (New York, 1911).

[69] But see the analysis of the personnel of Southern secession conventions by Ralph A. Wooster, in various state periodicals, summarized in his *The Secession Conventions of the South* (Princeton, 1963). Also note references to the studies by Schultz and Cauthen on South Carolina, mentioned previously.

[70] Ramsdell, "Lincoln and Fort Sumter," *Journal of Southern History*, III (August, 1937), 259–88. Tilley, *Lincoln Takes Command* (Chapel Hill, 1941).

sion were not serious, as well as from a completely realistic observation that the South was not united (eight slave states were still in the Union two months after the formation of the Southern Confederacy).[71] I argued that Lincoln planned to avoid a showdown, and to await a unionist reaction in the South, but that the unforeseen necessity of feeding Major Anderson's garrison at Fort Sumter frustrated his plan. Richard N. Current, in *Lincoln and the First Shot* (1963), has taken a view similar to Stampp's, but has added an emphasis on the fact that, in any case, the first blow was struck not by Lincoln but by the Confederates. For further discussion of this issue see Chapter IX below. Also, for a vivid general—but detailed—account of the period just before the war, see Bruce Catton, *The Coming Fury* (1961), the first volume of his centennial history of the Civil War.

In the history of the final stages of the crisis, as in the general record of this entire period, much of the most valuable historical work appears in studies of particular men. This is true for the Buchanan administration in Philip Shriver Klein's biography *President James Buchanan* (1962), and for the compromise efforts in Albert D. Kirwan's *John J. Crittenden: The Struggle for the Union* (1962), as well as in a study of the Washington Peace Conference by Robert Gray Gunderson, *Old Gentlemen's Convention* (Madison, 1961). Two volumes of essays, *Politics and the Crisis of 1860*, (1961) edited by Norman A. Graebner, and *The Crisis of the Union, 1860–1861* (1965), edited by George H. Knoles, also concentrate on the last months of crisis. But some of the best treatment is still to be found in studies of Abraham Lincoln, whose life has always been a focus for examining the civil conflict.

There was already a staggeringly large body of literature on Lincoln thirty years ago, but this has now been supple-

[71] Potter, *Lincoln and His Party in the Secession Crisis* (New Haven, 1942).

mented by four additional contributions of vital importance. In 1939 Carl Sandburg published his epic account of the war years, a work of great sweep and imagination and, incidentally, the longest biography—together with the earlier *The Prairie Years*—of any American.[72] In 1945, James G. Randall published the first two volumes of a four-volume study which, for the first time, gave a full, scholarly account of the problems and policies of Lincoln's Presidency.[73] In 1952, Benjamin P. Thomas published a one-volume biography which was a model of historical conciseness and balance.[74] In 1953, the Rutger's University Press issued Roy P. Basler's eight-volume edition of Lincoln's writings—a great advance over the previous edition by Nicolay and Hay which had been far from complete and not entirely accurate.[75] Other biographies for this period included, before 1960, on the Southern side, Lillian A. Kibler's life of Benjamin F. Perry, Robert D. Meade's study of Judah P. Benjamin, Rudolph von Abele's life of Alexander H. Stephens, and Hudson Strode's uncritical and excessively laudatory life of Jefferson Davis.[76] Since 1960,

[72] *Abraham Lincoln: The War Years* (4 vols.; New York, 1939.) *Abraham Lincoln: The Prairie Years* (2 vols.; New York, 1926).

[73] *Lincoln, the President: Springfield to Gettysburg* (New York).

[74] *Abraham Lincoln: A Biography* (New York). Two other books which are very important for the historical interpretation of Lincoln are Donald, *Lincoln Reconsidered*, and Richard N. Current, *The Lincoln Nobody Knows* (New York, 1958).

[75] Basler, *The Collected Works of Abraham Lincoln* (New Brunswick, 1953; Index, 1955). Other significant titles on Lincoln include the items by Jaffa and Fehrenbacher, mentioned above, and also Donald W. Riddle's *Lincoln Runs for Congress* (New Brunswick, N.J., 1948) and *Congressman Abraham Lincoln* (Urbana, 1957); William E. Baringer, *Lincoln's Rise to Power* (Boston, 1937); William B. Hesseltine, *Lincoln and the War Governors* (New York, 1948); and Reinhard H. Luthin, *The Real Abraham Lincoln* (Englewood Cliffs, N.J., 1960).

[76] Kibler, *Benjamin F. Perry, South Carolina Unionist* (Durham, 1946); Meade, *Judah P. Benjamin, Confederate Statesman* (New York, 1943); von Abele, *Alexander H. Stephens* (New York, 1946); Strode, *Jefferson Davis* (3 vols.; New York, 1955, 1959).

Ben H. Proctor has added a life of John H. Reagan (1962), William Y. Thompson has written about Robert Toombs (1966), F. N. Boney about John Letcher (1966), and Lillian Pereyra about James L. Alcorn (1966). Frontis Johnston has ably edited the papers of Zebulon B. Vance (1963), and Glenn Tucker has published a life of Vance (1965).

On the Northern side, more than a decade ago we had lives of John C. Frémont by Allan Nevins, of Thurlow Weed and of Horace Greeley by Glyndon G. Van Deusen, of Henry J. Raymond by Francis Brown, of Nathaniel P. Banks by Fred H. Harrington, of Salmon P. Chase and his family by Thomas G. and Marva R. Belden, of Gideon Welles by Richard S. West, Jr., of Simon Cameron by Lee Crippen, of Francis Lieber by Frank Freidel, of Edwin M. Stanton by Fletcher Pratt, of Lewis Cass by Frank B. Woodford, of John Wentworth by Don Edward Fehrenbacher, and a study of Greeley and the Republican Party by Jeter A. Isely.[77]

During the sixties, biographers have given us lives not only of Robert J. Walker and Charles Francis Adams, but of four of Lincoln's cabinet members (William H. Seward, Edwin Stanton, Edward Bates and Simon Cameron) and five senators who were prominent in the pre-war and war periods (William P. Fessenden, Charles Sumner, B. Gratz Brown, Lyman

[77] Nevins, *Frémont, Pathmaker of the West* (New York, 1955); Van Deusen, *Thurlow Weed, Wizard of the Lobby* (Boston, 1947); Van Deusen, *Horace Greeley, Nineteenth-Century Crusader* (Philadelphia, 1953); Brown, *Raymond of the Times* (New York, 1951); Harrington, *Fighting Politician: Major General N. P. Banks* (Philadelphia, 1948); Belden, *So Fell the Angels* (Boston, 1956); Pratt, *Stanton, Lincoln's Secretary of War* (New York, 1953); West, *Gideon Welles, Lincoln's Navy Department* (Indianapolis, 1943); Crippen, *Simon Cameron: Ante-Bellum Years* (Oxford Ohio, 1942); Freidel, *Francis Lieber, Nineteenth Century Liberal* (Baton Rouge, 1947); Woodford, *Lewis Cass, the Last Jeffersonian* (New Brunswick, 1950); Fehrenbacher, *Chicago Giant: A Biography of "Long John" Wentworth* (Madison, Wis., 1957); Isely, *Horace Greeley and the Republican Party, 1853–1861* (Princeton, 1947).

Trumbull, and Benjamin F. Wade).[78] The works on Adams, Seward, and Stanton were of outstanding importance.

The literature on all the varied questions which impinge directly or indirectly upon the Civil War is so vast that it almost defies the effort to view it together in any one focus. Perhaps the most pervasive quality which it all has in common is that it continues to be explicitly or implicitly controversial. Not only have historians failed to agree as to whether slavery furnished the basic motive for the war or whether it provided a smoke screen for concealing the basic motives; they have also disagreed as to the nature of the society of the Old South, the nature of slavery, the motivation and character of the antislavery movement, and the interpretation of every link in the chain of sectional clashes which preceded the final crisis. The irony of this disagreement lies in the fact that it persists in the face of vastly increased factual knowledge and constantly intensified scholarly research. The discrepancy, indeed, is great enough to make apparent a reality about history which is seldom so self-evident as it is here: namely that factual mastery of the data alone does not neces-

[78] James P. Shenton, *Robert John Walker: A Politician from Jackson to Lincoln* (New York, 1961); Martin Duberman, *Charles Francis Adams, 1807–1886* (Boston, 1961); Glyndon G. Van Deusen, *William Henry Seward* (New York, 1967); Benjamin P. Thomas and Harold Hyman, *Stanton: The Life and Times of Lincoln's Secretary of War* (New York, 1962); Marvin R. Cain, *Lincoln's Attorney General: Edward Bates of Missouri* (Columbia, Mo., 1965); Erwin Stanley Bradley, *Simon Cameron, Lincoln's Secretary of War: A Political Biography* (Philadelphia, 1966); Charles A. Jellison, *Fessenden of Maine: Civil War Senator* (Syracuse, N.Y., 1962—Fessenden was, of course, also a cabinet member, but for the period treated in this paper he was a senator); David Donald, *Charles Sumner and the Coming of the Civil War* (New York, 1960); Norma L. Peterson, *Freedom and Franchise: the Political Career of B. Gratz Brown* (Columbia, Mo., 1965); Mark M. Krug, *Lyman Trumbull, Conservative Radical* (New York, 1965); Hans L. Trefousse, *Benjamin Franklin Wade: Radical Republican from Ohio* (New York, 1963).

sarily lead to agreement upon broad questions of historical truth. It certainly narrows the alternatives between which controversy continues to rage, and this narrowing of alternatives is itself an important proof of objective progress. But within the alternatives the determination of truth depends more perhaps upon basic philosophical assumptions which are applied in interpreting the data than upon the data themselves. Data, in this sense, are but the raw materials for historical interpretation and not the determinants of the interpretive process. This is why the heavily researched field of the coming of the Civil War still remains, and seems likely ever to remain, subject to what we call reinterpretation—by which we mean the application of individual philosophical views to the record of the past.

APPENDIX

Review of *An Historian and the Civil War* by Avery Craven, from the *Journal of Southern History*, XXXI (1965), 207–10.

An Historian and the Civil War is a collection of fourteen essays by Avery Craven, one published in 1928, four in the thirties, one in the forties, four in the fifties, and four in the sixties. Two are extracted from full-scale books; one is published for the first time; the rest are from the quarterlies or from previous collections of essays. Several were first prepared as lectures and two were presidential addresses to the Mississippi Valley Historical Association and the Southern Historical Association. Five first appeared in this journal.

Two deal with Southern agriculture and agricultural reformers (especially John Taylor of Caroline and Edmund Ruffin), one with the applicability of Turner's frontier hypothesis to the South, and one with the pleasures of historical research. But the other ten all treat the background of the Civil War. Historians will be glad to have these ten, especially, gathered between two covers, for including as they do both periodical articles and selections from *The*

Repressible Conflict (1939) and *Civil War in the Making, 1815–1860* (1959), they bring together virtually all that Craven has published on the origins of the Civil War except what he wrote in his two readily accessible books, *The Coming of the Civil War* (1942) and *The Growth of Southern Nationalism, 1848–1861* (1953).

A detailed analysis of Craven's interpretation would go far beyond the limits of a review, and all that will be attempted here is to point out certain conclusions that stand out clearly from reading the essays in the sequence in which they were written.

First, Craven has been consistent throughout in asserting that the causes for antagonism between North and South (slavery, geography, economic differences, and so on; see pp. 82–83) were obvious, and hardly worth elaborate historical analysis, but that the reasons for the failure of the American people to handle these antagonisms as they have handled other antagonisms, within the framework of democratic procedures, are not obvious and need to be explained. "The breakdown of the democratic process" is a recurrent phrase. Thus, Craven has never attempted, primarily, to show what caused ill will between North and South; instead he has tried to show why the ordinary procedures for the resolution of conflict failed to operate in this particular case.

Second, Craven's thinking on this subject has clearly gone through an evolution which can be traced in these essays. During the thirties he placed heavy stress on the view that the basic difficulty was that men's ideas had lost touch with reality—that the antagonists created fictitious and exaggerated images of one another, thus generating unrealistic "fear and hate" and producing a crisis which was an "artificial creation of inflamed minds." In this analysis, he never reckoned sufficiently with the question whether artificially generated hatreds produced an antagonism or whether the antagonism produced what may be called functional hatreds—functional in the sense that if an adversary is to be dealt with as adversary, it may be psychologically necessary or at least helpful to hate him.

This emphasis found its most unqualified expression in writings between 1936 and 1939, and was still clearly apparent in *The Coming of the Civil War* (1942). As late as 1947, I can detect no clear turning in another direction. But in 1950, in "The 1840's and the Democratic Process," Craven began to emphasize a new theme: North and South were torn asunder by the onrushing forces of the "Industrial Revolution," or the "Modern Age," which swept the two sections in opposite directions. Industrialism drove the North forward to adapt to a system where work was done by machines and where men must be free and mobile, if for no other reason, so that they might adjust more readily to the constant changes of a volatile and dynamic economy. But industrialism forced the South backward, as it were, to specialize in producing fibers to feed the spindles and looms of Old and New England. The economy demanded that this function be performed by cheap and unskilled labor, and thus it reinvigorated the archaic system of chattel servitude, and reinforced the static elements in Southern society. Subsequently, Craven reasserted this theme in at least seven essays in 1952, 1959, 1961, and 1964.

Most of the historiographical discussion of "revisionism" (a term which Craven rejects) has not given adequate recognition to this latter phase of his thought. But this phase presents interesting comparisons with his earlier thought. These two stages of his interpretation appear to be poles apart on the question of inevitability, for the earlier view seemed to say that the precipitants of the war were superficial, arising from poorly grounded emotions, while the latter seemed to say that they were implicit in the basic technological and economic tendencies of the age. One view seems to deny determinism and to blame the agitators, while the other is about as deterministic as an explanation can be. But despite their conspicuous dissimilarity in this respect, the two periods of his thought resemble one another in two other features. (1) Both phases denied that the slavery issue *in itself* was basic, and though he did say in 1952 that "it is probably true that Negro slavery was the fundamental factor in producing the American Civil War," he quickly qualified this statement by speaking of slavery as a "symbol and carrier of *all* sectional differences." Earlier he saw slavery as a focus of false excitements, later as an intersection at which primal forces came into collision; never as a generative cause of conflict in itself. (2) Both phases denied that the South bore any unique guilt. First, he blamed troublemakers, North and South. Later he blamed no one, and argued that the South did not choose a slave labor system any more than the North chose a free labor system; blind forces determined both.

"Revisionism" is not a very precise concept and its usefulness in characterizing Craven's thought is questionable to say the least. If it implies a reaction against the idea of "irrepressibility" and a belief that the war could have been and ought to have been avoided, Craven has not been a revisionist for the past fifteen years. If it asserts that other factors were more important than slavery in causing the war, Craven makes no such assertion; he does, to be sure, treat the slavery issue as an expression of complex cultural forces rather than as a simple clash between good men and evil ones, but he is far from suggesting, as did Charles Beard, that it was a mere rationalization for other, hidden motives. If revisionism is an effort to shift the guilt of the war from the South to the North, he certainly minimizes the guilt of the South, but he does this less for purposes of fastening it upon the North than because he is dissatisfied with the guilt question as an aid to real understanding. In a larger sense, perhaps the most distinctive and most valuable quality of Craven's treatment lies not in his specific conclusions on contested points but in his awareness of the conflict as a tragedy transcending categorical verdicts. His gathered essays are distilled from a lifetime of reflection upon this tragedy. No brief summary can do justice to his controlled but deeply felt sense of the human aspects of his theme. A single blunt sentence on next to his last page tells more about his position than does the term revisionist: "The sight of any people drifting toward Civil War calls for much more than the distribution of blame."

CHAPTER V

The Lincoln Theme and American National Historiography

This chapter was originally a lecture delivered at Oxford University early in 1948. It was not an attempt to review the status of scholarship on Abraham Lincoln. Readers who are interested in that aspect will find Chapter IV more to their taste. Rather, I was trying to show how almost all of the important trends in American historical writing have been reflected in the interpretations placed upon Lincoln and his career. Since that was my purpose, the present republication did not seem to require the working in of recent titles, and I have let the essay stand as it was first written. For some of the more recent literature on Lincoln, I refer the reader to pages 101, 106, 144.

WHENEVER ANY scholar is invited, from whatever quarter, to a chair at Oxford, he must come to his post acutely mindful of the unique position of that university among the seats of learning in the Western world. His delight at his own good fortune must accordingly be balanced by a sense of the responsibility which he has incurred. For an American, appointed to the Harmsworth Chair, this feeling might well be accentuated by two unusual features of the professorship: it is reserved for an occupant who is, at least in point of law, an alien, and it is, I believe, the only professorship of the history of a single modern nation. Other professors take as their province certain broad periods—ancient history, modern history—or certain phases of human development—ecclesiastical history, the history of war, political economy, government, international relations, economic history, social and political theory, and European archaeology. There

151

is, it is true, a chair for the history of the British Empire, but this transcends purely national limits. The Harmsworth Chair, therefore, seems to be unique in its exclusive concern with the history of but one modern nation.

This point would seem less significant in actuality, I suppose, than it does nominally, especially when one considers how much the historical literature of Great Britain would be impoverished without the scholarship of Oxford, but even as a nominal arrangement it still seems paradoxical that the only nation whose history monopolizes a professorship at Oxford is not the British nation, and that a nationalistic preoccupation which is not accorded to any national citizen is sanctioned for an alien appointee.

Quite apart from this little anomaly, the historian of a single nation, living in an age when extreme nationalism has done immeasurable harm, may well ponder what his obligation is. Certainly if he dwells egocentrically upon his national culture as a thing apart, if he treats the character or the problems or the destiny of his nation as something separable and unique, he becomes at best the accomplice and at worst the mentor of the political isolationist. But although he must be constantly mindful of the forces which link his nation to the world community, it would be an act of blindness to ignore the historic power of national forces and the degree to which world forces have flowed through national channels. Consequently, it would seem that national history, as such, retains a vital importance, but that it requires to be fitted into a broader human context—that the historian dealing with one nation ought always to balance what is distinctive in the national life against what is universal in it.

Like a taxonomist, working with zoological or botanical specimens, he must ever be alert to note the specific differences which distinguish one strain—or one nation—without permitting the points of distinction to blind him to the generic similarities which link one species with its congeners or one nation with other kindred peoples.

Thinking how seldom such a balance has been maintained, and, indeed, how difficult it is to apply, I have sought for a theme which would touch upon the vividly distinctive aspects of American history—the frontier heritage, the broad social democracy, the optimistic faith in progress—and which would at the same time illustrate the generic qualities that link the United States with Western and especially with English civilization—the devotion to principles of self-government, the respect for constitutional forms and the tendency to find political solutions within the framework of these forms, the emphasis upon freedom. For this dual purpose, it seems to me, there are few general subjects in American history so well suited as the Abraham Lincoln theme. Not only does Lincoln's own career illustrate a humane nationalism with implications of universal value, but also the treatment of his life by historians shows admirably the transition in American historical writing from a narrow to a broader, more mature nationalism.

The history of Lincoln's reputation illustrates very strikingly the tendency of American historians of an earlier period to emphasize those phases of the national record which seemed unique, and the gradual development, more recently, of a less restricted outlook stressing the factors which mark America as part of the Western world. With these considerations in mind, I propose to discuss the Lincoln theme as a touchstone of American historiography.

Before one can approach Lincoln purely as a historical figure, it is pertinent to recall that every country seems to need for its cultural nourishment both a folklore and a history. In countries with an ancient tradition, it is possible to separate the folklore from the history proper by an interval of several centuries, and to draw the folk heroes from a remote period, half obscured by the shadows of a distant past. It is hard to imagine, therefore, that the tales which cluster about Alfred the Great or William Wallace could have originated in the age of the telegraph, the penny press, or the limited liability company; it is difficult to conceive of their being ascribed to a contemporary of Mr. Gladstone. But for the United States, the national past was foreshortened; the Golden Age was telescoped into the Industrial Revolution; and this meant that, if the United States were to develop a national folk hero at all, he must be not a figure of legend but some person in public life whose physical appearance and exact utterances were recorded literally and without idealization by the camera and by shorthand. Yet he must be able to transcend these disenchanting testimonies.

Lincoln was such a man, and thus it happened that this contemporary of Charles Darwin and of Karl Marx assumed in the national memory a place which belonged at the dawn of history. He became the object of fabulous tales such as had hardly been told since the days of the monastic chroniclers, and national legend began to endow him with qualities that one would associate with the hero of a saga. In epic terms such as Homer might have used, this legend stressed his great physical strength, coupled with the tenderest compassion for the weak, his brooding wisdom, his infinite patience and humility. Soon it raised him to a level which surpasses the human altogether and partakes of the divine. Hence emerged a figure born in a log cabin as lowly as any manger, growing up to bear the sorrows of the race and to suffer vicariously for all humanity. At last, on Good Friday, 1865, his life on earth was sacrificed for the redemption of the Union, and on Easter Sunday the people met in churches throughout the land to mourn the Savior of the states.

Nor has the veneration then offered to Lincoln's memory ever been withdrawn. For a long period the farmers of Illinois continued to tell that no Brown Thrush sang for a year after his death. This, one may recall, was precisely the same tribute which the nightingales of the New Forest paid to the memory of Edward the Confessor. Even today, anyone who visits the Lincoln Memorial at Washington senses that he is entering a temple, and men still think of the spirit of Lincoln as brooding over the republic. When Sir James Frazer wrote *The Golden Bough* he might well have included a chapter on Abraham Lincoln.

It is because of this legendary and semireligious quality that the Lincoln theme occupies so central a place in the American memory and in American letters. For every biographer who wished soberly to record the events of Lincoln's career there have been scores of poets—both in verse and prose—who wished to add their sprig of laurel, worshipers intent on burning their pinch of incense, moralists desirous of preaching from a Lincolnian text, and interpreters who felt the same compulsion to explain this fathomless personality which tragedians feel to render their own version of the Prince of Denmark. Perhaps the most striking evidence of the vigor of the cult of Lincolnolatry, however, is the body of apocryphal writings which it has inspired. No account of Lincoln's birthplace or of his paternity has been too fantastic to win credence —and publication. No explanation of his melancholy, or of his physical constitution, no rumor about body snatchers at his tomb, Jesuit conspiracy at his assassination, or spiritualistic communication from "Captain, my Captain" on another shore, has lacked spokesmen and believers.

Amid such a literature and such a tradition, the writings which have some pretension to historical merit occupy a limited and somewhat anomalous position. Yet they exist in sufficient number to illustrate changing trends in the interpretation of American history.

At the time of Lincoln's death American historical writers

were prone to explain events in moral terms. George Bancroft, at that time the dean of American historians, had written an account of the origins of the republic, in which he detected the hand of Providence intervening in the affairs of men, with great frequency, with clear visibility, and with uniform partiality toward the United States. Probably in his studies at Gottingen, Bancroft had absorbed the Germanic view of the nation as a kind of supernatural entity, and he was now applying this concept in his interpretation of the American past. However this may be, he and others like him had established a mode which, regardless of circumstances, would probably have predisposed the interpreters of the Civil War to present their leader as holding a divine mandate and their national cause as enjoying a divine sanction. Insofar as any such tendency existed, the character of events greatly reinforced it. At that time there was little awareness of the nature of sectionalism as such, or of the importance of economic and social forces in shaping the course of sectional rivalries. If an awareness had existed, men would still have been reluctant to apply any such detached and objective criteria in an analysis of their great conflict with the South. It was far more satisfying emotionally to regard the struggle as a clear-cut contest between righteousness in the form of freedom and iniquity in the form of slavery. For this purpose, it was altogether logical to put Lincoln forward as the Great Emancipator, and to make him, in every way, the symbol of the force that struck the shackles from the slaves.

In a very profound sense it was, of course, entirely true that Lincoln was the great man of the antislavery cause. Throughout his mature life he repeatedly asserted, without anger, without stridency, and yet with a stark, immutable distinctness, that he regarded slavery as socially, morally, and politically wrong. Also, it is clear, he took the lead in a movement to terminate it by reducing it to a static form which would ultimately fail of survival. In the end, waiting with a relentless patience until the institution occupied an untenable position, he struck it a blow more decisively fatal than all the abolitionist zealots, with their combined enthusiasm, could ever have delivered. Yet with full recognition of these important facts, one must recall that he did not at any time dedicate himself to the cause with single-minded devotion, and he always regarded the perpetuation of the Union as more important than the abolition of slavery. He maintained a scrupulous respect for the vested rights which were involved, and for the guarantees which slavery enjoyed under the Constitution. Unlike the typical reformer, he never permitted himself the self-indulgence of assuming superior righteousness or of pursuing his objective without regard for contingencies and consequences. He shrank from the prospect of extending full citizenship and equality to the Negro. He accepted the obligation to return fugitive slaves to their bondage. As late as 1861 he was willing to amend the Constitution to guarantee slavery in the states. During the first year and a half of the war he not only refrained from an act of emancipation but he also revoked the orders of two of his generals who sought to apply emancipation in their own military districts. When, at last, he issued the Emancipation Proclamation, it was not the act of a man fulfilling a lifelong plan, but rather of one who reluctantly accepted this recourse after the failure of the plan which was nearest to his heart—a plan of gradual compensated emancipation.

During Lincoln's lifetime the fervent abolitionists were acutely conscious of these facts, and most of them did not forget at the moment of the assassination. William Lloyd Garrison had sneered at Lincoln as a "wet rag"; Wendell Phillips had stigmatized him as "the slave-hound of Illinois";

and antislavery zealots in general had agreed that, as an abolitionist saint, Lincoln had to be "kicked into the Calender."

In 1866, when Josiah G. Holland, novelist and editor of the Springfield *Republican*, wrote the first serious biography of Lincoln's career as a whole, he included, with perfect candor, those events which showed Lincoln's reluctance to declare the slaves free.

In 1872, Henry Wilson, in his *Rise and Fall of the Slave Power in America*, declared that some of Lincoln's assertions "betrayed too much of the spirit of caste and prejudice against color." But while a few hard-headed individualists persevered in remembering the limits and qualifications in Lincoln's antislavery record, the majority, who chose to regard the war as a crusade against slavery, resolutely set themselves to create for Lincoln a record as Chief Crusader. If this placed history upon a Procrustean bed, so much the worse for history.

Many ephemeral writings contributed to this interpretation which pictured Lincoln as being, before all else, the Emancipator. Publications about him bore titles such as *Lincoln the Emancipator, Abraham Lincoln the Liberator, Lincoln the Great Emancipator, Abraham Lincoln, Reformer*. Among writings of substantial merit also, this same theme received stress. One finds a striking example of this in an otherwise quite objective biography by Isaac N. Arnold. Arnold, as an active leader in the Republican Party in Illinois, had known Lincoln personally for twenty-five years. In the same year in which Holland wrote, Arnold had also published a rather hasty biographical account, heavily larded with general history and bearing the significant title, *History of Abraham Lincoln and the Overthrow of Slavery*. Nineteen years later he returned to his theme with a *Life of Abraham Lincoln* which remains one of the best of the early biographies. In it, however, one would look almost in vain for any recognition that Lincoln was not an abolitionist. As Arnold develops his story, one of the incidents related is that of Lincoln's visit as a youth to New Orleans, where he met, it is asserted, an old Voodoo prophetess who predicted to him, "You will be President and all the Negroes will be free." Throughout the remainder of the volume frequent allusion is made to this story, and the reader is led to suppose that Lincoln constantly shaped his career to fulfill the prophecy. Accordingly, when the Lincoln-Douglas debates are described, no mention is made of Lincoln's assurance that he did not propose to tamper with slavery in the states, nor of his statement that, if he were vested with absolute power in the slavery question, he would not know what action to take. Arnold also ignores Lincoln's initial reluctance to join the Republican Party. Similarly, in dealing with the first Inaugural, he quotes most of the document, but by excisions which might be regarded as willful distortion, he omits the passages in which Lincoln asserted his intention to uphold the Fugitive Slave Law and expressed willingness to accept a constitutional amendment protecting slavery in the states. If a reader were left with no account of Lincoln except Arnold's, he would never suspect the ill will with which the abolitionists regarded Lincoln; indeed he would scarcely recognize that Lincoln was not an abolitionist himself. Such a reader would also suppose that the Emancipation Proclamation, at one stroke, abolished Negro slavery in America, for Arnold's account leads up with great dramatic effect to the issuance of the Proclamation, and then gives not a word of explanation of the contents of the document. The unwary reader would never suspect that the Proclamation applied only to a limited class of slaves—those in areas which remained in arms against the government at a specified future time—that it invited all slave states to avoid emancipation by returning to the Union, and that even when it went into effect it left slavery undisturbed in the loyal slave states: Delaware, Maryland, Kentucky, and Missouri.

In a sense, the stereotype of Lincoln the Emancipator represents nationalistic interpretation in its most extreme form, for it implies that the American republic enjoyed the unique favor of God, that God gave the American people a divinely inspired leader, as He had also done for His chosen people in Biblical times, and that it was reserved for the United States, peculiarly, to work out the divine plan. Such a view, becoming firmly entrenched, did not yield readily to new interpretations, and the concept of the single-purposed Emancipator retains much vigor even today.

Before the end of the nineteenth century, however, historians in general had begun to lean toward more secular interpretations of history: the theory of economic determinism had been clearly articulated and had begun to win adherents; and Henry Thomas Buckle and others had broadened the concept of history to include the cultural analysis of society as a whole.

National historians no longer made overt claims of priority in the divine favor, but they did quite legitimately seek to discover the factors which made their respective nations distinctive, and, having established such factors, they did emphasize them to a disproportionate extent.

In the United States, Frederick Jackson Turner was first to recognize and to state clearly the distinctive American factor. Historically, Americans were simply transplanted Europeans, but they had developed such non-European qualities as to make them, in the truest sense, a separate nation. In his famous paper in 1893 entitled "The Significance of the Frontier in American History," Turner advanced the thesis that the frontier had caused this distinctive evolution—that the existence, at the edge of settlement, of an undifferentiated society, where the individual was not overshadowed by established institutions, where status had little meaning, where all were reduced to a common level by the quest for survival, had engendered the qualities of individualism, social equalitarianism, and aggressive, materialistic energy which characterized the American. For a generation Turner's ideas were to dominate the writing of American history.

It would be an error to suppose that the writers on Lincoln preceded Turner in grasping this thesis. They did not possess enough historical philosophy for such a generalization. But it is certainly a significant fact that even before the Turner interpretation was enunciated, they began to replace Lincoln the saintly Emancipator with Lincoln the robust Frontiersman. Since this particular frontiersman had risen from a log cabin to the Presidency, he also embodied the typical American success story.

In the concept of the Frontiersman, as in that of the Emancipator, there was, of course, a great measure of validity. Lincoln was, in fact, born in a cabin of logs in a frontier community. He was reared in conditions that were, materially and culturally, extremely meager. He received virtually no formal education. It is true that he lived one entire winter in a half-faced camp—a dwelling open on the south side to every rigor of the elements. He did split rails, and his father, like many pioneers, did tend to be migratory, moving his Kentucky-born offspring first into the wilderness of Indiana and then into Illinois. He shared fully in the equalitarian and individualistic heritage. With facts like these, there was, of course, no need to falsify or even to distort. Mere emphasis would have sufficed. During Lincoln's lifetime such emphasis appeared when he was dubbed the Railsplitter, and he himself pointed out to the men in an Ohio regiment, visiting the White House, that he was "a living witness that any one of your children may look to come here as my father's child has." Even before his death a biography for youths had borne the title, *The Pioneer Boy and How He Became President*, and later popular accounts had embraced in their titles or their subtitles the designations the Forest Boy, the Backwoods Boy, the Farmer's Boy, the Self-made Man, and the Toiler, while another was entitled *Log Cabin to White House*.

The works which had the effect, historically, of establishing the concept of Lincoln the Frontiersman were none of these fugitive items but were three books that appeared between 1872 and 1892 by men all of whom had known Lincoln well in Illinois, who had know him less well or not at all in Washington, and who wrote primarily about Lincoln the pioneer rather than Lincoln the President. The first of these was Lincoln's personal companion, more stalwart of body than of mind, Ward H. Lamon, who went to Washington with the President and continued in association with him, half as bodyguard, half as friend; the second was Lincoln's law partner, William H. Herndon; and the third was an associate at the Bar, Henry C. Whitney, who had enjoyed the intimacy of riding circuit with Lincoln in the Eight Judicial District of Illinois.

Each one of these men tended not only to give the frontier aspect of Lincoln's life the heavy emphasis which it deserved, but further, to treat his career and personality as if it could be explained wholly in frontier terms, which it could not. Their perspectives were also, for diverse reasons, false. Whitney simply wrote, with artless candor, that part of the truth which he knew: he had observed that some of Lincoln's wittiest stories were unprintable and he duly recorded the fact. Lamon, a Virginian, formed a curious literary partnership with an enthusiastic Democrat, Chauncey F. Black, whose father had been Secretary of State under Buchanan. The Virginian and the Democrat as collaborators wished to correct the Republican, antislavery image of Lincoln as a man devoid of human frailty; if so, they corrected it by smashing it. As for Herndon, he wrote with an obsessive passion for the whole truth, and a comprehensive lack of capacity to distinguish the truth from flimsy rumor and garbled reminiscence. Lord Charnwood, with engaging ironic restraint, says that Herndon was, "like Boswell, of opinion that a great man is not best portrayed as a figure in a stained-glass window."

Although frontier forces played a powerful part in shaping Lincoln's career, they were, in the eyes of these writers, not powerful enough until they had been exaggerated. Not content, for instance, to show that Lincoln shared the hardships, the hazards, and the cultural privations which were borne alike by all frontier youths, Lamon awarded to him the additional handicap of illegitimate birth and a shiftless, ne'er-do-well father. Thomas Lincoln was described as "idle, thriftless, poor, a hunter, and a rover," and his marriage to Lincoln's mother was alleged to exist only "by mutual acknowledgment and cohabitation." Truth did not overtake either of these stories for more than a generation.

To illustrate further, the frontier certainly imparted to Lincoln robustness, earthiness, and a kind of primal strength, but there is no reliable evidence that it engendered in him any of the callousness or the slyness which appeared in so many frontiersmen. Apparently, he was an extraordinarily gentle person throughout his life—he could not even discipline his children. Yet Herndon tells stories of his lashing a a horse, and of his sewing a little dog into a coon skin, with the unforeseen result that it was set upon and killed by other dogs.

Apparently, also, Lincoln was as honest at the Bar as he was in all other phases of life. Despite this fact, Lamon, in describing the famous episode where Lincoln used an old almanac to confound a witness who claimed to have seen an

act of murder committed by moonlight, asserts that the almanac used was of the wrong year. This version of the story
is offered in the frontier spirit of admiration for the clever
rogue. At Lamon's hands Lincoln becomes almost the pic-
aresque hero.

Still another illustration: when Lincoln, as a youth,
whipped the frontier bully Jack Armstrong and later commanded Armstrong's friendship, the episode demonstrated
forcefully the excellence of Lincoln's physical and social adjustment to pioneer ways. But Lamon is not content to leave
it at that: he must magnify the sequel into a kind of David-
and-Jonathan affinity between Lincoln and Armstrong, with
Lincoln staying "for days and weeks together at Jack's cabin."

In short, so vividly and so intently do Herndon and Lamon
sketch the half-faced camp in the wilderness, the frontier
bullies, and the rail-splitting and river-boating days, that one
forgets that Lincoln also lived for many years in a house in
Springfield, that he practiced law far longer than he split rails,
and that by his marriage and his legal connections he was associated with men of enough education, social standing, and
knowledge of the world to get themselves distrusted as aristocrats.

To some extent, Herndon and Lamon presented their
image of Lincoln the Frontiersman because this was the
Lincoln they knew, the Lincoln they could best appreciate,
the Lincoln who appeared most picturesque. But in the case
of Herndon, at least, it must be added that if he did not
articulate the frontier thesis, he sensed it, and he was deliberately striving to explain Lincoln as the product of frontier
forces. For this purpose, he often digressed from the story of
Lincoln's life, in order to describe frontier revival meetings,
social functions, etc.; he characterized Lincoln's maternal
relatives, the Hanks family, as "peculiar to the civilization of
early Kentucky," and, after describing pioneer conditions at

some length, he observed that these "surroundings helped to create that unique character which in the eyes of a great portion of the American people was only less curious and amusing than it was august and noble."

For a quarter of a century, while those two Lincolns, the Emancipator and the Frontiersman, were assuming their definite form, American scholarship did not produce any adequate treatment of Lincoln as President, nor did it provide any comprehensive edition of his writings. These two gaps were filled, and the Lincoln literature was launched upon a third phase, as a result of the work, published in 1890 and 1894, of Lincoln's two personal secretaries, John G. Nicolay and John Hay. Nicolay and Hay possessed an incomparable personal knowledge of the President, they were the only writers, up to 1947, who enjoyed access to his private papers, and they were, in this field, the first writers of really superior talent and capacity. With such a combination of advantages they were able to advance historical knowledge of Lincoln more, perhaps, than would ever be possible for any subsequent scholar. In 1890 they published, in ten volumes, *Abraham Lincoln, A History,* which, with the exception of Sandburg's *Lincoln,* remains probably the longest biography of any American. As the title implies, the work included the broad panorama of the whole Civil War, and it sometimes left Lincoln standing in the wings for chapters at a time. It is seldom read today; in view of its imposing bulk it was probably never widely read; and the impression has got about, to some extent, that it is a mere protracted eulogy written in a spirit of Oriental deference to the wishes of Lincoln's son, Robert Todd Lincoln. This view is unduly severe. John Hay, soon to be Secretary of State, was too important a figure to be browbeaten by the son of a great man, and the reader has only to examine the objective account of Lincoln's marriage and the treatment of his love for Ann Rutledge to perceive that filial piety did not tyrannize over the authors. In many respects the fullness and the candor of the record is astonishing. Lincoln's balanced position on slavery—deploring the institution but conceding its rights—is set forth *in extenso,* and without any concealment whatever. His difficulties with intransigent cabinet ministers are exposed utterly frankly, despite the fact that Hay was a high priest of Republicanism and might have been expected to suppress episodes that were discreditable to the great men of the party.

But though Nicolay and Hay escaped many of the pitfalls of "official biography," they by no means escaped them all. Although they seldom distorted the record, seldom misrepresented Lincoln's position, they always defended that position whatever it might be. For other writers apology took the form of suppressing what they could not approve—if it was wrong, Lincoln did not do it; for Nicolay and Hay, apology lay in approving with no attempt at suppression—if Lincoln did it, it was not wrong. Their extended narrative, therefore, is one of virtually unbroken approbation, and at times their bias is extreme. For instance, Hay wrote privately to Nicolay that, in their treatment of General McClellan, "it is of the utmost moment that we should seem fair to him, while we are destroying him."

If Nicolay and Hay's account was not critical, nor free from bias, it was at least the first balanced treatment—no one aspect of Lincoln's career or personality was permitted to overshadow all other aspects—and it was comprehensive. Its most important ultimate value lay in the fact that it made a vast amount of new information available. It was based upon documents, of which it made explicit citation. This documentary contribution was further expanded in 1894 when the same authors edited two volumes of the writings of Lincoln. In 1905, with the assistance of Francis D. Tandy, they expanded the original collection and reissued it in a twelve-volume edition. Although apparently six times as voluminous, the later edition owed much of its bulk to padding in the format, and the number of items in the later edition exceeded those in the first only by about twenty percent. Since 1905, one may add, a considerable number of new items by Lincoln have come to light and have been published from time to time by various editors. Ida Tarbell, Gilbert Tracy, the Brown University Library, Paul M. Angle, Emanuel Hertz, and Rufus Rockwell Wilson have all contributed supplementary sheaves, while Roy P. Basler has rendered more accurately the text of some of the documents already known; but despite these additions, Nicolay and Hay's collection remains the basic compilation of Lincoln's works.

Writing at the end of the nineteenth century, Nicolay and Hay may be said to mark the culmination of a period in which the approach was essentially noncritical. They were the last of the major writers who had known Lincoln personally—henceforth posterity would take up the pen. Also, their work showed definitely the potentialities and the limitations of a noncritical approach. It provided a knowledge of Lincoln's career which was comprehensive, factually accurate, and reasonably well balanced in its proportions. It rested on documentary evidence, and will continue to give a reasonably good account of itself when tried by the canons of scholarship. But as a work of analysis and interpretation, it was negligible, and indeed one can scarcely be contradicted for saying that no mature interpretation of Lincoln's greatness was offered for half a century after his death. In terms of American nationalism, therefore, to return to my theme, it would seem justifiable to say that by the beginning of the century American scholarship had begun to apply disciplined methods of investigation and of documentation—methods which are conducive to rigorous thinking—but that it had not yet developed any appreciable capacity for self-criticism. When Nicolay and Hay portrayed the national hero, they did not insist that he was performing a divine mission, as Lincoln the Emancipator, nor that he was primarily an exponent of qualities uniquely American, as Lincoln the Frontiersman, but they did maintain, implicitly, that he was flawless in character and faultless in his actions. When they appraised his achievements in ending American slavery and in preserving the Union, they scarcely measured these values in terms broader than the national interest. It remained for future writers to consider what Lincoln's ideas of freedom implied for others besides the four million slaves, and whether the principle of Union possessed any broader meaning than considerations of American political welfare gave to it.

The first decade of the twentieth century witnessed several more biographies. Of the number, two deserve to be mentioned: Ida Tarbell's in 1900 because it was the first account which combined scholarly research with broad popular appeal, and Ellis Paxson Oberholtzer's in 1904 because it was the first treatment by a professional historian. The performance, however, was not one to win laurels for the academic world. The lack of mature interpretation was still conspicuous. Consequently it remained for an English writer, Lord Charnwood, in 1915, to write the first genuinely contemplative biography. In addition to its notable literary excellence, Charnwood's treatment of Lincoln possessed two especial merits. First, it questioned certain assumptions which had previously been treated as taboo: Did Lincoln temporize too much on slavery? Was there a quality of "cheap opportunism" in his political record? Did his policy at Fort Sumter differ from Buchanan's enough to justify the customary practice of gibbeting the silly old man while leaving Lincoln free from criticism? Was he, in the last analysis, responsible for precipitating the Civil War? These questions and others like them, which Nicolay and Hay refused even to treat as controversial, fairly burned to be discussed, and Charnwood discussed them. He concluded that although Lincoln was very fond of political maneuver he sacrificed his personal interest on several occasions as no opportunist would have done. He concluded also that, by throwing his weight against the Crittenden Compromise, Lincoln caused the war. Yet he still found in Lincoln a greatness of the first order, and by finding greatness despite fallibility he certainly placed Lincoln's reputation on a sounder basis than did those writers who treated the greatness as contingent upon infallibility.

The second factor of especial merit in Charnwood was that he was perhaps the first to grasp the universality of Lincoln's significance. He rejected the concept of Lincoln the Emancipator, saying, "it is not in the light of a crusader against this especial evil [Slavery] that we are to regard him," and he also rejected the concept of Lincoln the Frontier Democrat. Lincoln was a citizen, he said, "of that far country where there is neither aristocrat nor democrat." The few books which, as a youth, Lincoln read so eagerly, and so receptively, were in themselves quite alien to the frontier, and as for their limited number, "there is . . . great advantage in having one's choice restricted to good books." Lord Charnwood did not reject the concept of Lincoln the defender of the Union, but, while accepting it, he pointed out that this was more than a purely national concept, for loyalty to union had a "larger aspect than that of mere allegiance to a particular authority." Lincoln himself had shown a deep awareness of this larger significance, and, as Charnwood observed, "his affection for his own country . . . is curiously dependent upon a wider cause of human good." Lincoln himself had said of the American Revolution that the cause which nerved the Americans "was not the mere matter of separation of the colonies from the motherland, it was the sentiment in the Declaration of Independence which gave liberty, not only to the people of this country, but, I hope, to the world for all future time. It was that which gave promise that in due time the weight would be lifted from the shoulders of all men."

Charnwood made brilliant use of the Lincoln literature that had been accumulating for fifty years. His biography is a superb example of what can be done simply by thinking deeply about what others have written without deep thought. It interpreted anew, but it did not investigate anew, and the fully matured biography still required, as a prerequisite, a vast amount of fresh and detailed investigation.

The beginnings of such investigation in the 1920's gave evidence of an objectivity which marked a new phase in American historical writing. Insofar as this implies a mere technique of detailed research, it was, of course, not entirely new and it did not, on the face of it, embody any principle inconsistent with the earlier emphasis upon an America made unique by divine favor or by environmental conditions. But the spirit of such investigation was hardly compatible with the concept which treated the American nation as an isolated entity, unrelated to areas beyond the horizon. It was a spirit eminently conducive to self-criticism, and, for the first time it now became true that the most intelligent—and in many cases the most severe—criticism of America came from within the United States rather than from a Tocqueville, a Bryce, or other less gifted and less friendly analysts from the Old World. At its lowest level, this self-criticism took the crass form of indiscriminate disparagement of any men or institutions that had ever incurred indiscriminate praise. In its monotonous repudiation of all conventional ideas, it itself became quite conventionalized, and was known as "debunking." But the meritorious aspects of the new self-appraisal were far more significant, if less spectacular, and the re-examination of a great many topics in the American past yielded fruitful results because of the rejection of shibboleths. More-

over, if the spirit of investigation was conducive to self-criticism it was also conducive to a broader view of the United
States as part of North America, and North America as part
of the Western world. For the first time, the colonization of
the present United States was placed in its proper setting as
part of a general planting of European settlements in North
and South America. Similarly, the history of the colonies that
became the United States was recognized as a part of the history of the British Empire, and not a mere prologue to the
drama of the republic. Cultural historians began to sense that
study of the frontier alone would never provide a key to many
American ideas and institutions.

In this present phase of American historical writing, as in
previous ones, the treatment of the Lincoln theme has been
a sensitive barometer. During the decade when "debunking"
biographies were most prevalent, Edgar Lee Masters wrote a
characteristic one. At a time when Freudian interpretations
were freely dispensed by everyone who had acquired a smatter-
ing of Freud's terminology, Nathaniel W. Stephenson gar-
nished his *Lincoln, An Account of His Personal Life*, with psy-
choanalytical speculation. It must be added, in fairness, however, that Stephenson was also one of the first writers to
attempt an appraisal of the meaning of Lincoln's preservation
of the Union. To Stephenson, present and future developments constantly reveal new meanings in past events. Thus,
Lincoln's preservation of the Union acquired new significance
as the unfolding of world events revealed the increasing importance of the American republic in the history of the twentieth century. Asserting that the United States had become
"the most powerful and probably the most distinctive country
in the world," Stephenson suggested that

because we are what we are, the world during the next chapter
of its history will be what it will be. If the result should prove
unfortunate, then Lincoln's achievement was in the nature of a

tragic victory. If the outcome should prove beneficent, then Lincoln's achievement is one of the greatest in history. But whatever the eventual result, the enormous significance is not to be questioned. The statesman who determined the course of American development, who guided the Republic past its turning point, is one of the prime factors of modern experience. His work contributed to establishing a new balance of power among the social forces in his country. Out of this has resulted a new balance among the social forces of the world.

Although Stephenson could not foresee Hitler or Stalin, Lake Success or Hiroshima, the Truman Doctrine or the Marshall Plan, his analysis seems today more cogent than ever.

Stephenson's biography, like Charnwood's, was primarily a brilliant reinterpretation of information provided by others, but soon after its publication the long array of detailed revisions based upon new investigation began. The first genuinely great specimen of this new scholarship, appearing in 1928, was Albert J. Beveridge's study of Lincoln's life up to the time of the debates with Douglas. Before undertaking this project, Beveridge had enjoyed a distinguished career as United States Senator and as the writer of one of the few major American biographies—his life of Marshall. His skill in research, his art as a writer, and his unsurpassed knowledge of the subtleties of American politics equipped him for the achievement of the definitive biography. But all expectations were disappointed by Beveridge's sudden and untimely death. His work, so far as it extended, is, therefore, only a fragment, though a splendid one. Despite this limitation it embodied what still remains far the best account of Lincoln's political career up to the moment of his entry upon the national stage, and it effectively rehabilitated Stephen A. Douglas, who had long been stereotyped as a mere dramatic foil for Lincoln. Indeed, one may say of Beveridge's account that it was the first biographical treatment which combined extensive original investigation with critical capacity of a high order. But

other scholarly works, applying both research and criticism
in the treatment of special phases of Lincoln's career, were
beginning to appear with a frequency that is not yet diminished. In 1926 James G. Randall produced an analysis of the
constitutional aspects of Lincoln's Presidency; it showed that
however loyal Lincoln may have been to the spirit of the
Constitution, many of his wartime measures expanded the
executive power enormously and virtually ignored constitutional limitations. In the same year a study of Lincoln's child-
hood by Louis A. Warren demonstrated that the Lincoln
family were not, as Lamon and Herndon had implied, impoverished wretches, reduced to social degradation by the
ne'er-do-well qualities of Thomas Lincoln, but on the contrary
that Thomas Lincoln possessed a creditable record and that
the hardships which his wife and children experienced were
those which every frontier family expected to encounter. This
was not the first blow to the legend of Lincoln's lowly origins:
William E. Barton had already established the legitimacy of
Lincoln's birth by subjecting no less than seven alleged patern-
ities to an analysis more rigorous than they could withstand.
Nor did the impression that Lincoln knew only frontier surroundings remain unchallenged: Benjamin P. Thomas and
Paul M. Angle, in their respective studies of New Salem and
of Springfield, showed the diversity of elements in Lincoln's
environment. These studies struck indirectly but very forcibly
at the frontier legend, and they were followed by others which
re-examined critical phases of Lincoln's political career. William E. Baringer, tracing the growth of Lincoln's political influence, showed that he owed much of his success to artful
planning, adroit maneuver, and practical "organization."
T. Harry Williams, reviewing Lincoln's relations, as President,
with his party in Congress, revealed that the opposition which
Nicolay and Hay had represented as the work of a few mal-
contents was, in fact, almost a party revolt against the Presi-

dent. David M. Potter scrutinized again the sequence of events leading to the outbreak of war, and concluded that, far from being master of the situation, Lincoln in fact misapprehended the character of the secession movement and found himself unable to deal with the crisis in the way he had planned. Harry Carman and Reinhard H. Luthin analyzed Lincoln's use of the patronage and showed him to be a skillful and a not unwilling practitioner of the spoils system.

With the Lincoln legend rapidly yielding to these and other analyses, the historical treatment of this major American theme began to approach genuine maturity, though it appears unlikely ever to approach completion. As it did so, the subject reached a stage at which it was most fitting for the legend itself to be restated in its ultimate form, with a full artistic development of its epic qualities. Simultaneously, the opportunity appeared for a new, thoroughly scholarly synthesis which would assemble all the scattered monographic investigations and bring them to converge, thus producing for the first time a comprehensive, thorough, and critical treatment of Lincoln's career as a whole.

Both of these great opportunities have been superbly met: one by the literary artistry of Carl Sandburg and the other by the discerning scholarship of James G. Randall. Sandburg and Randall offer striking evidence of the breadth of spirit in which American historians are now capable of interpreting the dominant figure in the history of American nationalism. At the hands of Sandburg, Lincoln as a human personality becomes more universal, perhaps, than any other political leader in world history. Though he remains the Frontiersman, the Emancipator, the Savior of the Union, the pure and ultimate American, his intrinsic qualities as a man are evoked in a way that links him to men everywhere. The American aspects cease to be particular ones, and become general aspects in a vividly American manifestation. At the hands of Randall the political issues of Lincoln's career cease to be narrowly or explicitly American problems, and become universal problems in an American form. The question of slavery is treated not simply as a matter of chattel bondage in the Southern states of the American Union, but as an American manifestation of the general human problem of reconciling idealistic purpose with existing conditions. Of all the significant figures of history, Lincoln emerges as the one least willing to justify the means by the end. The question of Fort Sumter is treated not simply as a matter of constitutional and military crisis, but as an American manifestation of the general problem of the causation of war. Lincoln's own liberalism is treated not as that of a Northerner who shared in the sectional dislike of Southern slavery, but as that of one who opposed nativism, rebuked anti-Semitism, concerned himself with the welfare of industrial workers, and evinced a lively sympathy for the cause of freedom wherever it appeared and in whatever form.

If, as I have tried to indicate, American national history has begun to demonstrate a significant capacity to transcend narrow national concepts in its treatment of this peculiarly nationalistic theme, it is in fitting accord with the character of Lincoln that it should do so. For the great merit of Lincoln's nationalism lay in the fact that he never for a moment regarded national sovereignty and power as an end in themselves. Always he sought to make the national state a medium for the conservation of universal human values. His words of eulogy on Henry Clay expressed exactly his own spirit: "Mr. Clay," he declared, "loved his country partly because it was his own country and mostly because it was a free country. . . . he burned with a zeal for its advancement . . . because he saw in such the advancement . . . and glory of human liberty, human right, and human nature. He desired the prosperity of his countrymen . . . chiefly to show to the world that free men could be prosperous." When Lincoln fought to save the Union, it was not merely for the purpose of preserving a specific government at Washington, but for "the necessity that is upon us of proving that popular government is not an absurdity."[1]

Abraham Lincoln lived in a century which was marked preeminently by extreme, jingoistic, saber-rattling nationalism—nationalism in an advanced stage of egocentrism and resorting to every device of deceit, repression, and mass violence to achieve its ends. He lived in a country acutely convinced of its own national superiority. It is, therefore, perhaps one of the most striking features of Lincoln's greatness that, as Professor Randall observes, he fused the cause of nationalism with that of freedom. The other great nation-builders of the century—Napoleon, Cavour, Bismarck—sacrificed mankind at large for the enhancement of French, or Italian, or German power. Amid such developments it is a happy reflection for the United States that the most distinctively American figure in the national history, and the major leader in the consolidation of American national power, bore a significance least narrowly American.

[1] Like everyone who writes on Lincoln, I must acknowledge my indebtedness to J. G. Randall. His *Lincoln, the Liberal Statesman,* provided me with the quotations in this paragraph.

CHAPTER VI

Depletion and Renewal in Southern History

The following essay, written for a conference on the future needs of Southern studies at Duke University in 1966, repeats some of the information in Chapter IV, but essentially it represents the opposite side of the coin. Pages 119–33 of Chapter IV were devoted to accomplishments in the field of Southern history; this chapter is devoted to pointing out some of the things that need to be accomplished, and how one accomplishment in a given area calls attention to the neglected condition of adjacent areas. Successful research in a given field, instead of exhausting the field, often stimulates further work, the need for which was not previously visible. By this I do not mean to argue, however, that it is never possible for a field to become genuinely exhausted.

When this paper was presented at the conference, Professor George Tindall provided a thoughtful and searching comment, which is published in Edgar T. Thompson (ed.), Perspectives on the South: Agenda for Research *(see pp. 89–93), which contains the full conference proceedings.*

T̲HE HISTORY of the South has flourished as one of the most intensively cultivated branches of American history for many decades. In the earliest stages of its development, it was preoccupied almost exclusively with the Southern Confederacy, the slavery conflict as a prologue to the Confederacy, and Reconstruction as an epilogue to the Confederacy. The original Southern Historical Society, chartered four years after Appomattox, had as its founders high officials of the Confederate government and general officers of the Confederate Army. For a generation, no Southerner apparently could write history without rehearsing over again a legalistic defense of the constitutional right of secession. Raphael Semmes, for instance, in his *Service Afloat*, prefaced his rousing narrative of swashbuckling adventure on the high seas with a long, arid, and tedious exegesis on the metaphysics of secession.

If the history of the South, so-called, had remained as it began, merely a recital of the valor and rectitude of the Lost Cause, it would probably have withered on the academic vine early in the twentieth century. It would hardly have become a vital component in a Center for Southern Studies, such as was launched at Duke University exactly a century plus one year after Appomattox. But it acquired a new dimension when Frederick Jackson Turner and others brought forward the concept of the "section" as an important factor in American history. Turner specifically repudiated the popular idea that "the word section applies only to the struggle of South against North on the questions of slavery, state sovereignty, and eventually disunion." On the contrary, he insisted, rivalries between East and West were often crucial. The United States,

unlike such countries as France and Germany, . . . has the problem of the clash of economic interests closely associated with regional geography on a huge scale. . . . Economic interests are sectionalized. . . . We have become a nation comparable to all Europe in area, with settled geographic provinces which equal great European nations. We are in this sense an empire, a federation of sections, a union of potential nations. . . . There is and always has been a sectional geography in America, based fundamentally upon geographic regions. There is a geography of political habits, a geography of opinion, of material interests, of racial stocks, of physical fitness, of social traits, of literature, of the distribution of men of ability, even of religious denominations. . . . The significance of the section in American history is that it is the faint image of a European nation, and that we need to examine our history in the light of this fact.

Turner's formulation provided a supremely effective charter for a Southern history broadly conceived. Here was a concept which regarded the South as the faint image of a nation and which recognized that there were distinctive elements in Southern economic life, Southern social life, Southern literature, Southern religion, Southern ideology and popular attitudes and values—enough themes to provide a multiplicity of justifications for a center. Hence, any complete history of the South would embrace not only the Lost Cause, but also economic history, social and cultural history, intellectual history, and religious history, as well as the political and institutional history of a time span of more than three and a half centuries from Jamestown to Cape Kennedy. Such a view foreshadowed the broad concept of regionalism which men like Howard Odum and Rupert Vance were to develop with such fruitful effect in the 1930's. Turner himself, as the quotation has just shown, used the term "region" as well as the term "section."

Does this broader concept mean that anything which happens anywhere south of the Mason-Dixon line is within the province of Southern history? Are Southern historians entirely at the mercy of a geography which makes them responsible for all that occurs within an arbitrarily defined area? Not if they follow Turner, for his sectional or regional theory would confine Southern history to phenomena which have some kind of regional distinctiveness. This would exclude the history of things which are purely local on the one hand, or merely manifestations within the region of national phenomena, on the other. Thus, for instance, a history of the adoption of the commission form of municipal government in Galveston, Texas, would hardly seem to be a part of Southern history, unless regional conditions had impinged on the affairs of the city in a distinctive way. A good part of the experience of any community is likely to be shaped by purely local circumstances, with regional factors playing a minimal part. At the other end of the spectrum, the South now shares increasingly in a standardized national life and national way of doing things, which again reduces the factor of regional distinctiveness in certain areas to negligibility. For instance, dentistry is probably about the same in Durham as in Duluth; the use of structural steel for office buildings about the same in Winston-Salem, North Carolina, Salem, Massachusetts, and Salem, Oregon; television programs do not differ appreciably from New Orleans to Minneapolis-St. Paul. I am not sure that all these illustrations are well chosen, but it seems safe to assert that there are a good many features of American life in 1966 which have been so thoroughly standardized or homogenized on a national basis that nothing is gained by applying a regional perspective to their study.

These features have already grown immensely, to extend over a broader and broader range within the spectrum of our lives; and the indications are that they will continue to crowd out the features of regional distinctiveness until, conceivably, regionalism may become vestigial, just as the mule and the use of chewing tobacco have already become vestigial. The diminishing prominence of regional features within the South has already induced in almost all white Southerners moments or moods of regretful nostalgia, and it has prompted Harry Ashmore to write *An Epitaph for Dixie*. Ashmore says that the historical identity of the South consisted in one peculiar institution—slavery—and in a triad of successor institutions—the tenancy system in agriculture, the one-party system in politics, and the system of caste and legal segregation in race relations. All of these, says Ashmore, are now perishing institutions, and when they have finally expired, Dixie will become historic only.

If Dixie is ultimately to disappear, it will only follow the destiny of all things in human history; meanwhile, there are other writers who tell us that no society can be understood purely in terms of its current material circumstances, but that the past lives in the present and the present will live in the future. With no specific reference to the South, Seymour

Martin Lipset, in *The First New Nation*, has made this point with regard to Canada and the United States. The two countries have had very similar physical or material circumstances —the same ratios of men to land, the same high standard of living, the same frontier movement; but the United States repudiated the principle of authority and expelled the Tory elite in 1775–76, while Canada received the Tory Loyalists who fled from New England and absorbed them and their values into the Canadian system. That happened nearly two centuries ago, but the resulting differentials between society in the United States and in Canada still remain conspicuous. Lipset's observations on Canada might be regarded as paralleling C. Vann Woodward's observations, in *The Burden of Southern History*, upon distinctive factors in the past which may have a persisting effect in preserving a factor of Southern identity. As Woodward has suggested, the experience of military defeat in the Civil War, the long decades of poverty and stagnation in the Southern economy, the corroding psychological effects of the sense of guilt and evil which accompanied the caste system—these things were all features which other Americans did not share. Hence the characteristically American confidence of success, the shallow optimism, the bland conviction of the superior virtue and moral innocence of Americans did not strike root quite as deeply in the South. The residual survival of these attitudes might continue to make for cultural differentiation even after all the physical and material factors of distinctive Southernism have been eroded away.

I am really trying to say two things here: The first is that Southern studies, and especially Southern history, should not be concerned indiscriminately with everything that occurs within the South; rather, they should focus their analysis at points where the conditions of the Southern region differ from those of other regions and should concentrate their attention upon historical developments which are relevant to these differences. The second is that these differential factors may arise directly from prevailing natural or physical conditions at present, but they may also persist as survivals from the material or physical conditions of the past, and historians must be alert to both the continuing difference and the survival. To put this proposition into more concrete terms, the Southern historian has an anomalous job. His is the task of tracing the history of a region that never possessed clearly defined limits and only for four years possessed an organizational and structural identity as the Confederate States of America. For the rest of the time, he is dealing with an entity—the South—whose boundaries are indeterminate, whose degree of separateness has fluctuated historically over time, whose distinctiveness may be in some respects fictitious. His job in this complex of uncertainties is to identify and investigate the distinctive features of Southern society.

On the whole, this is what professional historians of the South have sought to do, and they have done it intensively and successfully for several decades now. They were quick to grasp the reality that one of the basic sources of sectional distinctiveness was the system of Negro slavery and plantation agriculture before the Civil War. After the war, the dominant tendencies lay in the bitter struggle to determine what social system should replace slavery and the continued dominance of the cotton economy, as well as the subordination of the Negro. All the while, both before and after the war and during Reconstruction, the political rivalries and battles which grew out of these conditions were also part of the essence of sectional identity.

Southern historians have recognized all of these themes and have cultivated them with an intensity which has not been paralleled in the historical study of any other American region. On some topics it has been worked to a point where diminishing returns now seem about to set in, and this is why, in the title of this paper, I have alluded to "depletion" in Southern history. Many of the golden nuggets in the streambed of Southern history have already been panned.

Some of the fields of investigation are closely worked indeed —so much so, in fact, that few of us would encourage a graduate student to embark on further intensive study. On the theme of slavery, for instance, there have been the state monographs by Jeffrey Brackett on Maryland, by James C. Ballagh on Virginia, by John Spencer Bassett and Rosser H. Taylor on North Carolina, by Ralph B. Flanders on Georgia, by Charles S. Davis and by James B. Sellers on Alabama, by Charles S. Sydnor on Mississippi, by V. A. Moody and by Joe G. Taylor on Louisiana, by Orville W. Taylor on Arkansas, by Chase Mooney on Tennessee, by Winston Coleman on Kentucky, and by Harrison Trexler on Missouri. There have also been the general works of Ulrich B. Phillips, Kenneth Stampp, and Stanley Elkins. On plantation agriculture, we have the irreplaceable work of Phillips, the magisterial volumes by Lewis C. Gray, the important monographic studies of rice by J. Harold Easterby and by Albert V. House, Jr., of sugar by Carlyle Sitterson, and of tobacco by Joseph C. Robert and Nannie M. Tilley, of hemp by James H. Hopkins, and on other aspects of Southern agriculture by J. C. Bonner, Cornelius Cathey, Avery Craven, John Hebron Moore, Edwin A. Davis, Alfred G. Smith, and others. On the political sectionalism between tidewater and frontier within the South, there are volumes by Charles H. Ambler on Virginia, John Spencer Bassett on North Carolina, William A. Schaper on South Carolina, Ulrich B. Phillips on Georgia, Thomas P. Abernethy on Tennessee, and Theodore H. Jack on Alabama, as well as Richard O. Curry's recent and notable study of West Virginia. On the secession movement, there have been studies for almost every state and more than one study for some states: Henry T. Shanks for Virginia, J. Carlyle Sitterson for North Carolina, Philip Hamer, Chauncey Boucher, Harold S. Schultz, and Charles E. Cauthen for South Carolina, George V. Irons for Georgia, Clarence P. Denman and Austin Venable for Alabama, Cleo Hearon and Percy Lee Rainwater for Mississippi, Willie M. Caskey for Louisiana, Earl Fornell and Edward M. Maher for Texas, Elsie M. Lewis for Arkansas, Walter H. Ryle for Missouri, and E. Merton Coulter for Kentucky.

It is a temptation to go on with a catalogue of this kind, perhaps too far; there are studies of state after state for the South during the Confederacy, such as those of T. Conn Bryan for Georgia, John K. Bettersworth and James W. Silver for Mississippi, and Jefferson D. Bragg for Louisiana. In addition to these, there are the broader works on the Confederacy by E. Merton Coulter, Clement Eaton, and Charles P. Roland, and many special studies of special topics such as morale, economic conditions, foreign relations, loyalty, social conditions, and so forth. There are studies of Reconstruction for literally every state. There are monographs on Populism in the South for various states, including Georgia (Arnett), Virginia (Sheldon), North Carolina (Delap), Alabama (Clark), Tennessee (Robison), Missouri (Clevenger), and Texas (Martin). On top of these, we have Noblin's life of Leonidas Polk and Woodward's revealing study of Watson. There are excellent studies of the progress of industrialization and economic change in the South by Calvin Hoover and Benjamin U. Ratchford, by Avery Leiserson, by Allen P. Sindler, by Thomas D. Clark, and by Robert H. Highsaw; and within the last year John C. McKinney and Edgar T. Thompson's wide-ranging and comprehensive collection of more than twenty scholarly papers on various aspects of Southern life and economy has appeared under the title *The South in Continuity and Change.*

But for three reasons, I must not go on with this listing: first, the recital is so long it would grow tiresome; second, if I attempted a fuller inventory, I would inevitably do an injustice to many significant studies which space prevents my mentioning. And most important, Professor Fletcher M. Green's former students have recently presented him with a *Festschrift* consisting of seventeen extensive historiographical essays which, with great thoroughness and learning, evaluate the present status of historical study in almost every phase of Southern history. Entitled *Writing Southern History* and edited by Arthur S. Link and Rembert W. Patrick, this *Festschrift* is perhaps the most searching and comprehensive inventory that has ever been made of any field of American history. It provides us with an unparalleled criterion for detecting what have been the more heavily worked and the more sketchily researched areas within the field of Southern history.

As we focus our attention upon the vast body of research which has been thus inventoried, we may be struck with a question as to how much of significance is left to be done. Or, to put it in familiarly Southern terms, we may wonder whether excessive historiographical "cropping" has "worked out" the soil still available to other historical cultivators. No doubt there are important areas in which it has. Where these exist, we should be glad of them, not regret them. But what I should like especially to suggest here is that, along with the depletion in some areas, there has been a recognition or discovery of other areas, so that the tasks of Southern history still present a wide range of opportunity for the historian. Very often, the completion of research at one level has simply exposed the need for work at another, deeper level. Work in one area has provided a new perspective on the problems that need to be worked out in another area. There is a saying that the increase in the diameter of our knowledge also increases the circumference of our ignorance, or, as the frontiers of our knowledge are pushed back, new contiguous areas, which have not been explored, are brought within the range of our inquiry.

This interplay between depletion of opportunity at one point and renewal at another is suggested at many points in Southern history. For instance, consider the theme of slavery. Our earliest monographic studies of slavery by men like James C. Ballagh and John Spencer Bassett, coming out of the school of history at Johns Hopkins, dealt with slavery in institutional terms, but did not seriously explore its economic aspects. The depletion of institutional studies paved the way for studies which were primarily economic (such as those of Ulrich B. Phillips, Lewis C. Gray, and Ralph B. Flanders), and for the numerous writers who have recently analyzed the question of the profitability of slavery. By the time that most of the economic possibilities had been worked out, other aspects in turn came into focus. Chase C. Mooney recognized the importance of demographic analysis, and he explored important questions of slave distribution which had never previously been analyzed. Clement Eaton and Richard C. Wade perceived that a focal point in the modification of the slave system was the employment of slaves as the equivalent of wage workers in the towns of the South. Hence they, and especially Wade, wrote about slavery in the cities. Kenneth Stampp and other modern writers insisted that it was not enough merely to ask how slavery worked as an economic system; we must also ask what it meant to the slave. But scarcely had they formed their answer in social and material terms before Stanley Elkins came forward with the contention that what slavery meant to the slave in terms of physical hardships, major or minor, was less important than what it meant in terms of psychological dependence and impairment of personality. Thus, the depletion of any one aspect of the topic of slavery has, up to now, always brought new aspects into focus.

Sometimes, as in the study of slavery, the development of

one aspect has prepared the way for moving on to another. But also, sometimes changes in our basic outlook have created a need for us to rework subjects which we once felt had been completely examined. About four decades ago, for instance, there was scarcely any subject which seemed to offer less promise for a new investigation than Reconstruction. There was a complete battery of monographs—one for every state, all fully documented, and all reflecting a strong political emphasis and a point of view that was either inspired by or sympathetic to the interpretation of William Archibald Dunning. As a field for historical investigation, Reconstruction seemed entirely depleted. But in 1932 Robert H. Woody and the late Francis B. Simkins showed how many latent possibilities still remained in the study of Reconstruction. In effect, their massive book *South Carolina During Reconstruction* demonstrated, without asserting, that all the older studies of the so-called "Dunning school" were at least partially out of date. Then, between 1938 and 1940, A. A. Taylor, Francis B. Simkins, and Howard K. Beale all published papers in which they called for a revision of the traditional interpretation. The field of Reconstruction had again become one of the most fruitful areas for research.

Although the need was agreed upon, the actual work of revision was a long time in gestation. As David Donald has recently said, "Except for works on Tennessee by T. B. Alexander (in 1950) and on Texas by W. C. Nunn (in 1962), no full-scale study of the postwar era in any Southern state has been published in the last twenty years." Roger Shugg in 1939 and Garnie McGinty in 1941 filled some of the gaps for Louisiana, and Vernon L. Wharton's study, *The Negro in Mississippi, 1865–1890* (1947), did something of the same sort for the Magnolia State; but the shelf of state studies of Reconstruction is still mostly where the Dunning school left it, although this school is now widely regarded as obsolete.

It is true that we have had a notable and quite recent harvest of significant books on Reconstruction in general, or on particular aspects of Reconstruction, including those by W. R. Brock, La Wanda and John H. Cox, Eric L. McKitrick, James M. MacPherson, Kenneth M. Stampp, Willie Lee Rose, David Donald, Rembert Patrick, Harold Hyman, and Selden Henry (forthcoming). These studies have given new vitality to what had become a stereotyped theme, and they have intensively explored a number of important topics. But the late Vernon Wharton observed that "for the Reconstruction period there has been no general study of Southern Negroes, carpetbaggers (including Negro carpetbaggers), scalawags or Southern 'redeemers.' " David Donald remarks that "There are no good books on the politics of any Northern state during Reconstruction. . . . A study of the Federal Army in the postwar South is badly wanted, as is a major work on the constitutional issues of the whole period. Andrew Johnson still lacks a good biographer, and there is no perceptive account of Grant's presidency."

This last point seems to me especially salient, for the works of Brock, the Coxes, McKitrick, MacPherson, Stampp, Rose, and Donald all concentrate heavily on the period of Lincoln and Johnson, with little attention to the period of Grant. Yet the Grant administration spanned nearly two-thirds of the so-called era of Reconstruction. The overthrow of the carpetbag regimes and the activity of Southern resistance organizations such as the Ku Klux Klan took place almost entirely during the Grant regime. Much of the period of Reconstruction has not been revised by the "revisionist" historians, even a quarter of a century after the doctrine of revisionism won acceptance at the ideological level. The brilliance of Vann Woodward's treatment of the electoral contest of 1877 in his *Reunion and Reaction* does not really qualify this statement. It is true that we have had some recent publications on the Ku Klux Klan, but Carl N. Degler, in a recent review, concludes by asserting that we still lack an adequate history of the role of the Klan, not to mention other similar organizations, during the later stages of Reconstruction.

A paper such as this is hardly the place to attempt to summarize what it took seventeen authors to recapitulate in *Writing Southern History*. My discussion of the literature of slavery and of Reconstruction has been intended rather to illustrate how the traversing of one subject leads us to the threshold of another, and how the apparent depletion of historiographical opportunities at one point is followed by a renewal of such opportunities at another. But in using these illustrations, I have fallen back to a consideration of the traditional themes—the themes of the prologue and epilogue of the Lost Cause—the very themes which Turner said we ought not to allow to narrow too much our recognition of the total sweep of the region as a realistic unit for the study of all kinds of social, cultural, and even, if you please, psychological phenomena.

The distinctiveness of the South may have been rooted, as Ulrich B. Phillips asserted, in the biracial system, and it may have manifested itself with maximum visibility in connection with the slavery conflict, the Civil War, and Reconstruction, but it has also appeared in a multitude of other forms. Southern Populism, as we all know, was unlike Western Populism; Southern Democrats have frequently been at odds with Northern Democrats on a multitude of issues other than civil rights. Southern attitudes on prohibition, Southern attitudes on women's suffrage, Southern attitudes on immigration restriction, Southern responses to the question of child labor, Southern attitudes toward intervention in World War II prior to December, 1941, Southern responses to modernism and secularism in the church have all been conspicuously different from the responses of other regions. Of course, as we all recognize, some of these differentials may reflect the simple fact that the South is more rural than other regions and we should try to avoid confusing ruralism in general with Southernism in particular. But the real point here is that the opportunities for the historian of the South are as broad as the social, cultural, intellectual, and economic differentials of the region. Here let me revert again to Turner's sweeping statement that there is a geography of political habits, of opinion, of material interests, of racial stocks, of physical fitness, of social traits, of literature, and even of religious denominations. Let me also suggest again that wherever there is a distinctive or formative geography, there is material for a distinctive history of each of these elements which Turner mentioned, and for others which he could have mentioned if he had chosen to extend his list.

The field of Southern history still presents many and fundamental challenges, and these challenges remind us, in a sense, of how little we know with certainty, despite all the scholarly labor that has been devoted so intensively to research. In this connection, I will say nothing about the continued and apparently insoluble differences in point of view about slavery; but let me suggest how far we are from agreeing about so basic a question as the nature of antebellum society. To some writers it was an aristocratic enclave in a democratic republic —a region dominated by planter grandees, few in number, but great in wealth and influence. These planters monopolized the best acreage, set the social tone, and imposed their leadership upon the only truly deferential society which existed in the United States. Their ownership of other human beings, as slaves, confirmed and sanctioned, as it were, their ascendancy, and committed the South to conservative and traditional modes of life and thought. For these writers Calhoun was the symbolic Southerner. Yet to other writers, including notably Fletcher M. Green and the late Frank L. Owsley, the

Old South partook rather fully of American democracy. The planters were only cotton farmers on a larger scale; their fortunes rose and fell; they gained political leadership only by displaying affable and democratic manners; and they held it only by a steady sequence of concessions to democracy in matters of the franchise, banking, land policy, and the like. The Whiggish party of the gentleman was ever on the defensive against the Democratic party of the common man. There was as much bumptiousness as there was deference, as much landgrabbing and speculation as there was tradition and gentility, Jefferson—not Calhoun—was the Southerner par excellence. The Negro slave was not the representative symbol and essential feature of a system of hierarchy and fixed status, but a great and unfortunate exception, the only person excluded from the benefits of democracy in a society which was essentially democratic.

Confronted by a choice between two such diverse images, both upheld by eminent authority, how shall we picture the Old South? We have, I believe, some scholarly work to guide us. Fabian Linden, in a long and much neglected paper in the *Journal of Negro History*, has shown that there was a considerable amount of euphoria in Professor Owsley's statistics (something which Rupert B. Vance also suggested more briefly). Moreover, we all know that the democratic manners of political leaders are not an infallible proof of democratic purposes. Yet, even if these qualifications are accepted and allowance is made for them, the interplay of aristocracy and democracy in the Old South remains a subtle problem, and all the simple answers seem suspect.

Another dimension of the intricacy of this problem has been most effectively pointed up by Eugene D. Genovese's recent book, *The Political Economy of Slavery*. Genovese rejects two interpretations of the Old South which have won wide acceptance, and he offers a third, which is a most arrest-

ing intellectual construct, though it would require a great
deal of testing before we could accept it with confidence. In
sum, says Genovese, we have customarily been presented with
an option between two explanations of the Old South. One
explanation, fairly well represented by the Owsley version, says
that the agrarian factor dominated—the South was a land of
small farmers who lived primarily by producing their own subsistence, and for whom money income was a subsidiary,
though of course an essential, factor. This was the South
of the Jeffersonian dream, and, of course, even a large plantation might be a subsistence plantation, with much of its
activity devoted to production for use. Such an image of the
Old South subtly discounts the importance of the slave, and
that is perhaps why many Southerners, embarrassed by slavery, have accepted it; it is also why Genovese, convinced of
the focal importance of slavery, rejects it.

The alternative view has been put forward chiefly by the
more stringent critics of the slavery system, of whom Kenneth
Stampp is the best known, but by no means the harshest.
These writers tend to minimize both the agrarian and the
feudal aspects of Southern life and to insist that the ante-
bellum Southern agricultural system was an integral part of
the American capitalist economic system—more folksy, more
rural than industrial capitalism, but just as committed to production for the market, just as preoccupied with money income and credit facilities, just as impersonal in its mechan-
isms, and, of course, just as exploitative in its quest for cheap
labor. This view minimizes the cultural distinctiveness of the
South and reduces the region to not much more than an area
of agricultural specialization, producing one particular market
commodity—cotton—by the techniques of one particular
mode of labor exploitation—slavery—all within a capitalistic
orbit.

Genovese rejects this view also. To him capitalism is, as I

read him, a whole cultural system, an attitude toward the relationship between production and other life values. Therefore, the fact that a society produces for the market, uses a money and credit economy, or exploits its labor is not an adequate index to the degree to which it participates in the capitalist culture. As he suggests, Saudi Arabia, India, and other countries have adopted many capitalistic devices without being culturally capitalistic. The diagnostic feature of life in the Old South, as he sees it, is neither agrarianism nor cotton capitalism, but the stark, unqualified direct relationship of mastery and dependence that inhered in the system of slavery. Such a system had a paradoxical double effect. It gave to the slaveholder a sense of responsibility which the employer might never feel, and at the same time it released in the slaveholder the impulses which absolute power may generate, and which, again, the employer never knew.

Again, if I may construe Genovese further, I think he is saying two things especially. First, the South really did not care about capitalism in its dynamic and mobile aspects—the aspects that transform a society. It cared only about those features of capitalism necessary to the perpetuation of the cotton-based society. Southern banks, he says, were not trying in an innovative way to stimulate all kinds of economic expansion; they were trying to service the cotton economy. If this is true, it should lend itself to testing. If it is verified, it should sharpen our focus upon the Old South. Second, the system of psychological relationships in a society depends upon the institutional and operative relationships. The institutional and operative relationships of a slaveholding system were wholly different from those of a wage-labor system, and the South therefore operated under a wholly distinctive system of psychological relationships. This system must not be sentimentalized as an agrarian system, which it was not, nor categorized simply as a peculiarly brutal form of capitalism,

which it was not either; it must be understood as something
very distinctive, in terms of its own.

It is, of course, not in order for me here to attempt to weigh
the relative validity of any of these conflicting views. What
I seek to point out is this: the opportunities of study in
Southern history cannot have been very seriously depleted
when we are still debating the basic questions, and when
the essential character of Southern society still presents different appearances to different viewers. The tasks of Southern
history are constantly being depleted and renewed at the
same time, and this fact stands true even without reference
to the immense and even revolutionary changes of the years
since *Brown* v. *Board of Education*. Parenthetically, I would
mention that a student of mine, Hugh D. Graham, has
written a thesis on the attitudes of the Tennessee press toward desegregation and related questions during these years,
and his thesis suggests to me that there are many, many
opportunities for study in this period, especially if we firmly
reject the stereotype of the South as a monolith and recognize
the importance of newspapers as well as legislatures, church
bodies as well as political parties, and differences between
urban and rural attitudes, as distinguishing features within
the framework of the almost universal reluctance of the white
South—which ought not to be denied—to accept desegregation.

This observation, in turn, leads me to one final comment
on the present tasks and opportunities of Southern history.
We have come into an era when, in the profession generally,
historians are increasingly dissatisfied with the adequacy of
their traditional methods, and are concerned to bring to
bear upon history the knowledge now at the command of
other disciplines. What do sociologists know about the social
structure of classes which historians might utilize in their
study of specific conflict between groups? What do economists

know about the factors conducive to rapid development or to stagnation which historians need to know in order to understand the prolongation of poverty in one country and the sudden recovery from economic reverses in another? What do psychologists know about human motivation which will enable historians to understand what impels human action? There is much evidence today that the important frontiers of Southern history are interdisciplinary frontiers. There are a number of comments by the authors of *Writing Southern History* which corroborate this view: For instance, Bennett H. Wall says, "The most intellectually stimulating and challenging essays on slavery in recent years have been written by historians interested in sociology and economics and by economists. One of them, apparently little known and rarely cited, is Edgar T. Thompson, 'The Natural History of Agricultural Labor in the South.' " Herbert Doherty observes that one can learn more about the history of the Negro church from Benjamin Mays, a sociologist, than from the formal history by Carter Woodson. George Tindall points out that for future historians the mid-twentieth century should be a "happy hunting ground in terms of the history of changes in race relations." With some spirit, Tindall asserts that there is much deficiency along with the achievements in Southern history. He mentions a number of neglected political topics, and then continues. "Business and labor history offer infinite possibilities, and Negro institutions of all kinds—social, economic, educational, and religious—provide ground that is not yet even plowed. Folk history may be too exotic for the common academic drudge but is there no writer who can do for Southern Negroes what Howard Odum did for Southern white folk in his *American Epoch*, or Wilbur Joseph Cash in his *The Mind of the South?* Is there none who can do for the Negro migrant what Handlin did for the European in *The Uprooted?*"

Handlin, it may be noted, is a historian, but in *The Up-rooted* he is not writing quite as a historian would usually write. Odum and Cash were not historians at all. What Wall and Doherty and Tindall are all asking for is history written with an infusion of what related fields of learning may impart. When the historian studies the poverty of the six decades after Appomattox and the relatively rapid economic growth of the South today, he needs to know not only about the New Deal and twenty-odd years of a war economy, but he must be able to apply what economists know about what retards some economies and enables others to become airborne. To deal with the history of Negro-white relations—the changes and the slowness of change—he must know not only about slavery, and Appomattox, and Reconstruction, and *Plessy* v. *Ferguson*, and Booker T. Washington's Atlanta Address, but he must know what a psychologist can tell him about the sources and nature of prejudice. He must, in fact, ask questions which up to now have been asked by social scientists but not by historians. To what extent does the rigidity of the segregation system arise from personal insecurities in members of the Southern white population? Do such insecurities have a higher incidence statistically among segregationists than among those who are not rigid about segregation? This is a tricky question, for, on the face of it, it seems unlikely that the people in one whole block of states would have greater personal insecurity than people in another whole block. To what extent is segregation supported not primarily because of "prejudice," or specific attitudes toward Negroes, but because of a desire, shared by all people everywhere, to do what their community, or at least what their reference group in the community, expects of them? To what extent in other words, has the support of segregation been, for many Southerners, merely a peculiarly compulsive type of conformity? To what extent is it rooted in sheer psychic inertia, to what extent

in the fact that men who treat other people badly need psychologically to believe that these others deserve to be treated
badly, to what extent in the fact that it is entirely realistic
for men to fear those whom they have wronged? But also,
to what extent is the impulse of separateness related somehow to the sense of identity, wholly apart from any animus
against the group toward whom separateness is maintained?
And are minorities, whose identity seems less secure than that
of majorities, more sensitive about this identity? The white
South has seen itself as a minority since almost two decades
prior to the Civil War, and it almost lost its identity at
Appomattox. The fierceness of the resistance of Southern
whites to Reconstruction was partly the result of a desperate
sense that their identity inhered partly in their Southernism
and their whiteness and that this identity must not be lost.
Is the bitterness of resistance to desegregation perhaps in
part an aspect of this same identity concept?

Questions like these lie ahead of us, and the historian can
hardly do justice to his themes if he avoids these questions.
Viewing the problem in these terms, it seems safe to say
that while several decades of intensive research in Southern
history have yielded a vital and extensive body of knowledge,
they have not depleted the field, but have left the investigator
of today with two challenges in which he may rejoice. First,
they have left him with a number of vital questions still to be
resolved; second, they have confronted him with the need, in
handling these questions, to work in a broader context of
sharing what other disciplines have to offer both in the way
of answers, and also of questions. This is to say that he needs
to work in just such a context as a well organized and well
integrated center for Southern studies both in the social
sciences and in the humanities would be able to offer. The
history of the South is more suffused with these interdisciplinary questions than, perhaps, most other fields of history,

and historians of the South should welcome the establishment of an interdisciplinary center proportionately. Through such a center, they might more readily find means for vitalizing many depleted themes in the study of Southern history.

Part 3

THE CRISIS OF THE UNION

CHAPTER VII

John Brown and the Paradox of Leadership among American Negroes

For a long time, one of the relatively neglected aspects of the problem of race relations in the United States has been the constraint that seemed to inhibit the personal interaction between Negroes and even those whites who were, in their ideals, most full of good will toward Negroes taken collectively. This condition may be somewhat mitigated in the present, though the rejection of whites by some blacks presents the same thing in another dimension. In any case, it was a conspicuous feature of the past. Reflecting upon this inhibition, I was led to ask what actual personal relationships existed between Negroes and the man who was, in some respects, the most militant white champion of Negro freedom in the nineteenth century.

ONE OF THE anomalies in the history of American Negroes is that, as a group, they have had only very limited opportunity to choose their own leadership. Historians agree, more or less, on a selected list of men who have been Negro leaders—Frederick Douglass, Booker T. Washington, W. E. B. Du Bois, Marcus Garvey, Martin Luther King. Of course, there have also been other very distinguished figures—Thurgood Marshall, Ralph Ellison, James Baldwin, Walter White, Roy Wilkins, *et al.*, but they have not commanded large mass followings; and there have been still others like Elijah Muhammad, Malcolm X, and Stokeley Carmichael whose role is or was controversial even within the Negro community. But none of these men was ever chosen to leadership by an election in which the body of American Negroes voted for what might be called "the Negroes' choice." Despite the wide-

spread growth of organized groups of Negro activists in recent years, there has never been an organization which we can
designate with assurance as expressing the attitudes of the rank
and file of American Negroes, unless it was Marcus Garvey's
Universal Negro Improvement Association. Most of the others
have appealed either to the middle class, as the NAACP has
done, or to ideological radicals, and not to the run-of-the-
mill American Negro.

This absence of an organizational basis for the selection
of leaders has meant that the positions of leadership were
gained in special ways, sometimes in arbitrary or, as it were,
fictitious ways. For instance, Frederick Douglass received his
license as spokesman for four million slaves from a small
coterie of abolitionists who later quarrelled with him. True,
he was an excellent choice and he proved a very able leader
indeed—perhaps as able as any American Negro—but the
choice was nevertheless a historical accident, as the choice
of many excellent leaders has been. Booker T. Washington,
also an able man, did not owe his eminence to the recognition
that Negroes gave him, but was appointed to the political
leadership of American Negroes by Theodore Roosevelt, and
to the economic leadership by Andrew Carnegie. W. E. B.
Du Bois received his investiture in an especially ironical way
—the anomaly of which he felt as keenly as anyone else. He
was made the key figure in the NAACP by a wealthy, highly
respectable, and I think one can say smug, self-appointed
committee of upper-class white moderate reformers; later, he
owed his more or less posthumous canonization to academic
Marxist intellectuals whom most Negroes had never heard
of. Today some of the militant types whose names flash like
meteors across the headlines—Carmichael, Rap Brown, Le-
Roi Jones—have been fobbed off on American Negroes partly
by social revolutionaries who care nothing for civil rights or
Negro welfare within our existing society, and partly by the

mass media which need sensational and extravagant material to galvanize the attention of a jaded public. If one looks for Negroes who owed their positions of leadership primarily to the support accorded them by other Negroes, the most authentic names are those of Marcus Garvey and Martin Luther King, and perhaps Roy Wilkins, despite the attacks which he has sustained from the left. At a more limited level, I think one should add Elijah Muhammad and Malcolm X.

These comments may seem extraneous indeed to a consideration of the career of John Brown, but indirectly they may have a certain pertinence because though Brown was not a Negro, he probably went farther in plans for launching a Negro revolution in the United States than anyone in history. He intended to become the commander-in-chief of an army of Negroes. Yet he had no Negro lieutenants; he took almost no advice from Negroes and acted in defiance of such advice as he did take; and most paradoxical of all, he completely concealed his intended insurrection from the Negroes who were expected to support it. His was the classic case of a man who acted in the name of American Negroes and relied upon them to follow him, but never really sought to represent them or to find out what they wanted their leader to do.

Historians of the antislavery movement have already complained, with considerable justice I think, that the Negro was neglected even by the abolitionists. Many abolitionists could not see the Negroes, as it were, for the slaves. Thus even the underground railroad became, historiographically, the first Jim Crow transportation in America. Traditional accounts pictured the railroad as an operation in which heroic white conductors braved dangers unspeakable in transporting fugitives from one hideout to the next, while the helpless and passive Negroes lay inert in the bottom of the wagon bed, concealed under a layer of hay. We now know that a good many respectable Yankee families who had never worked on the railroad later decided that they had intended to, or they would have if there had been a fugitive handy, and gradually translated this sentimental ex post facto intention into the legend of a fearless deed. But that is beside the point. What is relevant to the theme of this paper is that historically there was an anomalous relationship between the Negro slaves and their white sympathizers, and the paradox of this relationship shows up in its most striking form in the story of John Brown and Harpers Ferry. The paradox lay in the fact that the white abolitionists believed that the Negroes were all on the brink of a massive insurrection, yet they seldom consulted any Negro for corroboration and they conducted their own abolitionist activities—even John Brown's insurrectionary activities—as if Negroes could be regarded abstractly, like some sort of chemical element which at a certain heat would fuse into a new compound, and not concretely as a plurality of diverse men and women, each one with a temperament and aspirations of his own.

What were John Brown's specific relations with Negroes? It cannot be said that Negroes were entirely an abstraction to him, as they have been to some civil rights enthusiasts, for he knew Negroes, worked with them, and included them, on terms of seeming familiarity, in the intimacy of his little band of followers. But let us examine the record in more detail.

John Brown was apparently reared from an early age to hate slavery. The details may have been overdramatized, as they have been in the story of the early life of Lincoln, but the fact appears clear. As early as the 1830's he assisted in the escape of at least one fugitive; he made plans to rear a Negro child with his own children in his home; and he also thought of conducting a school for Negroes. His systematic activity in behalf of Negroes and his actual association with Negroes, however, began in the late 1840's when he agreed to move to North Elba, New York, where Gerrit Smith proposed to make him responsible for a colony of Negroes for which Smith was prepared to give 120,000 acres. At North Elba, Brown tried to help the Negro settlers, including at least one known fugitive. He gave them advice about farming and took some into his home, where they worked and shared the Spartan life of his family. But the North Elba project failed, primarily because the region never has been good farm country; it was frigid and rigorous in a way that made adaptation by Southern Negroes especially difficult. Moreover, Brown's own financial difficulties in the wool business made it impossible for him to stay at North Elba on a regular basis, and compelled him to spend much of his time at Springfield, Massachusetts, instead. At Springfield in 1847, he invited Frederick Douglass to visit him, and there he revealed to Douglass the first version of the plan which ultimately took him to Harpers Ferry. This was a scheme to organize a band of about twenty-five men, who would operate from hideouts in the Southern Appalachians. These men would induce slaves to run away and would assist them in their escape. Douglass had been a fugitive slave himself, had lived among slaves, had known the South at first hand; but there is no evidence that Brown asked him for his opinion about the practicability of the plan or about any aspect of the operations. Douglass probably knew a great deal that might have been useful to Brown, but Brown took no advantage of this potential information. This was characteristic of him throughout his life.

By the time of the enactment of the Fugitive Slave Act in 1850, Brown was in Springfield most of the time. In response to the act, he organized a League of Gileadites, as he called it, to offer physical resistance to the enforcement of the act. He drew up an "Agreement" and nine resolutions for the League, with an emphasis upon encouraging Negroes to be brave and not to resort to halfway measures: "When engaged, do not do your work by halves, but make clean work with your enemies and be sure you meddle not with any others. . . . All traitors must die, whenever caught and proven to be guilty." Brown wrote to his wife in November, 1850: "I, of course, keep encouraging my colored friends to 'trust in God and keep their powder dry.' I did so today at a Thanksgiving meeting, publicly." Forty-four black men and women of Springfield signed Brown's agreement, but their commitment was never put to the test, for no efforts were made by Federal officials to arrest fugitives in the Springfield area. Still, the League is of great interest, for it was the only case in which this man—who gave so much of his energy while living and finally his life itself to the Negro cause—relied primarily upon Negroes in his work.

As the focus of the slavery controversy shifted to Kansas, Brown shifted his activities to that arena, and the plans which he had revealed to Douglass fell into abeyance. But ultimately it was the Kansas diversion which led him back to the Virginia project. Kansas fed his impulse toward violence, his appetite for leadership, and his hatred of slavery. It also unfitted him for his former prosaic pursuits in the wool trade. If Kansas had continued as a scene of violence, he might have ended his career as a Jayhawker on the Kansas prairies, but by 1857 Kansas was becoming pacified. Robert J. Walker had replaced Geary as governor and was giving the Free-Soilers fair treatment; the Free-Soilers had won control of the legislature when Walker threw out fraudulent proslavery votes. The antislavery party had nothing whatever to gain by a resumption of the border wars. They remembered, unpleasantly, the murders committed by Brown along Pottawatomie Creek (something which Easterners did not know about), and they regarded Brown as a troublemaker—trigger-happy and too much of a lone wolf. Brown began to perceive that his career as a Kansas guerrilla was played out, and though he still talked about organizing a crack military unit for Kansas, his thoughts were turning increasingly toward the old idea of some kind of operation in the Southern Appalachians.

Brown left Kansas twice, first in October, 1856, with a divided mind as to whether he ought to return and continue active in the border wars; and again in November, 1857, knowing that his path would lead to Virginia. It is significant that, on both occasions, he stopped off at Rochester to see Douglass (in December, 1856, and in January, 1858). What meaning the visit in 1856 may have had, no one now can tell; at least it showed, as Douglass testifies, that the relationship formed nine years previously had been kept very much alive. But the visit in 1858 lasted for three weeks, and during this time Brown unfolded in full, perhaps for the first time, his second version of a plan for operation in Virginia. Douglass did not, at that time, disassociate himself from the plan, and indeed he later helped Brown to raise funds among well-to-do Negroes. But having been both a slave and a fugitive, Douglass perceived defects in the realism of Brown's plan, and he warned Brown of the pitfalls which were involved. John Brown did with this advice what he always did with all advice—he ignored it.

An interval of twenty months was to elapse between these conferences with Douglass and the final action at Harpers Ferry. This represented a delay of over a year in Brown's original plans. The delay resulted from two things: first, lack of money; and second, the fact that a soldier of fortune named Hugh Forbes, whom Brown had taken on as a military adviser, became disaffected because he did not receive the pay which he thought he had been promised, broke confidence, and revealed much of the plot to Senators Henry Wilson and William H. Seward. This breakdown in security greatly alarmed Brown's financial supporters, who virtually ordered him to suspend his plans.

Thus, during most of 1858 and 1859, Brown, who wanted only to smite the slaveholders, discovered that he had to be a salesman and a fund-raiser first. So long as he was soliciting for funds for aid to Free-Soilers in Kansas, he was able to make public appeals. But as his insurrectionary scheme developed, it required the utmost secrecy, and he could appeal only to trusted sympathizers including principally the Secret Six—Gerrit Smith in Peterboro, New York, and five backers in Boston: George L. Stearns, Franklin B. Sanborn, Thomas Wentworth Higginson, Theodore Parker, and Samuel Gridley Howe. These men had been moderately generous since 1857, but they tended to want more action before they gave additional money, and Brown wanted additional money as a preliminary to the action. Often he was actually reduced to asking for handouts, and he never did obtain anything approaching the financial support which was needed for an operation on the scale which he projected.

Somehow, nevertheless, he weathered all these difficulties. Meanwhile, he had been looking to a means of formalizing his plans and raising recruits; and to this end he had made a curious pilgrimage with twelve of his followers, all of them white men except Richard Richardson, to Chatham, Ontario, in May, 1858. Ontario at that time had a population of upwards of thirty thousand Negroes, a vast proportion of whom were former slaves who might be expected to support a campaign against slavery in the South. Among these people, Brown had determined to make his appeal, to relax secrecy, and to seek the sanction and support of the Negro community for his daring plan. He had invited Gerrit Smith, Wendell Phillips, "and others of like kin" to be on hand.

Accordingly, on May 8, 1858, Brown presented to a secret "convention" at Chatham, consisting of twelve of his own followers and thirty-four resident Negroes, a plan of organization entitled "A Provisional Constitution and Ordinances for the people of the United States." This document condemned slavery, defined slavery as war, thus asserting for the slaves a legal status as belligerents, and provided for a provisional government, with a commander-in-chief of the army, an executive, a legislature, and a judiciary. This government was to act against slavery—indeed, to make war against it—and in explaining it Brown stated where the army would get its troops. "Upon the first intimation of a plan formed for the liberation of the slaves," he said, "they would immediately rise all over the Southern states." By "flocking to his standard" they would enable him to extend his operations outward and southward from the mountain country in which he would begin, until he could operate upon the plantations of the lower South. They could defeat any militia, or even Federal troops sent against them, and "then organize the freed blacks under this provisional Constitution." What John Brown was planning was not a raid but a revolution.

The convention politely voted for the proposed Constitution, and on the next day it elected John Brown commander-in-chief and members of his party Secretaries of State, of the Treasury, and of War. Two men were elected as members of Congress, and one of these, Osborn P. Anderson, was an Ontario Negro. All the others were whites.

But Gerrit Smith was not there; Frederick Douglass was not there; and Wendell Phillips was not there. And when John Brown left Ontario, only two new Negro recruits went with him, one of whom, fearing arrest, soon returned to Canada. This was the only real effort Brown ever made to organize Negro support, and it had failed completely. It indicated clearly that the most famous project for a Negro insurrection in the history of the United States did not have the full support of even a corporal's guard of Negroes. There must have been hundreds of Negroes in Ontario who heard all about Brown's "secret" plan, but they had learned in a realistic school, and far more shrewdly than Emerson and Thoreau, and the litterateurs of Boston, they recognized that there was something unrealistic about this man. What was wrong was that he was recruiting members of a supporting cast for a theatrical melodrama in which the protagonist and principal actor was to be John Brown.

Only a month after the Chatham "convention" Brown sent one of his very earliest recruits, John E. Cook, to Harpers Ferry, Virginia, to live as a spy and to reconnoiter the environs. Cook found employment as a lock-tender on the canal and maintained his mission for over a year, but Brown was very apprehensive that he would talk too much, and this apprehension must have increased greatly when Cook married a local Harpers Ferry girl.

Fourteen months after the Chatham convention, Brown and a small band of followers began to converge on a farmhouse in Maryland which was to be their rendezvous. At first there were twenty of them, including sixteen whites and four Negroes—two of whom were born free and two of whom had run away from slavery. After they had gathered, Frederick Douglass came down to Chambersburg, Maryland, with a friend of his, Shields Green, who was, like himself, an escaped slave. Brown and Douglass had a final conference, which must have been a strained affair on both sides. Brown now revealed a new and even more alarming design—his purpose to seize the arsenal at Harpers Ferry. To this Douglass instantly took exception. He warned Brown that the position would be a trap from which escape would be impossible, and also that an attack on Federal property would turn the whole country against Brown's plans. He said that this was such a complete change of purpose that he would no longer participate. Brown urged him not to withdraw, saying, "I want you for a special purpose. When I strike, the bees will begin to swarm, and I shall want you to help me hive them." But Douglass still refused, and turning to his friend he asked what Green intended to do. Green's reply was, "I b'lieve I'll go wid de ole man."

Green was later accused of lack of courage, but there was in fact something supremely heroic about his action. His remark showed little confidence in Brown's plan but much loyalty to Brown personally; and he later died on the gallows because he had subordinated his judgment to his sense of personal devotion.

On the evening of October 16, 1859, after waiting three months for additional men, money, and munitions, most of which never arrived, John Brown marched with nineteen of his band, now grown to twenty-two, down to Harpers Ferry. There he seized the Potomac River bridge, the Shenandoah River bridge, and the Federal armory and rifle works. He also sent out a detail to bring in two of the slaveholders of the neighborhood with their slaves. This mission was accomplished. Then he settled into the arsenal and waited, while first the local militia and later a small Federal force gathered to besiege him. Within thirty-six hours, his hopes were blasted and his force was destroyed—five men had escaped, but ten were dead or dying, and seven were in prison, all to die at the end of a rope.

Technically, Brown's operation had been such an unmitigated disaster that it has lent color to the belief that he was insane. Certain aspects were indeed incongruous. After making melodramatic gestures in the direction of secrecy, he had left behind him on the Maryland farm a large accumulation of letters which revealed all his plans and exposed all his secret supporters among the elite of Boston. As Hugh Forbes wrote, "the most terrible engine of destruction which he [Brown] would carry with him in his campaign would be a carpet-bag loaded with 400 letters, to be turned against his friends, of whom the journals assert that more than forty-seven are already compromised." After three and a half months of preparation, he marched at last without taking with him food for his soldiers' next meal, so that, the following morning, the Commander-in-Chief of the Provisional Army of the North, in default of commissary, was obliged to order forty-five breakfasts sent over from the Wagner House. For the remaining twenty-five hours, the suffering of Brown's besieged men was accentuated by the fact that they were acutely and needlessly hungry. His liaison with allies in the North was so faulty that they did not know when he would strike, and John Brown, Jr., who was supposed to forward additional recruits, later stated that the raid took him completely by surprise. If this was, as is sometimes suggested, because of the disordered condition of young Brown's mind rather than because of lack of information from his father, it still leaves a question why such a vital duty should have been entrusted to one whose mental instability had been conspicuous ever since Pottawatomie. Finally, there was the seemingly incredible folly of seizing a Federal arsenal and starting a war against the state of Virginia with an army of twenty-two men. This latter folly was probably the strongest factor in the later contention that he was insane. In layman's terms, anybody who tried to conquer a state as large as one of the nations of Western Europe with less than two dozen troops might be regarded as crazy. Was John Brown crazy in these terms?

Without trying to resolve the insanity question, to which C. Vann Woodward, Allan Nevins, and others have given extensive attention, let me just make two brief comments: first, that insanity is a clear-cut legal concept concerning a psychological condition which is seldom clear-cut; second, that the insanity concept has been invoked too much by people whose ulterior purposes were too palpable—first by people who hoped to save Brown's life by proving him irresponsible; then by Republicans who wanted to disclaim his act without condemning him morally; and finally by adverse historians who wanted to discredit his deeds by saying that only a madman would do such things. The evidence shows that Brown was very intense and aloof, that he became exclusively preoccupied with his one grand design, that he sometimes behaved in a very confused way, that he alternated between brief periods of decisive action and long intervals when it is hard to tell what he was doing, that mental instability occurred with significant frequency in his family, and that some who knew him believed he had a vindictive or even a homicidal streak with strong fantasies of superhuman greatness. Also, Pottawatomie should be borne in mind. From all this, one may clearly infer that Brown was not, as we would now term it, a well-adjusted man.

But withal, the heaviest count in the argument against Brown's sanity is the seeming irrationality of the Harpers Ferry operation. Yet Harpers Ferry, it might be argued, was irrational if, and only if, the belief in a vast, self-starting slave insurrection was a delusion. But if this was a fantasy, it was one which Brown shared with Theodore Parker, Samuel Gridley Howe, Thomas Wentworth Higginson, and a great many others who have never been called insane. It was an article of faith among the abolitionists that the slaves of the South were seething with discontent and awaited only a signal to throw off their chains. It would have been heresy for an orthodox abolitionist to doubt this, quite as disloyal as for him to entertain the idea that any slave owner might be a well-intentioned and conscientious man. Gerrit Smith believed it, and two months before Brown's attempted coup he wrote, "The feeling among the blacks that they must deliver themselves gains strength with fearful rapidity." Samuel

Gridley Howe believed it, and even after Brown's failure and
when war came, he wrote that twenty to forty thousand volunteers could "plough through the South and be followed by
a blaze of servile war that would utterly and forever root out
slaveholding and slavery." Theodore Parker believed it, and
wrote in 1850, "God forgive us our cowardice, if we let it
come to this, that three millions of human beings . . . de-
graded by us, must wade through slaughter to their inalien-
able rights." After Harpers Ferry, Parker said, "The Fire of
Vengeance may be waked up even in an African's heart, especially when it is fanned by the wickedness of a white man;
then it runs from man to man, from town to town. What
shall put it out? The white man's blood." William Lloyd Garrison was apparently inhibited from making such statements
by his opposition on principle to the use of violence, but his
Liberator constantly emphasized the unrest and resentment
among the slaves; and he had once declared that, but for his
scruples, he would place himself "at the head of a black army
at the South to scatter devastation and death on every side."
As J. C. Furnas has expressed it, there was a widespread
"Spartacus complex" among the abolitionists, a fascinated
belief that the South stood on the brink of a vast slave uprising and a wholesale slaughter of the whites. "It is not easy,
though necessary," says Furnas, "to grasp that Abolitionism
could, in the same breath warn the South of arson, rape, and
murder and sentimentally admire the implied Negro mob
leaders brandishing axes, torches, and human heads." This
complex arose from the psychological needs of the abolitionists and not from any evidence which Negroes had given to
them. No one really asked the Negroes what they wanted,
or just how bloodthirsty they felt. There is much evidence
that they wanted freedom to be sure, but again there is not
much evidence that anyone even asked them how they
thought their freedom could best be gained, and how they

would like to go about getting it. Certainly John Brown did not ask, when he had a really good opportunity at Chatham, Ontario. All he did was talk. He did not listen at all. In fact there is no evidence that he ever listened at anytime, and this is perhaps the most convincing proof that he lived in the "private world" of an insane man.

But Brown's idea that the South was a waiting torch, and that twenty-two men without rations were enough to put a match to it, far from being a unique aberration, was actually one of the most conventional, least original notions in his whole stock of beliefs. Thus the Boston *Post* spoke much to the point when it said, "John Brown may be a lunatic but if so, then one-fourth of the people of Massachusetts are madmen."

The *Post* certainly did not intend to shift the question from one concerning Brown's personal sanity to one concerning the mass delusions of the abolitionists. A historian may, however, regard the latter as a legitimate topic of inquiry. But if he should do so, he must recognize at once the further fact that the Spartacus delusion—if delusion it was—was not confined to the abolitionists. The Southerners, too, shared this concept, in the sense that they were ever fearful of slave insurrections and were immensely relieved to learn that the slaves had not flocked to Brown's support. Clearly they had felt no assurance that this would be the outcome.

This is no place for me to go into either the extent or the realism of Southern fears of slave insurrection. The only point to make here is that John Brown, believing in the potentiality of a slave insurrection, only believed what both abolitionist and slaveholders believed. But Brown needed to know the specifics of that potentiality as others did not. He needed to know how strong it was, how it could be cultivated, how it could be triggered. The lives of himself and his men depended upon knowing. Yet there is no evidence that he ever even asked the questions. He merely said, "When I strike, the bees will swarm." But Negroes are not bees, and when figures of speech are used in argumentation, they are usually a substitute for realistic thinking.

Brown may have been right, at a certain level and in a certain sense, in believing that the Negroes might revolt. But he was completely wrong in the literal-minded way in which he held the idea, and this indiscriminate notion about Negro reactions probably led him to what was really his supreme folly. He supposed that the Negroes of Jefferson County would instantly spring to the support of an insurrection of which they had not been notified—that they would, of their own volition, join a desperate coup to which they had not even been invited. Brown evidently thought of Negroes, as so many other people have done, as abstractions, and not as men and women.

It was not as if he had not been warned: his English soldier of fortune, Hugh Forbes, told him that even slaves ripe for revolt would not come in on an enterprise like this. "No preparatory notice having been given to the slaves," he said, "the invitation to rise might, unless they were already in a state of agitation, meet with no response, or a feeble one." But Brown brushed this aside: he was sure of a response, and calculated that on the first night of the revolt, between two hundred and five hundred slaves would rally to him at the first news of his raid. Again later, when John E. Cook was keeping his lonely and secret vigil for more than a year as Brown's advance agent at Harpers Ferry, and even after Brown had moved to the farm in Maryland, Cook pleaded to be allowed to give the slaves at least some inkling of what was afoot. But Brown sternly rejected this idea. Thus, when the "Negro insurrection" began, the Negroes were as unprepared for it, as disconcerted, and as mystified as anyone else.

Brown, in his grandiose way, boasted of having studied the

slave insurrections of history—of Spartacus, of Toussaint. But one wonders what those two, or even Denmark Vesley, would have had to say about John Brown's mode of conducting an insurrection. Abraham Lincoln, with his usual talent for accuracy of statement, later said, "It was not a slave insurrection. It was an attempt by white men to get up a revolt among slaves, in which the slaves refused to participate." But in a way Lincoln understated the case. The slaves were never asked to participate. Brown's remarkable technique for securing their participation was to send out a detail in the middle of the night, kidnap them, thrust a pike into their hands, and inform them that they were soldiers in the army of emancipation. He then expected them to place their necks in a noose without asking for further particulars.

Yet he was so supremely confident of their massive support that all the strange errors of October 16 and 17 sprang from that delusion. This was why he marched without rations; it was why thirteen of his twenty-one followers carried commissions as officers in their knapsacks, though none of his five Negro followers was included in this number—thirteen officers would hardly suffice to command the Negro troops who would swarm like bees to his headquarters; it was why he wanted the weapons at Harpers Ferry although he already had several times as many weapons as were needed for the men at the Maryland farm. Finally it was why he sat down at Harpers Ferry and waited while his adversaries closed the trap on him. He was still waiting for the word to spread and for the Negroes to come trooping in.

John Brown wanted to be a leader for the Negroes of America. He dwelled upon this idea almost to the exclusion of all others. Ultimately he died with singular bravery to vindicate his role. Yet he never thought to ask the Negroes if they would accept him as a leader, and if so, what kind of policy they wanted him to pursue. Of course he could not ask them all, but he never even asked Frederick Douglass or the gathering of Negroes at Chatham. He knew what he wanted them to do and did not really care what they themselves wanted to do. John Brown occupies and deserves a heroic place in the gallery of historic leaders of American Negroes. Yet, like many other prominent and less heroic figures in that gallery, he was a self-appointed savior, who was not chosen by the Negroes, who had no Negro following of any magnitude, and whose policies in the name of the Negro were not necessarily the policies of the Negroes themselves.

Horace Greeley and Peaceable Secession

In May, 1941, this paper on Horace Greeley and his attitude
toward secession appeared in the Journal of Southern History.
Ten years later Thomas N. Bonner published a paper, "Horace
Greeley and the Secession Movement, 1860–1861," in which he
offered an interpretation that was fundamentally different from
mine. Any scholar concerned with the question should, of
course, read both papers. But since I have never responded to
Professor Bonner's paper, I take this opportunity to summarize
in a Postscript my comment upon our points of disagreement.

*T*HE VICTORY of Abraham Lincoln in the presidential
election of November 6, 1860, marked the end of a campaign that had preoccupied the public mind for some months.
Under normal circumstances the long period of tenseness
would have been followed by a reaction, as tired cam-
paigners relaxed and successful ones exulted. For this electoral
harvest, however, there was to be no festival. Even before the
votes were counted, the legislature of South Carolina had
ominously chosen to remain in session in order that it might
instantly set the secession ball rolling if the "Black Republicans" should be the victors. True to its purpose, the legislature, within four days of the election, passed an act providing
for a state convention to meet in December. Thus the secession crisis followed instantly upon the excitement of the
campaign. Instead of affording a respite, the election height-
ened the tenseness. Republican leaders who had expected
four months of grace in which to prepare for their direction of
national policy were confronted by an exigent and rapidly moving crisis.

In the circumstances they appeared at their worst. For four months they evaded, equivocated, shifted, blundered, and sought refuge in fantasy. Of their chief leaders, William H. Seward gave incessant and prolix expression to a somewhat mystical conviction that the portentous and explicit acts of the South were evidences of a passing frenzy which would subside of itself. Meanwhile, Lincoln resorted to a complete, impenetrable, and alarming silence. Lesser Republicans, for the most part, met the crisis no more effectively than their two foremost leaders, and thus throughout the winter their tone was generally either blustering or vacillating, and, in either case, unrealistic.

Out of this welter of confusion one voice rose above the din with promptness and emphasis, and, as it seemed, with clarity. This was the voice of Horace Greeley. Before the crisis was three days old he wrote off, in his characteristic illegible hand, the most quoted sentence that his New York *Tribune* ever carried to a waiting public: "if the Cotton States shall become satisfied that they can do better out of the Union than in it, we insist on letting them go in peace."

Greeley did not know it, but he had contributed a footnote to history. For decades since he sent his startling pronouncement to the composing room, historians have pictured the general confusion as the secession movement got under way, and have scrupulously mentioned that a respectable minority of Northerners, unwilling to plunge the nation into war, sought peace by separation. To those who detect such a willingness to separate, the *Tribune* is, of course, the perfect illustration. Horace Greeley is the personification of this sentiment, and his editorial of November 9 is their perennial footnote. His facile assertion that "we insist on letting them go in peace" has become an accepted stage property in the drama of history. In whole or in part, *verbatim*, or in most literal paraphrase, his vivid declaration has passed from tome to textbook. Greeley himself started it upon the road to repetition by republishing his entire editorial in *The American Conflict* (1864).[1] Within the same year it was abridged and distorted by the excision of all reservations and conditions, so that it appeared to give unqualified acceptance to secession;[2] and in this deleted form it has been making the rounds ever since. It appears in the *American Nation* series[3] and in the *Chronicles of America*;[4] it is used in standard older works such as those of James Ford Rhodes,[5] Edward Chan-

[1] Horace Greeley, *The American Conflict* (2 vols.; Hartford, 1864–66), I, 358–59.

[2] See S. D. Carpenter, *Logic of History* (Madison, Wis., 1864), 86. The writer does not mean to say that other authors have quoted Carpenter, but only that the editorial has been abridged constantly since the war.

[3] "The New York *Tribune*, which held the position of leadership among Republican journals, and which was a power throughout the north, was proclaiming that 'if the Cotton States shall become satisfied that they can do better out of the Union than in it, we insist on letting them go in peace.' . . . Nor was Greeley alone in his views; the abolitionists professing anxiety to accomplish the extinction of slavery were arguing that the South should be permitted to secede. Governor Moore of Alabama was hailing them as 'our best friends.'" French E. Chadwick, *Causes of the Civil War* (New York, 1906), 164–65.

[4] "What strikes us most forcibly, as we look back upon that day, is the widespread desire for peace. . . .

"Horace Greeley said in an editorial in the *New York Tribune*: 'If the cotton states shall decide [Greeley said "shall become satisfied," not "shall decide"] that they can do better out of the Union than in it, we shall insist [Greeley said "insist," not "shall insist"] on letting them go in peace. . . . Whenever a considerable section of our Union shall deliberately resolve to go out, we shall resist all coercive measures designed to keep them in [Greeley said "it in," not "them in"]. We hope never to live in a republic where [Greeley said "whereof"] one section is pinned to the residue by bayonets.'" Nathaniel W. Stephenson, *Abraham Lincoln and the Union* (New Haven, 1921), 90.

[5] "Another phase of opinion was both represented and led by Horace Greeley. Three days after the election, the New York *Tribune*, in a leading article, said: 'If the cotton States shall decide [Greeley

ning,[6] and Albert Bushnell Hart;[7] it appears also in more recent interpretations by Arthur C. Cole[8] and James Truslow Adams;[9] it is employed similarly by Samuel E. Morison and Henry S. Commager,[10] by Charles and Mary Beard,[11] by

said "shall become satisfied," not "shall decide"] that they can do better out of the Union than in it, we insist on letting them go in peace.'" James F. Rhodes, *History of the United States from the Compromise of 1850 to the Final Restoration of Home Rule in the South in 1877* (7 vols.; New York, 1893–1906), III, 140.

[6] "Horace Greeley, in the New York 'Tribune' wrote that if the Southern States want to leave the Union, they have an absolute moral right to do so." Edward Channing, *A History of the United States* (6 vols.; New York, 1905–25), VI, 292.

[7] "The belief that the Union was no union was not confined to Breckinridge Democrats, for the Republican journalist and leader, Horace Greeley, was in the clearest tones preaching non-resistance; on November 9, 1860, his New York 'Tribune' declared that 'if the cotton States shall decide [Greeley said "shall become satisfied," not "shall decide"] that they can do better out of the Union than in it, we insist on letting them go in peace.'" Albert B. Hart, *Salmon Portland Chase* (Boston, 1899), 199.

[8] "Other Northerners of the 'hopelessly abolitionized' type rejoiced with Greeley at the opportunity to 'let the erring sisters depart in peace.' If some of these talked of the South's right to self-government and self-determination, it is clear that their deeper motive was to rid the nation of responsibility for an undesirable institution." Arthur C. Cole, *The Irrepressible Conflict, 1850–1865* (New York, 1934), 304.

[9] "Three days after the election Horace Greeley wrote in *The Tribune* advising that if the Southern States should secede, although the movement would be a revolutionary one, they should be allowed to go in peace. 'We hope never to live in a Republic, whereof one section is pinned to the residue by bayonets.'" James T. Adams, *America's Tragedy* (New York, 1934), 147–48.

[10] "Horace Greeley of the New York *Tribune* and General Winfield Scott struck the key-note of Northern sentiment in January with the phrase 'Wayward sisters, depart in peace!'" Samuel E. Morison and Henry S. Commager, *The Growth of the American Republic* (2 vols.; New York, 1937), I, 539. In attributing these attitudes to Greeley and Scott as of January, the authors ignore the facts that Greeley had begun to qualify his "go in peace" utterances as early as December, and that General Scott, although inclined to accept seces-

Arthur M. Schlesinger,[12] John Spencer Bassett,[13] Harold U. Faulkner,[14] and by uncounted others. It is stock in trade. Horace Greeley has been identified with peaceable separation just as thoroughly as Henry VIII with matrimony or Machiavelli with duplicity.

If this interpretation had been a palpable fraud, it could never have achieved such currency. It was necessarily based upon a half-truth at least—a half-truth which could slip by the unwary, secure admittance in good academic society, and,

---

sion as early as October, 1860, did not use the phrase "Wayward sisters, depart in peace" until March 3, 1861. Even then he did not actually propose to address the seceding states thus, but only enumerated this as one of four alternative policies which might be adopted toward the South.

[11] "Horace Greeley wrote in the Tribune: 'If the cotton states shall decide [Greeley said "shall become satisfied," not "shall decide"] that they can do better out of the Union than in it, we insist on letting them go in peace. The right to secede may be a revolutionary one but it exists nevertheless.'" Charles A. Beard and Mary R. Beard, *The Rise of American Civilization* (2 vols.; New York, 1927), II, 63.

[12] "Antislavery radicals, for their part, declared publicly that the departure of the slave states was good riddance. 'If the cotton States shall decide [Greeley said "shall become satisfied," not "shall decide"] that they can do better out of the Union than in it,' asserted the *New York Tribune*, 'we insist on letting them go in peace.'" Arthur M. Schlesinger, *Political and Social Growth of the United States, 1852–1933* (New York, 1936), 50.

[13] "At the same time the New York *Tribune* and abolitionists generally, were asserting plainly that the North could not conquer the South and that the South, if it so wished, should be allowed to 'depart in peace.'" John S. Bassett, *A Short History of the United States* (New York, 1939), 512.

[14] "In addition to the economic interests there were many abolitionists who evidently believed the Union would be as well off without the slave states. 'If the cotton states shall decide [Greeley said "shall become satisfied," not "shall decide"] that they can do better out of the Union than in it,' said Greeley in December [*sic!*], 'we shall insist [Greeley said "insist," not "shall insist"] on letting them go in peace,' and this sentiment was echoed by Wendell Phillips and Henry Ward Beecher." Harold U. Faulkner, *American Political and Social History* (New York, 1938), 331.

when challenged, present its veracious side to view. Thus if Greeley had never said "we insist on letting them go in peace," he could scarcely have been identified with peaceable separation. But once he had uttered that single, misquotable phrase, it made no difference that he had previously taken a most belligerent tone, and, after a brief interlude, was to revert to it; it did not matter that his editorials both previously and during the crisis suggested quite plainly that expediency caused him to pretend to offer a separation which he did not expect the South to accept; it was of no consequence that the vivid phrase and others like it were surrounded by conditions and reservations and ambiguities that went far to nullify the apparent meaning. The *Tribune* said "go in peace," and that was plain enough. History has been content to leave it at that.

Historians who rely on this passage and depict Greeley in the role of a pacifist must recognize, of course, that his words in November, 1860, conformed ill with his position a few months before or a few months after that time. For he had been, and was in the future to be, quite bellicose; so aggressive an editor was rare, even in that day of ink-stained pugnacity. In the previous January, shortly after John Brown went to the gallows, the *Tribune* warned "Democratic Disunionists" that Virginia had no "monopoly of the hanging of traitors." [15] During the campaign for Lincoln's election Greeley declared that if South Carolina should "undertake to repeat in 1861 the tantrums of 1833," she would be "treated as she was then

[15] The New York *Tribune*, January 5, 1860, said: "It is striking how gentle the fire-eaters have become since the Republicans have caused it to be understood that they do not think that Virginia ought to have a monopoly of the hanging of traitors. It is perhaps as well, however, for them to understand that the future Republican administrators of Federal power will not try and execute the Democratic Disunionists, who may hereafter fall into their hands with the indecent haste exhibited by Virginia in the case of John Brown."

—kindly but firmly." [16] After the election he dropped this menacing tone completely for a time, but within eight months he was goading the administration into a premature and bloody battle on the Plains of Manassas.[17] Clearly, the abhorrence of force which is attributed to Greeley as of November, 1860, was, if sincere, both brief and out of character.

Scholars have tended to dismiss this inconsistency with the facile explanation that Greeley was utterly erratic.[18] This, indeed, he was. It is also sometimes assumed that he was transparently sincere. But no entirely sincere person could have practiced the adroit treachery which he used to prevent the nomination of Seward in 1860. He had not spent his life among the New York politicians for nothing, and he did not publish everything that crossed his mind. The columns of the *Tribune* were not his confessional. Like other newspaper editors less angelic of countenance, less innocent of manner, he was writing not for self-expression, but for designed effect upon definite groups of people.

Before examining whether Greeley's motives coincided with his words, it is essential to inquire whether his words coincided with the interpretation which history has assigned to them. The famous editorial was not nearly so clear-cut as historians have left their readers to suppose. The editor of the *Tribune* used emphatic words, but, like Humpty-Dumpty, he

[16] *Ibid.*, July 25, 1860.

[17] On June 26, 1861, and thereafter until First Manassas, the *Tribune* carried the cry, "*Forward to Richmond! Forward to Richmond! The Rebel Congress must not be allowed to meet there on the 20th of July!* BY THAT DATE THE PLACE MUST BE HELD BY THE NATIONAL ARMY!" Charles A. Dana, the managing editor, phrased this outburst, but it could not have continued to appear in the *Tribune* unless Greeley so willed.

[18] Rhodes, *History of the United States*, III, 141, remarks that others besides Greeley supported peaceable secession, and that the proposal was not "merely the erratic outburst of an eccentric thinker."

thoughtfully inserted a provision that they should mean whatever he wished them to mean.

After certain preliminary observations the editorial turned to the question of northern policy with reference to secession:

if the Cotton States shall become satisfied that they can do better out of the Union than in it, we insist on letting them go in peace. The right to secede may be a revolutionary one, but it exists nevertheless; and we do not see how one party can have a right to do what another party has a right to prevent. . . . And whenever a considerable section of our Union shall deliberately resolve to go out, we shall resist all coercive measures designed to keep it in. We hope never to live in a republic whereof one section is pinned to the residue by bayonets.

Thus far the *Tribune* was bold, sweeping, and, as the textbooks testify, quotable. It was, of course, not very explicit; it did not say what would be accepted as proof of a deliberate resolve to go out, nor what Federal instrumentality should recognize secession; it did not specify whether the President might suspend operation of the laws, nor what attitude it would take if the northern people refused to recognize the right of secession, which, it agreed, "might be revolutionary"; it left room for several difficulties. But such details seem trifles in the presence of Greeley's forceful and dramatic language —language which produces a much more vivid mental impression than the passages which follow.

The first of these continued:

But while we thus uphold the practical liberty if not the abstract right of secession, we must insist that the step be taken, if it ever shall be, with the deliberation and gravity befitting so momentous an issue. Let ample time be given for reflection; let the subject be fully canvassed before the people; and let a popular vote be taken in every case before secession is decreed. Let the people be told just why they are urged to break up the confederation; let them have both sides of the question fully presented; let them reflect, deliberate, then vote; and let the act of secession be the echo of an unmistakable popular fiat. A judgment thus rendered, a demand for separation so backed, would either be acquiesced in without the effusion of blood, or those who rushed upon carnage to defy and defeat it would place themselves clearly in the wrong.

In brief the *Tribune* now insisted that secession was acceptable only as a deliberate and orderly execution of the clearly expressed popular will. This was reasonable; but any dialectician will suspiciously observe that the *Tribune* had tacitly reserved full jurisdiction in deciding what was deliberate, what was orderly, and what was an authentic expression of public opinion. It hastened to exercise this jurisdiction in the very next paragraph:

The measures now being inaugurated in the Cotton States with a view (apparently) to Secession, seem to us destitute of gravity and legitimate force. They bear the unmistakable [*sic*] impress of haste—of passion—of distrust of the popular judgment. They seem clearly intended to precipitate the South into rebellion [N. B.!] before the baselessness of the clamors which have misled and excited her can be ascertained by the great body of her people[.] We trust that they will be confronted with calmness, with dignity, and with unwavering trust in the inherent strength of the Union and the loyalty of the American People.[19]

Thus ended the famous "go in peace" editorial. It might fairly be summarized as follows: First, the South may depart in peace. Second, she must observe certain forms in doing so. Third, she is not, in the present movement, observing these forms. This was equivalent to saying: we concede in the abstract a certain right of withdrawal, but that has nothing to do with the present case. Far from agreeing to actual secession, this merely shifted the ground on which secession would be opposed. It was not so much surrender as it was strategic retreat.

The fictitious nature of Greeley's "acquiescence" in seces-

[19] New York *Tribune*, November 9, 1860.

sion was made even more transparent in later editorials. In the ensuing weeks he constantly reiterated his declaration that an authentic secession ought to be permitted, and, with equal constancy, appended some form of joker to neutralize any practical applicability which might have crept into his generalizations. At one time he specified that secession must be ratified by a popular vote; at another time he insisted that it must be the act of "six or eight contiguous states." Again, it must be adopted by the "pretty unanimous . . . resolve" of the Southern people; it must not be done with any view to securing inducements to return to the Union; the seceding states must first demonstrate their potential ability to "form an independent, self-subsisting nation"; they must show "due regard for the rights and interests of those they leave behind." [20]

At times the verbal tricks and dodges of the *Tribune* were a travesty upon the word "secession." Thus: "If she [Florida] will only pay back the money which she has cost the Union, and take herself off quietly, we will warrant Uncle Sam never

[20] *Ibid.*, January 14, 1861: "If they [the cotton states] will . . . take . . . a fair vote by ballot of their own citizens, none being coerced nor intimidated, and that vote shall indicate a settled resolve to get out of the Union, I will do all I can to help them out."

On December 17, 1860, the *Tribune* said: "But if seven or eight contiguous States shall present themselves authentically at Washington, saying, 'We hate the Federal Union; we have withdrawn from it . . . ,' we could not stand up for coercion."

On December 8: "whenever six or eight contiguous States shall have formally seceded from the Union, and avowed the pretty unanimous and earnest resolve of their People to *stay* out, it will not be found practicable to coerce them."

On December 24: "whenever a portion of this Union large enough to form an independent, self-subsisting nation, shall see fit to say authentically to the residue, 'We want to get away from you,' we shall say . . . 'Go!'"

On December 28: "should they [seek separation] . . . with . . . due regard for the rights and interests of those they leave behind, we shall feel bound to urge and insist that their wishes be gratified."

The Crisis of the Union 229

to offer even One Cent Reward for her return." [21] Similarly,
"No Southern republic could be allowed to take or possess
the mouth of the Mississippi." [22] Or, as a final example of
naked duplicity: "Let South Carolina secede as far as she
wishes so long as she pays the duties and respects the
forts." [23]

About three weeks after its first declarations the *Tribune*
made a notable shift of ground. Still maintaining a show of
nonaggressive feeling, it subtly altered its definition of the
"right of secession," which it had ostensibly recognized. By
its new definition secession was not a matter of state action,
but was a process to be consummated by a Federal constitutional convention. In detail the procedure suggested was this:

We trust, therefore, that, if the Cotton States should resolve to
secede, they will quietly and inoffensively announce their determination to do so, asking Congress to call a Convention to arrange
the terms of separation. They must be aware that this is a work
of difficulty—that time is required to effect it—and that . . . [the]
President, will be constrained by his inauguration oath to collect
the revenue and enforce the laws throughout the entire area of our
country until such separation shall have been duly effected. But
if they really desire to go out, and will allow time to effect the
separation peacefully, we shall do what we can to persuade the
North to accede to their wishes.[24]

Holding fast to this position, Greeley rode out the crisis,
and when war came he insisted, as he continued to insist
throughout his life, that he had been prepared to accept the
decision of the people of the South.[25] Perhaps he actually be-

[21] *Ibid.*, November 24, 1860.
[22] *Ibid.*, November 19, 1860. See also, *ibid.*, November 30, 1860.
[23] *Ibid.*, December 21, 1860.
[24] *Ibid.*, November 26, 1860.
[25] Horace Greeley, *Recollections of a Busy Life* (New York, 1868),
398.

lieved this himself. But a detached spectator can hardly do so. The plain fact is that the *Tribune* editor said one thing and meant another, and that, to veil this inconsistency, he resorted to one of the oldest and simplest tricks of casuistry— an alteration in the definition of his words. The "secession" of which he spoke was antithetical to "secession" as it was generally understood. His doctrine of dissolution by general consent had no more to do with secession than philosophical anarchism has to do with bomb throwing. And his record as a whole tends to impair rather than sustain the historical tradition that there was a powerful and sincere movement for peaceable separation.

This conclusion, if it be accepted, entails an imperative question. If Greeley disliked peaceable secession, why did he feign approval of it? Why should he give lip service to a cause to which he was hostile? If his was the bellicose spirit which drove Irwin McDowell prematurely "On to Richmond," why did he at first make such a great show of reluctance to coerce the secessionists?

This query looks to a concealed motive, and it is not to be expected that such a motive can be categorically defined. But despite the presence of hidden factors it is possible to say, with some degree of assurance, that the motive was double, and that its duality consisted in a purpose to mollify the people of the South by avoiding threats against them, and a purpose to offer a fictitious alternative to frightened Northerners, who might otherwise choose concession as the only alternative to war.

With reference to the people of the South it was evident, on the face of it, that threats of coercion would only serve to inflame the Southern temper, "fire the Southern heart," and strengthen the Southern radicals; whereas a show of acquiescence might disarm the Southern fear of aggression, remind the South of the fellowship that had existed in the Union, and give Southern unionists an opportunity to rally their forces. Inasmuch as Southern anger flared up at every threat, it obviously behooved the friends of union to avoid threatening language.

Greeley was by no means unconscious of this consideration, nor was he unresponsive to its implications for his own policy. He knew that a denial of the right of secession would constitute a challenge to the South to assert it, whereas an acceptance of it would cause the South to consider more carefully the advantages of the Union and the self-inflicted penalties of destroying it. Historians should have been forewarned that Greeley was influenced by this aspect of the matter, and they should, accordingly, have discounted his literal words. For he himself stated the point, with directness and simplicity, as early as May 2, 1854, in an editorial which foreshadowed, and deciphered, as it were, his policy in the crisis six years later:

We would have the North, whenever the South shall cry out, "Hold me! hold me! for I'm desperate, and shall hurt somebody!" —coolly answer, "Hold yourself, if you need holding; for we have better business on hand,"—and this would be found after a little to exert a decidedly sedative, tranquillizing effect on the too susceptible nerves of our too excitable Southern brethren. Instead of bolting the door in alarm, and calling for help to guard it, in case the South should hereafter threaten to walk out of the Union, we would hold it politely open and suggest to the departing the policy of minding his eye and buttoning his coat well under his chin preparatory to facing the rough weather outside. And this, we insist, is the true mode of reducing his paroxysms and causing him to desist from such raw-head demonstrations in [the] future.[26]

This was a plain avowal of opportunism, and of course it could not be repeated too freely without defeating its own end at the crucial moment. But it is significant that six years before the crisis, Greeley outlined his plan for mollifying the

[26] New York *Tribune*, May 2, 1854.

South and scotching secession by offering free rein to the fire-eaters. This generous offer, he supposed, would disarm opposition, and, with equal generosity, be refused. Thus his acquiescence in separation was designed not to avert battle, but to avert separation. It is clear, too, that he continued to adhere to this view, for he suggested again at the height of the crisis that expediency, and not conviction, dictated his words. Thus:

But one thing we must firmly and always insist on—that there shall be no bribing, no coaxing, no wheedling those to stay in the Union who want to get out. Every step in this direction tends to confirm the Slave States in their mistaken notion that the Union is more advantageous to us than to them—that it is a contrivance to . . . enrich the North at the cost of the South. And this is to-day the chief source of National peril. It is because the Southern people have been persistently told that the Free States would be pecuniarily ruined by disunion . . . that we are eternally threatened with Secession. Let it be fully and fairly understood that the benefits of the Union are mutual—that we don't want the South to remain in the Union out of charity to us—and this eternal menace of Nullification and Secession will be hushed forever.[27]

All this suggests that Greeley used disunion to defend the Union, offered secession to defeat the secessionists, agreed to an abstract proposition to forestall its practical application. It does not suggest at all that he was sincerely committed to voluntary separation.[28]

But if Greeley was impelled partly by a desire to stay the secession movement in the South, he was governed scarcely less by a purpose to prevent a policy of "appeasement" at the North. If, in fact, he felt any real tolerance of disunion, it

[27] *Ibid.*, November 19, 1860.
[28] Another oblique motive with reference to the South appears in the *Tribune*, December 17, 1860: "We would expose the seceders to odium as disunionists, not commend them to pity as the gallant though mistaken upholders of the rights of their section in an uneven military conflict."

sprang not from his horror of war, but from his horror of slavery and of compromise with slavery. In his antislavery zeal he sometimes proclaimed that, as between slavery extension and disunion, he would choose disunion. Thus: "Let the Union be a thousand times shivered rather than we should aid you to plant Slavery on Free Soil." [29] But this did not argue that he was actually prepared to accept either disunion or slavery. Men who somewhat rhetorically choose "death before dishonor" usually do not seek either alternative, and it is safe to surmise that Greeley's "disunion before compromise" was analogous.[30]

In a sense the whole misconception of Greeley's position arises from a failure to perceive the alternatives in the light of which he acted. It is often tacitly assumed that he simply preferred secession to coercion—disunion to bloodshed—peace to war.[31] This assumption is in part justified by such phrases as the one in which the *Tribune* affirmed its aversion to a Union pinned together by bayonets. But the one alternative which did most to condition Greeley's response was that of compromise. Compromise was a familiar, recurrent experience, whereas fratricidal warfare remained a contingency often discussed but never realized. It was compromise which Gree-

[29] *Ibid.*, February 20, 1850.

[30] E.g., the *Tribune* of December 3, 1860, said: "Then 'let the winds howl on,' until it shall be settled . . . that the Free States will not surrender their convictions nor their principles even to a threat that the Union shall be dissolved if they do not."

[31] An example of such an assumption follows: "Men who had never before taken seriously the Southern threats of disunion had waked suddenly to a terrified consciousness that they were in for it. . . .

"The very type of these people and of their reaction was Horace Greeley. . . . He was wallowing in panic. He began to scream editorially. The Southern extremists were terribly in earnest; if they wanted to go, go they would, and go they should . . . . what was the Union compared with bloodshed? There must be no war—no war. Such was Greeley's terrified appeal to the North." Nathaniel W. Stephenson, *Lincoln* (Indianapolis, 1922), 109–10.

ley dreaded, and in preference to it any alternative, however obnoxious—even disunion—seemed the better choice. If he toyed with the idea of peaceable secession, it was not because brute conquest repelled him, but because the remaining alternative, "disgraceful compromise," seemed to him "the unpardonable sin." [32] He himself indicated, in a letter to Abraham Lincoln, how completely aversion to compromise overshadowed all other considerations in his mind:

"I fear nothing, care for nothing, but another disgraceful back-down of the free States. That is the only real danger. Let the Union slide—it may be reconstructed; let Presidents be assassinated, we can elect more; let the Republicans be defeated and crushed, we shall rise again. But another nasty compromise, whereby everything is conceded and nothing secured, will so thoroughly disgrace and humiliate us that we can never again raise our heads, and this country becomes a second edition of the Barbary States as they were sixty years ago. 'Take any form but that.' " [33]

And again, some ten years later, when war hysteria had died out, Greeley reaffirmed that his "controlling conviction from first to last" had been a resolute adherence to every point of the antislavery position; he did not mention his devotion to peace. For the obloquy which his policy had brought upon him, he found "consolation" in the fact that he had "done something toward arresting the spring-tide of Northern servility that set strongly in favor of 'conciliation'" rather than in the fact that he had tried to avert the slaughter. [34]

Quotations might be multiplied ad nauseam, but the mere

[32] New York Tribune, December 15, 1860: "Consenting to a disgraceful Compromise with Disunionists and traitors, will be the Unpardonable Sin . . . in the eyes of the Northern people."
[33] Greeley to Lincoln, December 22, 1860, in John G. Nicolay and John Hay, Abraham Lincoln, A History (10 vols.; New York, 1890), III, 258.
[34] Greeley, Recollections of a Busy Life, 397–98.

chronology of events renders quotations superfluous. As late as October 26, 1860, the *Tribune* spurned disunion.[35] Soon after that a crisis arose. Judging by previous crises, such as that of 1850, a compromise was likely to result. At once the *Tribune* fell away from its emphatic unionism. But as the possibility of compromise faded away, and the prospect of war grew imminent, the militant unionism of the *Tribune* returned. In other words, when confronted by a choice between compromise and peaceable secession, Greeley chose peaceable secession; but when confronted by a choice between war and peaceful secession, Greeley chose war. In the light of this it is hard to understand the persistence with which historians have represented him as a champion of voluntary dissolution.

In many respects the policy of the *Tribune*, like other policies of the same time, is inexplicable except in the light of the continued incredulity of secession. For thirty years the northern opposition had built up this incredulity like an antitoxin from the sterile germs of threat unsupported by act. So strong was the antitoxin now that the shock of actual and virulent secession could not break it down. Conventions might meet, ordinances be framed, flags fly, cockades blossom, and regiments march, without enforcing conviction upon the Republican mind.

Thus Greeley, on the very same day that he told the South to go in peace, assured his readers that "we are convinced that the agitation raised in the South will gradually and surely subside into peace," [36] and only the day before he still described the newspapers which predicted a crisis as "silly, gasconading journals." [37] Later, he found the threats of 1860

[35] On that day the *Tribune* said: "Mr. Lincoln's election may now be set down as certain; and it is quite time the Southern ultraists should be given to understand that they are to receive from this quarter no aid or countenance in their disunion and secession projects."

[36] *Ibid.*, November 9, 1860.

[37] *Ibid.*, November 8, 1860.

tame compared with those of 1832,[38] felt sure Carolina would shrink from the "solitary plunge," [39] and was certain that "the great majority do not . . . mean to break up the Union. They simply mean to bully the Free States into concessions." [40]

Here was the very heart and essence of the *Tribune* position. Greeley had no more idea of dividing the Union than Solomon had of dividing the infant; he depended on patriotism to refuse his offer, just as the wise king depended on maternal love to save the child. And when at last it dawned upon Greeley that he was confronted by a revolution and not by a maneuver in the game of party politics, he beat a retreat in haste behind a cover of equivocations, quibbles, and puns on the word secession.

History cannot search souls and it cannot declare with certainty what were the motives of Horace Greeley, or of any other man. But at least it can say that the evidence does not support the interpretation usually placed upon his acts, and that, indeed, it supports an interpretation which is very nearly opposite.

Considered from this aspect the significance of Greeley's vociferation is a curious one. Insofar as the cause of voluntary separation depended upon him, it was a phantom from the beginning. If his attitude was typical (as historians assume), the go-in-peace program was devoid of appreciable support and never achieved a place in the realm of practicable solutions. It was, in this sense, altogether illusory and undeserving of the notice which history has given it. But, like other illusions and red herrings, it bore an enormous importance. For it constantly obscured the clarity of the true alternatives—compromise and war. Could the great mass of people have

[38] *Ibid.*, November 12 1860.
[39] *Ibid.*, November 15, 1860.
[40] *Ibid.*, November 20, 1860. The writer has inverted the phrases in this quotation.

seen these alternatives in naked antithesis, they would hardly have rushed upon the sword. But the champions of compromise were never able, until too late, to convince the public that bloodshed would ensue upon the refusal of concessions. The delusion of peaceable secession always rose up to obscure the stern logic of the situation and to make Cassandras of those who sought for an adjustment. Like a smoke screen the talk of separation in peace concealed the fact that the choice was between compromise and war. The veil of smoke was not blown away until the cause of compromise had been rejected, and war alone remained, to be hailed perforce as the Irrepressible Conflict.

POSTSCRIPT

As mentioned in the headnote to this chapter, the purpose of this Postscript is to summarize the points of disagreement between Thomas N. Bonner ("Horace Greeley and the Secession Movement, 1860–1861," *Mississippi Valley Historical Review*, XXXVIII, 425–44) and myself regarding Greeley's attitude toward secession. Although at first glance it might appear that Bonner and I are entirely at odds, there is actually one important point on which we concur and where we differ from previous writers: we both recognize the fact that Greeley never did unequivocally concede the right of a state autonomously to withdraw from the Union and in fact he did not even make an unqualified concession of the right of the South to withdraw by unilateral action.[1] This agreement is signifi-

[1] Note my summary above of the editorial of November 9: "Thus ended the famous 'go in peace' editorial. It might fairly be summarized as follows: First, the South may depart in peace. Second, she must observe certain forms in doing so. Third, she is not, in the present movement, observing these forms. This was equivalent to saying: we concede in the abstract a certain right of withdrawal, but that has nothing to do with the present case."

cant, because previous writers, including notably James Ford Rhodes, had pictured Greeley as first whole-heartedly accepting the idea of separation in preference to war and then suddenly reversing himself. Both Bonner and I reject the idea of such a sudden reversal, and both of us recognize that Greeley was really not very squeamish about fighting a war (Bonner says: "But, said Greeley, if a sufficient number of states should undertake to establish their independence without the consent of the remaining states, it would be found impracticable to coerce them. This did not imply any moral repugnance to coercion on Greeley's part.")

But although we both emphasize the fact that Greeley never conceded a clear path to secession, we disagree as to his consistency, his sincerity, and most of all his motivation.[2]

As to consistency, Bonner believes that Greeley always held steadily to the view that disunion could be accomplished by the joint consent of all the states in a general convention. The phrase "we insist on letting them go in peace," as Bonner construes it, meant only: we will support action by a convention of states which will permit them to go. To Bonner, this was Greeley's position throughout ("Substantially, Greeley was consistent in his declarations." [p. 433]). In Greeley's editorial of January 14, which Rhodes saw as a reversal, Bonner feels that "there is no perceptible departure from earlier principles." [p. 439] Greeley "continued to offer to the South, in terms very similar to those employed in November, the possibility of a peaceable division of the Union." [p. 438] Yet, there was unmistakably such a conspicuous alteration in Greeley's tone that Bonner necessarily gives recognition to it, even if he does

[2] "The problem becomes, then, essentially one of motives. Why did Greeley expound the possibility of peaceable secession? Was he sincere in setting it forth as an alternative to coercion? Do the secession editorials show an inconsistency which could not be due to the actual trend of events, and if so, how may it be explained? These are some of the questions which suggest themselves." Bonner, p. 428.

not really take it into account: "As a result of the course secession was taking in the South, the *Tribune* counseled a firmer
policy. Less was said about the possibility of a peaceable breakup of the Union, and more emphasis was placed upon the
necessity of upholding the laws." [p. 436] Bonner speaks of
this as if it were only a change of emphasis. But before accepting such an understated conclusion, one might note that on
November 9, while insisting that withdrawal from the Union
must be accomplished in a regular and deliberative way, without undue haste, and with adequate steps to assure that it
represented the will of the majority of those involved in the
withdrawal, Greeley did not deny that withdrawal could be a
unilateral step and he even implied that it might be taken
unilaterally ("Let ample time be given for reflection; let the
subject be fully canvassed before the people; and let a popular
vote be taken in every case before secession is decreed. [The
phrase, "in every case," implies that a number of states might
properly arrive at such decrees separately—i.e., unilaterally.]).
Bonner denies that this language implied a recognition of unilateral action and says, "The phrase 'letting them go' is decisive however. . . . It implies that he expected any vote of
secession to be submitted in some way to the North for consideration and action—possibly to a national convention, or
perhaps to Congress." [p. 430, n 21] But if this was implied it
was such a cryptic and attentuated implication that millions
of Americans in 1860 and countless historians since then failed
to detect it, and Bonner, ninety years later, was the first person
with antennae super-sensitive enough to pick it up. Perhaps
Bonner is reading this implication backward from the later
editorial of November 26 in which Greeley did assert that the
consent of a national convention would be necessary to disunion [see p. 229, above]. And perhaps, as I argue in my paper,
Greeley was not consistent, but did shift between November
9 and November 26 from the position that separation could be

unilaterally accomplished to the position that it must be done with the multilateral consent of a convention of all the states.

The questions of consistency and sincerity are, of course, to some extent intermingled, for if Greeley were as consistent as Bonner contends, the question of his sincerity would hardly arise.[3] Sincerity is a tricky concept for the historian to deal with in any case. When I argue that Greeley was insincere, I mean primarily that in using the phrase "we insist on letting them go in peace," he appeared to make a concession to the South; but that he instantly began surrounding this concession with qualifications which neutralized it and made it fictitious [p. 228, above]. On November 9 he stated "The right to secede may be a revolutionary one, but it exists nevertheless; and we do not see how one party can have a right to do what another party has a right to prevent."[4] But by the end of the year, he had virtually "defined" secession out of existence and had asserted the right of a convention of states to prevent the exercise of the "right" of secession if it chose to do so. Thus, Greeley gained the credit for disclaiming any coercive purposes, without in fact giving up the option to exercise coercion. ("Let South Carolina secede as far as she wishes so long as she pays the duties and respects the forts." New York *Tribune*, December 21, 1860). Bonner's response to my argument that Greeley was playing tricks with the word secession is to say "Actually it is Potter who assumes secession to be something quite different than what was included in the term in 1860." [p. 443] He offers no evidence for this assertion, and it

[3] As Bonner himself says, p. 441: "The consistency of Greeley's secession policy having been determined, the question of his sincerity in offering peaceable secession becomes largely a superfluous one."

[4] On December 4, the *Tribune* made this point more explicit: "Admit a right to exist and you cannot well deny that there must be a proper time for and manner of exercising it." Presumably, this would not include waiting for the consent of those who denied the right.

is, perhaps, not the strongest point in his paper, though it is certainly one of the more crucial ones.[5]

Just as the question of consistency merges into the question of sincerity, the question of sincerity merges into the question of motivation. Bonner believes that Greeley's motive was straightforward and was what he stated it to be. "It is," Bonner says, "the writer's conviction that Greeley revived Jefferson's revolutionary doctrine only to strengthen the unionist's hands in the South [by avoidance of threatening language] and, that failing, to provide a means whereby the cotton states *en masse* could leave the Union without bloodshed." [p. 435]

On the urgency of Greeley's desire to strengthen the hands of the Southern Unionists, readers of my paper will see that Bonner and I are in agreement, and that there is no issue (p. 231, above). But as to the interpretation that Greeley wanted to find a viable means of disunion, we are in complete disagreement. Does not the evidence indicate instead that once the alternative of compromise was clearly eliminated, Greeley lost all interest in providing a means whereby the cotton states *en masse* could leave the Union without bloodshed, and lost all his aversion to living "in a republic whereof one section is pinned to the residue by bayonets"? Does it not also indicate that the fluctuations in Greeley's attitude toward disunion are

[5] Again, Bonner says, p. 442, "Potter calls attention to the qualifications which Greeley attached to his peaceable secession offers, but there is no evidence to support his contention that in his November 26 editorial Greeley began to alter subtly his definition of the right of secession, making it no longer a matter for state action." The best evidence is in the language of the editorials of November 9 and November 26 themselves. The former, though not explicit on the matter of unilateral action, seemingly suggests and certainly does not deny that secession could be unilaterally invoked by a state, if such state acted deliberately and democratically. The latter clearly denies that there can be any unilateral action, and admits of separation only by the consent of a convention of the states.

correlated not with the likelihood of bayonets but with the likelihood of compromise? A clear statement of what came foremost in Greeley's thinking appears in a letter which he wrote to Lincoln on December 22, 1860. Both Bonner and I quoted this statement but Bonner, as it seems to me, does not recognize how explicitly Greeley specified that there was one completely dominating reason which prompted him to temporize with the otherwise repulsive and unacceptable alternative of disunion: "I fear nothing, care for nothing, but another disgraceful back-down of the free States. That is the only real danger. Let the Union slide—it may be reconstructed; let Presidents be assassinated, we can elect more; let the Republicans be defeated and crushed, we shall rise again. But another nasty compromise, whereby everything is conceded and nothing secured, will so thoroughly disgrace and humiliate us that we can never again raise our heads, and this country becomes a second edition of the Barbary States as they were sixty years ago. 'Take any form but that.' "

Why the Republicans Rejected Both Compromise and Secession

In a conference at Stanford in March, 1963, on the Civil War, the papers read included Glyndon Van Deusen, "Why the Republican Party Came to Power"; Roy Nichols, "Why the Democratic Party Divided"; Avery Craven, "Why the Southern States Seceded," and my discussion of the Republican attitude toward secession, the chapter which follows.

Each of the papers had a commentator, and I was fortunate in receiving comment from Kenneth Stampp, who treated my essay with kind consideration and at the same time raised some vital and searching questions, especially about my insistence upon viewing the situation as the participants saw it. He offered the alternative that the historian must see the past bifocally, both as the participants saw it and also "with all the wisdom and perspective that experience and hindsight can give us." I regret that it is not feasible to reprint Professor Stampp's comment in full, but I thank him for it, and commend it to the reader, who will find it, with the other essays, in George H. Knoles, editor, The Crisis of the Union, 1860–1861.

H ISTORIANS HAVE a habit of explaining the important decisions of the past in terms of principles. On this basis, it is easy to say that the Republicans rejected compromise because they were committed to the principle of antislavery and that they rejected secession because they were committed to the principle of union. But in the realities of the historical past, principles frequently come into conflict with other principles, and those who make decisions have to choose which principle shall take precedence. When principles thus conflict, as they frequently do, it is meaningless to show merely that a person or a group favors a given principle: the operative question is what priority they give to it. For instance, before the secession crisis arose, there were many Northerners who believed in both the principle of antislavery and the principle of union, but who differed in the priority which they would go to one or the other: William Lloyd Garrison gave the priority to antislavery and proclaimed that there should be "no union with slaveholders." Abraham Lincoln gave, or seemed to give, the priority to union and during the war wrote the famous letter to Horace Greeley in which he said: "My paramount object is to save the Union and it is not either to save or to destroy slavery. What I do about slavery and the colored race, I do because I believe it helps to save the Union, and what I forbear, I forbear because I do not believe it would help to save the Union." Lincoln was always precise to almost a unique degree in his statements, and it is interesting to note that he did not say that it was not his object to destroy slavery; what he said was that it was not his paramount object—he did not give it the highest priority.

To state this point in another way, if we made an analysis of the moderate Republicans and of the abolitionists solely in terms of their principles, we would hardly be able to distinguish between them, for both were committed to the principle of antislavery and to the principle of union. It was the diversity in the priorities which they gave to these two principles that made them distinctive from each other.

A recognition of the priorities, therefore, may in many cases serve a historian better than a recognition of principles. But while it is important to recognize which principle is, as Lincoln expressed it, paramount, it is no less important to take account of the fact that men do not like to sacrifice one principle for the sake of another and do not even like to recognize that a given situation may require a painful choice between principles. Thus, most Northern antislavery men wanted to solve the slavery question within the framework of union, rather than to reject the Union because it condoned slavery; correspondingly, most Northern unionists wanted to save the Union while taking steps against slavery, rather than by closing their eyes to the slavery question.

In short, this means—and one could state it almost as an axiom—that men have a tendency to believe that their principles can be reconciled with one another, and that this belief is so strong that it inhibits their recognition of realistic alternatives in cases where the alternatives would involve a choice between cherished principles. This attitude has been clearly defined in the homely phrase that we all like to have our cake and eat it too.

Perhaps all this preliminary consideration of theory seems excessively abstract and you will feel that I ought to get on to the Republicans, the crisis, and the rejection of compromise and secession; but before I do, let me take one more step with my theory. If the participants in a historical situation tend to see the alternatives in that situation as less clear, less sharply focused than they really are, historians probably tend to see the alternatives as more clear, more evident, more sharply focused than they really were. We see the alternatives as clear because we have what we foolishly believe to be the advantage of hindsight—which is really a disadvantage in understanding how a situation seemed to the participants. We know, in short, that the Republicans did reject both compromise and secession (I will return to the details of this rejection later) and that the four-year conflict known as the Civil War eventuated. We therefore tend to think not only that conflict of some kind was the alternative to the acceptance of compromise or the acquiescence in secession, but actually that this particular war—with all its costs, its sacrifices, and its consequences—was the alternative. When men choose a course of action which had a given result, historians will tend to attribute to them not only the choice of the course, but even the choice of the result. Yet one needs only to state this tendency clearly in order to demonstrate the fallacy in it. Whatever choice anyone exercised in 1860–61, no one chose the American Civil War, because it lay behind the veil of the future; it did not exist as a choice.

Hindsight not only enables historians to define the alternatives in the deceptively clear terms of later events; it also gives them a deceptively clear criterion for evaluating the alternatives, which is in terms of later results. That is, we now know that the war did result in the preservation of the Union and in the abolition of chattel slavery. Accordingly, it is easy, with hindsight, to attribute to the participants not only a decision to accept the alternative of a war whose magnitude they could not know, but also to credit them with choosing results which they could not foresee. The war, as it developed, certainly might have ended in the quicker defeat of the Southern movement, in which case emancipation would apparently not have resulted; or it might have ended in the independence of the Southern Confederacy, in which case the Monday morning quarterbacks of the historical profession would have been in the position of saying that the rash choice of a violent and coercive course had destroyed the possibility of a harmonious, voluntary restoration of the Union—a restoration of the kind which William H. Seward was trying to bring about.

I suppose all this is only equivalent to saying that the supreme task of the historian, and the one of most superlative difficulty, is to see the past through the imperfect eyes of those who lived it and not with his own omniscient twenty-twenty vision. I am not suggesting that any of us can really do this, but only that it is what we must attempt.

What do we mean, specifically, by saying that the Republican party rejected compromise? Certain facts are reasonably familiar in this connection, and may be briefly recalled. In

December, 1860, at the time when a number of secession conventions had been called in the Southern states but before any ordinances of secession had been adopted, various political leaders brought forward proposals to give assurances to the Southerners. The most prominent of these was the plan by Senator John J. Crittenden of Kentucky to place an amendment in the Constitution which would restore and extend the former Missouri Compromise line of 36° 30′, prohibiting slavery in Federal territory north of the line and sanctioning it south of the line. In a Senate committee, this proposal was defeated with five Republicans voting against it and none in favor of it, while the non-Republicans favored it six to two. On January 16, after four states had adopted ordinances of secession, an effort was made to get the Crittenden measure out of committee and on to the floor of the Senate. This effort was defeated by 25 votes against to 23 in favor. This was done on a strict party vote, all 25 of the votes to defeat being cast by Republicans. None of those in favor were Republicans. On March 2, after the secession of the lower South was complete, the Crittenden proposal was permitted to come to a vote. In the Senate, it was defeated 19 to 20. All 20 of the negative votes were Republican, not one of the affirmative votes was so. In the House, it was defeated 80 to 113. Not one of the 80 was a Republican, but 110 of the 113 were Republicans.

Another significant measure of the secession winter was a proposal to amend the Constitution to guarantee the institution of slavery in the states. This proposed amendment—ironically designated by the same number as the one which later freed the slaves—was actually adopted by Congress, in the House by a vote of 128 to 65, but with 44 Republicans in favor and 62 opposed; in the Senate by a vote of 24 to 12, but with 8 Republicans in favor and 12 opposed.

While opposing these measures, certain Republicans, including Charles Francis Adams, brought forward a bill to admit New Mexico to statehood without restrictions on slavery, and they regarded this as a compromise proposal. But this measure was tabled in the House, 115 to 71, with Republicans casting 76 votes to table and 26 to keep the bill alive. Thus, it can be said, without qualification, that between December and March no piece of compromise legislation was ever supported by a majority of Republican votes, either in the Senate or the House, either in committee or on the floor. This, of course, does not mean either that they ought to have supported the measures in question, or that such measures would have satisfied the Southern states. It is my own belief that the balance between the secessionist and the nonsecessionist forces was fairly close in all of the seceding states except South Carolina, and that the support of Congress for a compromise would have been enough to tip the balance. But the Crittenden measure would possibly have opened the way for Southern filibustering activities to enlarge the territorial area south of 36° 30′—at least this was apparently what Lincoln feared —and the "thirteenth" amendment would have saddled the country with slavery more or less permanently. When we say, then, that the Republicans rejected compromise, we should take care to mean no more than we say. They did, by their votes, cause the defeat of measures which would otherwise have been adopted by Congress, which were intended and generally regarded as compromise measures. In this sense, they rejected compromise.

When we say the Republican Party rejected secession, the case is so clear that it hardly needs a recital of proof. It is true that at one stage of the crisis, many Republicans did talk about letting the slave states go. Horace Greeley wrote his famous, ambiguous, oft-quoted, and much misunderstood editorial saying that "if the cotton states shall become satisfied that they can do better out of the Union than in it, we insist on letting them go in peace." Later, when the situation at Fort Sumter had reached its highest tension, a number of Republicans, including Salmon P. Chase, Simon Cameron, Gideon Welles, and Caleb Smith, all in the cabinet, advised Lincoln to evacuate the fort rather than precipitate hostilities; but this hardly means that they would not have made the issue of union in some other way. Lincoln himself definitively rejected secession in his inaugural address when he declared: "No state upon its own mere motion, can lawfully get out of the Union. . . . I . . . consider that in view of the Constitution and the laws, the Union is unbroken; and to the extent of my ability I shall take care, as the Constitution itself expressly enjoins upon me, that the laws of the Union be faithfully executed in all the States." After the fall of Fort Sumter, he translated this affirmation into action by calling for 75,000 volunteers, and by preparing to use large-scale military measures to hold the South in the Union. The fact that no major figure in the North, either Republican or Democrat, ever proposed to acquiesce in the rending of the Union and that no proposal to do so was ever seriously advocated or voted upon in Congress, is evidence enough that the Republicans rejected secession even more decisively than they rejected compromise. They scarcely even felt the need to consider the question or to make an organized presentation of their reasons. It is true that some of them said that they would rather have disunion than compromise, but this was a way of saying how much they objected to compromise, and not how little they objected to separation. It was almost exactly equivalent to the expression, "Death rather than dishonor," which has never been understood to mean an acceptance of death, but rather an adamant rejection of dishonor.

Here, then, in briefest outline is the record of the Republican rejection of compromise and of secession. What we are concerned with, however, is not the mere fact of the rejection, but rather with its meaning. Why did the Republicans do this? What was their motivation? What did they think would follow from their decision? What did they believe the alternatives to be? Specifically, did this mean that the choice as they saw it was clear-cut, and that they conceived of themselves as opting in favor of war in a situation where they had a choice between secession and war? As I come to this question, I must revert to my comments earlier in this paper by pointing out again the tendency of historians to see the alternatives with preternatural clarity and the fallacy involved in attributing to the participants a capacity to define the alternatives in the same crystalline terms.

Peace or war? Compromise or conflict? Separation or coercion? These alternatives have such a plausible neatness, such a readiness in fitting the historian's pigeon holes, that it is vastly tempting to believe that they define the choices which people were actually making and not just the choices that we think they ought to have been making. We all know, today, that economists once fell into fallacies by postulating an economic man who behaved economically in the way economists thought he ought to behave. But even though we do know this, we are not as wary as we should be of the concept of what might be called an historical man who behaved historically in the way historians thought he ought to have behaved. It is very well for us, a hundred years later, to analyze the record and to say there were three alternatives, as distinct as the three sides of a triangle, namely compromise, voluntary separation, or war. Indeed this analysis may be correct. The error is not in our seeing it this way, but in our supposing that since we do see it in this way, the participants must have seen it in this way also.

Nothing can be more difficult—indeed impossible—than to reconstruct how a complex situation appeared to a varied lot of people, not one of whom saw or felt things in exactly the same way as any other one, a full century ago. But in the effort to approximate these realities as far as we can, it might be useful to begin by asking to what extent the choices of compromise, separation, or war had emerged as the possible alternatives in the minds of the citizens as they faced the crisis. Did they see the Crittenden proposals as embodying a possibility for compromise, and did a vote against these proposals mean an acceptance of the alternatives of war or separation? Did a policy which rejected both compromise and war indicate an acceptance of the alternative of voluntary separation? Did a decision to send food to Sumter and to keep the flag flying mean an acceptance of war? By hindsight, all of these indications appear plausible, and yet on close scrutiny, it may appear that not one of them is tenable in an unqualified way.

Did a vote against the Crittenden proposals indicate a rejection of the possibility of compromise? If Republicans voted against the Crittenden proposals, did this mean that they saw themselves as rejecting the principle of compromise and that they saw the possibilities thereby narrowed to a choice between voluntary separation or fierce, coercive war? If they repelled the idea of voluntary separation, did this imply that they were prepared to face a choice between political compromise or military coercion as the only means of saving the Union? If they urged the administration to send food to the besieged men in Sumter and to keep the flag flying there, did this mean that they had actually accepted the irrepressibility of the irrepressible conflict, and that they regarded peaceable alternatives as exhausted?

Although it makes the task of our analysis considerably more complex to say so, still it behooves us to face the music of confusion and to admit that not one of these acts was necessarily seen by the participants as narrowing the alternatives in the way which our after-the-fact analysis might indicate. To see the force of this reality, it is necessary to look at each of these contingencies in turn.

First, there is the case of those Republicans, including virtually all the Republican members in the Senate or the House, who refused to support the Crittenden proposals. To be sure, these men were accused of sacrificing the Union or of a callous indifference to the hazard of war; and to be sure, there were apparently some men like Zachariah Chandler who actually wanted war. (It was Chandler, you will recall, who said, "Without a little blood-letting, the Union will not be worth a rush.") But there were many who had grown to entertain sincere doubts as to whether the adoption of the Crittenden proposals, or the grant of any other concessions to the South, would actually bring permanent security to the Union. The danger to the Union lay, as they saw it, in the fact that powerful groups in many Southern states believed that any state had an unlimited right to withdraw from the Union and thus disrupt it. Southerners had fallen into the habit of asserting this right whenever they were much dissatisfied and declaring they would exercise it if their demands were not met. They had made such declarations between 1846 and 1850, when the Free-Soilers proposed to exclude slavery from the Mexican Cession. They had done so again in 1850 when they wanted a more stringent fugitive slave law. The threat of secession had been heard once more in 1856 when it appeared that the Republicans might elect a Free-Soiler to the Presidency. On each occasion, concessions had been made: the Compromise of 1850 made it legally possible to take slaves to New Mexico; the compromise also gave the slave owners a fugitive act that was too drastic for their own good; in 1856, timid Union-loving Whigs rallied to Buchanan and thus helped to avert the crisis that Frémont's election might have brought. Each such concession, of course, confirmed the Southern fire-eaters in their habit of demanding further concessions, and it strengthened their position with their constituents in the South by enabling them to come home at periodic intervals with new tribute that they had extorted from the Yankees. From the standpoint of a sincere unionist, there was something self-defeating about getting the Union temporarily past a crisis by making concessions which strengthened the disunionist faction and perpetuated the tendency toward periodic crises. This was a point on which Republicans sometimes expressed themselves very emphatically. For instance, Schuyler Colfax, in 1859, wrote to his mother about conditions in Congress: "We are still just where we started six months ago," he said, "except that our Southern friends have dissolved the Union forty or fifty times since then." In the same vein, Carl Schurz ridiculed the threat of secession, while campaigning for Lincoln in 1860: "There had been two overt attempts at secession already," Schurz was reported as saying, "one the secession of the Southern students from the medical school at Philadelphia . . . the second upon the election of Speaker Pennington, when the South seceded from Congress, went out, took a drink, and then came back. The third attempt would be," he prophesied, "when Old Abe would be elected. They would then again secede and this time would take two drinks, but would come back again." Schurz's analysis may have been good wit, but of course it was disastrously bad prophecy, and it had the fatal effect of preparing men systematically to misunderstand the signs of danger when these signs appeared. The first signs would be merely the first drink; confirmatory signs would be the second drink. James Buchanan recognized, as early as 1856, that men were beginning to underestimate the danger to the Union simply because it was chronic and they were too familiar with it: "We have so often cried wolf," he said, "that now, when the wolf is at the door it is difficult to make the people believe it." Abraham

Lincoln provided a distinguished proof of Buchanan's point in August, 1860, when he wrote: "The people of the South have too much of good sense and good temper to attempt the ruin of the government rather than see it administered as it was administered by the men who made it. At least, so I hope and believe." As usual, Lincoln's statement was a gem of lucidity, even when it was unconsciously so. He hoped and believed. The wish was father to the thought.

The rejection of compromise, then, did not mean an acceptance of separation or war. On the contrary, to men who regarded the threat of secession as a form of political blackmail rather than a genuine indication of danger to the Union, it seemed that danger of disunion could be eliminated only by eliminating the disunionists, and this could never be accomplished by paying them off at regular intervals. The best hope of a peaceful union lay in a development of the strength of Southern unionists, who would never gain the ascendancy so long as the secessionists could always get what they demanded. Viewed in this light, compromise might be detrimental to the cause of union; and rejection of compromise might be the best way to avoid the dangers of separation or of having to fight the disunionists.

If the rejection of compromise did not mean the acceptance of either separation or war, did the rejection of separation mean an acceptance of a choice between compromise and coercion as the remaining alternatives? This was the choice which history has seemed to indicate as the real option open to the country. But, though the unfolding of events may subsequently have demonstrated that these were the basic alternatives, one of the dominating facts about the Republicans in the winter of 1860–61 is that they rejected the idea of voluntary disunion and also rejected the idea of compromise, without any feeling that this narrowing of the spectrum would lead them to war. At this juncture, what may be called the

illusion of the Southern unionists played a vital part. Both
Lincoln and Seward and many another Republican were convinced that secessionism was a superficial phenomenon. They
believed that it did not represent the most fundamental impulses of the South, and that although the Southern unionists
had been silenced by the clamor of the secessionists a deep
vein of unionist feeling still survived in the South and could
be rallied, once the Southern people realized that Lincoln
was not an Illinois version of William Lloyd Garrison and that
the secessionists had been misleading them. Lincoln and
Seward became increasingly receptive to this view during the
month before Lincoln's inauguration. Between December 20
and February 4, seven Southern states had held conventions,
and each of these conventions had adopted an ordinance of
secession. But on February 4, the secessionists were defeated
in the election for the Virginia convention. Within four weeks
thereafter, they were again defeated in Tennessee, where the
people refused even to call a convention; in Arkansas, where
the secessionist candidates for a state convention were defeated; in Missouri, where the people elected a convention so
strongly antisecessionist that it voted 89 to 1 against disunion;
and in North Carolina, where antisecessionist majorities were
elected and it was voted that the convention should not meet.

It clearly looked as though the tide of secession had already
turned. Certainly, at the time when Lincoln came to the Presidency, the movement for a united South had failed. There
were, altogether, fifteen slave states. Seven of these, from
South Carolina, along the south Atlantic and Gulf Coast to
Texas, had seceded; but eight others, including Delaware,
Kentucky, and Maryland, as well as the five that I have already
named, were still in the Union and clearly intended to remain
there. In these circumstances, the New York *Tribune* could
speak of the Confederacy as a "heptarchy," and Seward could
rejoice, as Henry Adams reported, that "this was only a tem-

porary fever and now it has reached the climax and favorably passed it." The Southern unionists were already asserting themselves, and faith in them was justified. Thus, on his way east from Springfield, Lincoln stated in a speech at Steubenville, Ohio, that "the devotion to the Constitution is equally great on both sides of the [Ohio] River." From this it seemed to follow that, as he also said on his trip, "there is no crisis but an artificial one. . . . Let it alone and it will go down of itself." Meanwhile, Seward had been saying, ever since December, that the Gulf states would try to secede, but that unless they received the backing of the border states, they would find their petty little combination untenable and would have to come back to the Union. Again we owe to Henry Adams the report that Seward said, "We shall keep the border states, and in three months or thereabouts, if we hold off, the Unionists and the disunionists will have their hands on each others throats in the cotton states."

Today, our hindsight makes it difficult for us to understand this reliance upon Southern unionism, since most of the unionism which existed was destroyed by the four years of war; and it was never what Seward and Lincoln believed it to be in any case. But it seemed quite real when five slave states in rapid succession decided against secession. Thus, in terms of our alternatives of compromise, separation, or war, it is interesting to see that an editorial in the New York *Tribune* on March 27, 1861, specifically examined the alternatives and specifically said that there were only three; but the three which it named were not the three we tend to perceive today. The fact that this editorial, rather closely resembling one in the New York *Times*, was probably inspired by the administration gives it additional interest.

The *Tribune* began by saying that there were but three possible ways in which to meet the secession movement. One was "by prompt, resolute, unflinching resistance"—what I have been calling the alternative of war; the second was "by complete acquiescence in . . . secession"—that is, separation. But instead of naming compromise as the third alternative, the *Tribune* numbered as three "a Fabian policy, which concedes nothing, yet employs no force in support of resisted Federal authority, hoping to wear out the insurgent spirit and in due time re-establish the authority of the union in the revolted or seceded states by virtue of the returning sanity and loyalty of their own people." As the editorial continued, it explained the reasoning which lay behind the advocacy of this policy.

To war on the Seceders is to give to their yet vapory institutions the strong cement of blood—is to baptize their nationality in the mingled life-blood of friends and foes. But let them severely alone —allow them to wear out the military ardor of their adherents in fruitless drilling and marches, and to exhaust the patience of their fellow-citizens by the amount and frequency of their pecuniary exactions—and the fabric of their power will melt away like fog in the beams of a morning sun. Only give them rope, and they will speedily fulfill their destiny—the People, even of South Carolina, rejecting their sway as intolerable, and returning to the mild and paternal guardianship of the Union.

In behalf of this policy, it is urged that the Secessionists are a minority even in the seceded States; that they have grasped power by usurpation and retain it by terrorism; that they never dare submit the question of Union or Disunion fairly and squarely to the people, and always shun a popular vote when they can. In view of these facts, the Unionists of the South urge that the Government shall carry forebearance to the utmost, in the hope that the Nullifiers will soon be overwhelmed by the public sentiment of their own section, and driven with ignominy from power.

It seems reasonably clear that this editorial defined quite accurately the plan of action which Lincoln had announced in his inaugural. In that address, although affirming in general terms a claim of federal authority which, as the *Tribune* expressed it, conceded nothing, he made it quite clear that he would, as the *Tribune* also said, "employ no force" in the immediate situation. He specifically said he would not use force to deliver the mails—they would only be delivered unless repelled. He specifically said that federal marshals and judges would not be sent into areas where these functions had been vacated. "While the strict legal right may exist in the government to enforce the exercise of these offices, the attempt to do so would be so irritating that I deem it better to forego for the time the use of such offices." Without officials for enforcement, Lincoln's statement that he would uphold the law became purely a declaration of principle, with no operative or functional meaning. Finally, after having first written into his inaugural a statement that "all the power at my disposal will be used to reclaim the public property and places which have fallen," he struck this passage from the address as it was ultimately delivered. It was at about this time that Senator William P. Fessenden of Maine wrote that "Mr. Lincoln believed that gentleness and a conciliatory policy would prevent secession"—as if secession had not already occurred.

Finally, there is a question of whether even the decision to send supplies to Fort Sumter involved a clear acceptance of the alternative of war as well as a rejection of the alternatives of separation or compromise. Professor Stampp and Richard Current have both argued with considerable persuasiveness that Lincoln must have known that the Sumter expedition would bring war, since his informants from Charleston had warned him that such an expedition would be met with military force; and they have shown too that anyone with as much realism as Lincoln had in his makeup must have recognized that the chances for peace were slipping away. Yet I think their argument is more a reasoning from logic—that Lincoln must have seen the situation as we see it—and not an argument based primarily on expressions by Lincoln himself, showing that he had abandoned his belief in Southern unionism and accepted the alternative of war. Indeed, insofar as we have expressions from him, he continued to believe in the strength of Southern unionism. Even when he sent his war message to Congress on July 4, he said: "It may well be questioned whether there is today a majority of the legally qualified voters of any state, except perhaps South Carolina, in favor of disunion. There is much reason to believe that the Union men are in the majority in many, if not in every one of the so-called seceded states."

The crisis at Fort Sumter has possibly had almost too sharp a focus placed upon it by historians, and I do not want to dissect that question all over again in this paper. I will state briefly that, in my opinion, Lincoln pursued the most peaceful course that he believed was possible for him to pursue without openly abandoning the principle of union. That is, he assured the Confederates that food only would be sent into Fort Sumter, and nothing else would be done to strengthen the Union position unless the delivery of the food was resisted. While this may be construed, and has been construed, as a threat to make war if the food were not allowed, it can equally well be regarded as a promise that no reinforcement would be undertaken if the delivery of the food was permitted. Lincoln's critics, who accuse him of a covert policy to begin in an advantageous way a war which he now recognized to be inevitable, have never said what more peaceable course he could have followed that would have been consistent with his purpose to save the Union. Thus, they are in the anomalous position of saying that a man who followed the most peaceable course possible was still, somehow, a maker of war.

But as I suggested a moment ago, this focus upon Fort Sumter can perhaps be intensified too much. Even if Lincoln anticipated that there would be shooting at Sumter (and he must have known that there was a strong likelihood of it),

what would this tell us about the choice of alternatives leading to the American Civil War? We may again revert to the
somewhat arbitrary practice of answering this question in
terms of the alternatives as they appear to us now. If the
situation is viewed in this way, one would say we have three
options neatly laid in a row: separation, compromise, war.
If a man rejects any two of them, he is choosing the third;
and since Lincoln and the Republicans rejected separation
or compromise, this means that they exercised a choice for
war. As a statement of the way in which the historical process
narrows the field of possible action, this may be realistic; but
for illumination of the behavior of men it seems to me very
misleading. It assumes two things: first that choices are positive rather than negative; second that a choice of a course
which leads to a particular result is in fact a choice of that
result. Neither of these assumptions seems valid. What often
happens is not that a given course is chosen because it is
acceptable, but that given alternatives are rejected because
they are regarded as totally unacceptable; thus one course
remains which becomes the course followed, not because it
was chosen, but because it was what was left.

When Lincoln ordered the Sumter expedition to sail, it was
not because he wanted to do so; it was because he hated even
worse the contingency of permitting the Sumter garrison to
be starved into surrender. As he himself said, he had been
committed to "the exhaustion of peaceful measures, before
a resort to any stronger ones." But by mid-April at Sumter,
the peaceful measures had all been exhausted; and the course
that Lincoln followed was taken not because it was what he
had chosen, but because it was what was left. That course
resulted, as we now say, in the bombardment of Sumter, and
the bombardment of Sumter was followed by four years of
fighting which we call the Civil War. But even though the
sending of the expedition led to events which in turn led on

to war, it does not follow that the choice to send the expedition involved an acceptance of the alternative of war.

If deeds and consequences could be thus equated, our view of human nature would have to be more pessimistic than it is; and at the same time, our view of the future of humanity might perhaps be somewhat more optimistic. For it would imply that men have deliberately caused the succession of wars that have blotted the record of human history—certainly a harsh verdict to pronounce on humanity—and it would also imply that they have a certain measure of choice as to what forces of destruction they will release in the world—a proposition which would be comforting in the age of nuclear fission. But when we examine the situations of the past, how seldom does it appear that men defined the alternatives logically, chose the preferable alternative, and moved forward to the result that was intended? How often, on the other hand, do we find that they grope among the alternatives, avoiding whatever action is most positively or most immediately distasteful, and thus eliminate the alternatives until only one is left—at which point, as Lincoln said, it is necessary to have recourse to it since the other possibilities are exhausted or eliminated. In this sense, when the Republicans rejected both compromise and secession, thus narrowing the range of possibilities to include only the contingency of war, it was perhaps not because they really preferred the Civil War, with all its costs, to separation or to compromise, but because they could see the consequences of voting for compromise or the consequences of accepting separation more readily than they could see the consequences of following the rather indecisive course that ended in the bombardment of Fort Sumter. They did not know that it would end by leaving them with a war on their hands, any more than they knew it would cost the life of one soldier, either Rebel or Yank, for every six slaves who were freed and for every ten white Southerners who were held in the Union. When they rejected compromise, because they could not bear to make concessions to the fire-eaters, and rejected separation, because they could not bear to see the Union broken up, this does not mean that they accepted war or that they were able to bear the cost which this war would make them pay. It may really mean that they chose a course whose consequences they could not see in preference to courses whose consequences were easier to appraise.

Historians try to be rational beings and tend to write about history as if it were a rational process. Accordingly, they number the alternatives, and talk about choices and decisions, and equate decisions with what the decisions led to. But if we examine the record of modern wars, it would seem that the way people get into a war is seldom by choosing it; usually it is by choosing a course that leads to it—which is a different thing altogether. Although war seems terribly decisive, perhaps it requires less positive decision to get into wars than it does to avert them. For one can get into a war without in any way foreseeing it or imagining it, which is easy. But to avert war successfully, it has to be foreseen or imagined, which is quite difficult. If this is true, it means that the Republicans may have rejected separation and compromise not because they accepted the alternative, but precisely because they could not really visualize the alternative. When they took the steps that led them into a war, they did so not because they had decisively chosen the road to Appomattox or even the road to Manassas, in preference to the other paths; instead they did so precisely because they could not grasp the fearfully decisive consequences of the rather indecisive line of action which they followed in the months preceding their fateful rendezvous.

CHAPTER X

Jefferson Davis and the Political Factors in Confederate Defeat

> *In a conference at Gettysburg College in November, 1958, a number of participants discussed various reasons for the North's victory in the Civil War. Richard Current addressed himself to economic factors, T. Harry Williams to military factors, Norman Graebner to the determining effect of foreign policy, and David Donald discussed how the loose arrangements of a hyperdemocratic society had handicapped both sides. It fell to me to discuss the role of political factors, and the result was the essay below.*
>
> *I should like to note that at the end of this essay I remarked very briefly upon the fact that the Confederacy may have suffered from the lack of a party system, and I suggested that this idea might bear elaboration. I am glad to say that Eric McKitrick has developed the idea most effectively. As an extension of the theme of this paper, I commend to the reader McKitrick's "Party Politics and the Union and Confederate War Efforts" in William N.* Chambers and Walter Dean Burnham, editors, The American Party Systems (New York, 1967), 117–51.

THE QUESTION "Why did the North win the Civil War?" is only half of a question by itself, for the other half is "Why did the South lose the Civil War?" Was one side more crucial than the other? Did the North win because the South was a natural loser, or did the South lose because the North was a natural winner? Is one side of a watch crystal concave because the other is convex, or is one convex because the other is concave? Shall we explain the results in terms of what the North did to the South, as Kenneth P. Williams tended to do in *Lincoln Finds a General*, or in terms of what the South failed to do to the North, as Douglas S. Freeman tended to do in his studies of R. E. Lee and Lee's Lieutenants?

The answer to these questions is easier in theory than it is in application. In principle it is clear that the outcome of a contest between two parties results not from the qualities of either taken alone, but from the differentials between them. Yet to measure these differentials, one must give a kind of bifocal attention to both parties at the same time. This is an ambidextrous feat which historians of the Confederacy and historians of the Union have alike found hard to attain. Consequently, most of the answers come to us in terms of the strength of the Union or the weakness of the Confederacy, rather than of the relative qualities of the two.

Where differentials are examined, they can be measured more precisely in economic terms than in any other, and historians have long been impressed by the great economic superiority of the North. Here there are innumerable measurements—of manpower, of wealth, of railroad mileage, of industrial capacity—all of which point up the overwhelming advantage on the side of the Union. These comparisons have led many writers to conclude that the South was fighting against the census returns and that Northern victory was inevitable from the beginning.

One-sided as these statistical comparisons are, even they fail to reveal in full the economic handicaps of the South. No statistics can measure, for instance, how much the Confederacy suffered from the fact that it had the kind of economy that is prostrated by war, in contrast to the Union which had the kind of economy that flourishes under wartime conditions. War invigorated the Northern economy by stimulating a leading form of Northern economic activity, namely industrial production. Thus the conflict brought prosperity to the civilian population, and civilian morale remained good largely because civilians had nothing to be demoralized about. But in the Confederacy, war paralyzed the chief form of economic activity, which was the cultivation of cotton. As the flow of income from cotton dried up, the economy languished, the economic welfare of civilians suffered, and their morale deteriorated. In the end, the economic morale of the people collapsed before their military morale was exhausted.

In terms of economic logic, it can perhaps be demonstrated that the Confederacy, hopelessly overmatched by almost every measure of strength, was doomed to defeat. But history not only shows that in war the lighter antagonist sometimes defeats the heavier, it also shows that what seems logically certain often fails to happen. Thus, if we survey the course of the Civil War, we do not find that, in actuality, the Confederacy developed very formidable striking power—power impressive enough to make Lincoln doubt, even as late as 1864, that the Union would be saved? Do we not find the effective power of the opposing forces balanced so evenly that sometimes great results seemed to swing on the hinge of relatively trivial events? If a Confederate soldier had not shot Stonewall Jackson in the dusk at Chancellorsville, if Gouverneur Warren had not had a quick eye for Little Round Top, if a duplicate copy of Lee's plan of campaign in September, 1862, had not been used by someone on D. H. Hill's staff to wrap three cigars, might not a delicate balance have swung the other way in spite of all the statistics?

In weighing the question whether inescapable forces doomed the South in advance, it is well also to remember that the question is not what the South might have done during the last twenty-one months of the forty-eight-month war. For in fact, the result had been registered after Gettysburg and perhaps even after Sharpsburg, and all the South could hope for then was that the Northern people might fail to notice that they had won—as indeed the Northern Democrats did fail to notice in the election campaign of 1864. But for fourteen months before Lee came to high command, and for perhaps thirteen months after he did so, the result often appeared to be in real doubt, and it seems legitimate to question whether more effective political policies by the Confederates might at that time have made a crucial difference.

If the balance was, in fact, a delicate one, the analysis of forces must go far beyond the a priori arguments of economic determinism. While no one will deny that economic factors gave to the North an immense advantage, the precise question is whether other countervailing factors could possibly have offset it. For instance, could superior military and political skill on the Confederate side have done so? Reducing this question still further: Was there a differential in military performance in favor of the South which tended to offset, in part, the economic differential in favor of the North? The preponderance of historical opinion has agreed that the answer to this question is yes. For four long years, Lee's army did stave off defeat. But was the differential in political performance also in favor of the South? If it was, then one can say that Southern military and political prowess were hopelessly overmatched by the Union's sheer economic weight. But unless the effectiveness of the Confederate government equalled or surpassed that of the Union government, we cannot rest the evaluation of Confederate policy, as some historians have done, with the affirmation that Confederate leaders should not be blamed for their mistakes since the problems that they faced were insuperable. Instead, we shall have to say that economic and political factors, in conjunction, produced the final result, despite military factors which had a contrary tendency. Can we not go a step farther and ask whether the difference between Union and Confederate political performance was not as great as or greater than the economic disparities—whether in fact the discrepancy in ability between Abraham Lincoln and Jefferson Davis was not as real and as significant as the inequality in mileage between Union and Confederate railroad systems?

The danger of a question like this is that it tends to displace one explanation with another, and to minimize the truly immense handicaps of the Confederacy. No just appraisal would ever underestimate the dead weight of those handicaps, but on the other hand, an appreciation of the magnitude of the South's problems should not stand in the way of a recognition that Confederate policy sometimes aggravated these problems instead of diminishing them, and that mistakes of policy as well as the handicaps of given conditions weakened the Southern cause.

In a number of the situations in which the Confederacy failed, it is fairly evident both that the problems were essentially insurmountable and also that government policy made them even worse than they would otherwise have been. In the matter of raising public revenue and controlling inflation, for instance, it was inevitable that a new government with no gold reserves and no revenue laws would face financial crisis, and also that the scarcity of goods in a blockaded, nonindustrial country would cause an inflationary rise in prices. But while no government could have wholly averted these evils, almost any government could have done more than the Confederacy did. Hesitating to resort to taxation, it called on the states for funds, and they met the requisitions largely by borrowing. In the end, only about one per cent of Confederate revenue was raised by taxation, which is a smaller proportion than any modern government in wartime has raised in this way. In spite of this abuse, the Confederate dollar held up almost as well as the Union greenback during the first two years of the war, which suggests that a sounder financial policy might have sustained it somewhat longer.

A similar combination of unavoidable difficulties on the

one hand, and mistaken choices between policy alternatives on the other appears in the treatment of what had traditionally been the South's major economic asset—namely the cotton crop. In 1861, this asset was worth $225 million in gold, or nearly ten times as much as the actual gold supply in the Confederacy. Every one of the 4,500,000 bales, if exported and held in a European warehouse, would have helped to pay for vital Confederate purchases overseas. The loss of a considerable part of this value was inevitable, because shipping could not have been procured to export the whole crop before the Union blockade became operative. It was fantastic to suppose, for instance, as did Alexander H. Stephens, that fifty iron-bottomed boats could have been bought and used for the export of 4,000,000 bales. But while lack of shipping forced the Confederate leaders to keep a part of the cotton at home, they willingly embraced a fallacious belief—the King Cotton delusion—which caused them voluntarily to keep all of it at home. This belief that, by withholding their cotton, they would force Britain and France to intervene in the war, failed to face up to the question whether there were commodities which the Confederacy would need even more urgently than Britain and France would need cotton fibers.

There were realistic men in the Confederacy who perceived the fallacy in the cotton policy. As early as April, 1861, Secretary of the Treasury C. G. Memminger resolutely opposed the cotton embargo and expressed his disapproval "of any obstruction to commerce in our ports." During 1862, the Commissary Department faced the reality that supplies were vital and must be procured even if it meant trading cotton to the enemy—a far more serious matter than selling it abroad. According to R. G. H. Kean, in November, Commissary General Lucius B. Northrop reported that "he could not supply the Army unless allowed to purchase bacon from the enemy at Memphis with cotton," and the Quartermaster

General wanted to procure blankets in the same way. The Secretary of War, George W. Randolph, had already become convinced of the necessity of a cotton trade limited to the bureau in question. By April, 1863, Secretary of State Judah P. Benjamin broke sharply away from the King Cotton doctrine, asserted that it was a matter of primary importance to bring in army supplies at Confederate ports, and proposed a definite export of cotton "to be received by the merchant vessels of France at certain designated points." Before the end of the war, even General Lee strongly recommended to President Davis that the trade which was already bringing New York bacon to his army should be widely extended to secure other supplies.

These men perceived the point of a problem posed by Kean: "The question is simply whether they [the North or the British and French] suffer more for the . . . cotton . . . or we for the indispensable articles of salt, meat, clothing, medicines." But Kean also reported, "The President resisted it [the proposal for trade] in toto." In March, 1863, he noted in his diary that "the President has yielded at last on the subject of getting meat from the enemy for cotton"—this in connection with General Kirby Smith's trade at the mouth of the Río Grande. But Kean added, "Too late to do much good." Nearly a year later, he was still criticizing Davis for placing upon the cotton trade restrictions which made it almost impossible to conduct. As he reported, regulations for the trade were drawn very carefully in the War Office and sent to the President, but "they came back so modified as to destroy the trade by their stringency."

In the end, cotton responded to the laws of necessity, and a vast amount was traded through the lines. In fact, this trade became an important factor in sustaining the armies in the West, and Memphis took its place as "a greater outfitting point for Confederate armies than Nassau." Private families

—even patriotic ones—found that by smuggling out a single bale they might escape starvation, while quartermasters and commissaries and state officials learned that this was sometimes the only way to keep Southern armies in the field. Therefore, it cannot be said that Jefferson Davis succeeded in imposing a policy based upon the King Cotton doctrine. All that he did succeed in doing was to reduce the cotton situation to chaos. In this chaos, the Confederate government lacked control of the cotton in the South and lacked a constructive overall policy for utilizing such cotton as it did control. Consequently, private owners smuggled large amounts of cotton through the lines, thus breaking the partial embargo, demoralizing the citizens who were too patriotic to smuggle, and creating competition against their own government in bidding for the goods which cotton would buy. At the same time, the government itself survived by accepting, more or less unwittingly, the fruits of a trade conducted mostly on an unsanctioned basis by desperate or imaginative minor officials. But while permitting enough trade to break its own embargo, the government never faced the question how best to reap the potential advantage of the cotton supply as a whole. At the end of the war, 2,500,000 bales had been destroyed to prevent them from falling into the hands of the enemy; less than 1,000,000 probably had been exported through the blockade; and an incalculable amount had been smuggled through the lines, more for the gain of private parties than for the good of the cause. Such was the ultimate destiny of what everyone recognized as the greatest economic asset of the Confederacy.

The same pattern of initial handicaps compounded by mistaken policy appears in the procurement of supplies and foodstuffs for the Confederate Army. The initial handicap lay in the fact that there were many commodities, especially those produced abroad, which were inevitably scarce, or even unobtainable. The mistaken policy lay in the fact that even the goods which might have been produced in sufficient quantity became scarce because of restrictive economic measures. In this connection, it is important to recognize that, as the war developed, Southern farmers turned from the production of cotton to the production of grain, and there was no overall deficiency of food. But in procuring food for the army the Confederacy found itself in the dilemma that if it purchased supplies on the open market at an uncontrolled price, inflation would mushroom, while on the other hand, if it requisitioned supplies at an arbitrary price, productive output would be discouraged and the loyalty of the producers would be impaired. Caught between these alternatives, the government chose to give priority to avoiding inflation. Accordingly it set up a system of impressment, which partook of legalized confiscation, since it permitted military officers to seize draft animals or foodstuffs at a fixed price which was sometimes less than half of the market value. The net result of this was to encourage corrupt practices, to place civilian morale under an almost intolerable strain, and to discourage production without noticeably slowing the pace of inflation. As men either hoarded their crops, or stopped planting altogether, severe shortages developed. By March, 1863, these shortages were so acute that Kean wrote: "The Army will be starved and famine will ensue in the cities unless the Secretary changes his policy and buys in the market for the best price. The government will have to outbid the traders; else *neither* will get anything of the present scanty stock and no future stock will be produced."

The failures of the impressment system have received full recognition at the hands of historians, but another error in economic mobilization, which has largely escaped notice, was the failure of the Confederacy to assert control over the use of a labor force which constituted more than one-third of its manpower—namely that part which consisted of Negro slaves. Where manpower was white, the government did not hesitate very many months before adopting conscription laws which made the allocation of the labor of such men subject to public control. These laws drew most men of military age into the army, but they left others, whose occupations were deemed to be essential, in a civilian status. But where manpower was Negro, conscription did not bring it under similar control. Because of the *idée fixe* that slaves were property and not persons, the allocation of nearly 40 per cent of the Confederacy's total manpower was left to the whim and discretion of individual slaveholders. This produced great inequalities of sacrifice, for manpower meant earning power on the farms. Conscription had taken the manpower, and thus the earning power of the nonslaveholding families, who suffered great privations during the war. It left most of the manpower and thus the earning power of the slaveholding families, whose privations were usually much less severe.

It is an ironical comment on the blind refusal of the South to regard slaves as men that when resentment flared up against this system, it took the form of protest not against the failure to conscript slaves—whether for military or non-military service—but against the exemption from military service of one white man as overseer for every twenty slaves whose labor had to be supervised. The disgruntled men who said bitterly that this was "a rich man's war and a poor man's fight" resented deeply the fact that a limited number of white men were allowed to remain in noncombatant employment as overseers, yet they apparently did not resent at all the fact that the labor of several million black workers continued to be used for the benefit of their owners, while the labor of white workers was subject to the demands of the Confederacy. The failure to include Negroes in any over-all system of public allocation of labor was both a fundamental source of inequality of sacrifice on the part of the people and a basic flaw in the plan of economic mobilization. It is in some ways surprising that Jefferson Davis seems to have grasped this point, for in a message to Congress in November, 1864, he observed that slaves were sometimes treated as property, subject to impressment for short terms, but that "the slave . . . bears another relation to the state —that of a person. . . . In this [war] aspect, the relation of person predominates so far as to render it doubtful whether the private right of property can consistently and beneficially be continued and it would seem proper to acquire for the public service the entire property in the labor of the slave, and to pay therefor due compensation."

These failures, if failures they be—the failure to tax, the failure even to attempt an effective use of the cotton supply, the failure to achieve effective use of resources and manpower —all stemmed from attitudes which prevailed widely in the Confederacy. Insofar as they were errors, they were the errors of the South in general and not of the Confederate President nor any other one man in particular. In fact, the general level of political leadership in the Confederacy left much to be desired—as witness the parochialism of men like Governor Joseph E. Brown, who never really perceived that the defense of Georgia lay beyond the territorial boundaries of the state, or the negativism of men like Senator Henry S. Foote, whose futile ranting presented a painful anticlimax to the great tradition of Southern political excellence in the federal Congress in the decades before the war.

But in appraising the part which political factors played in the failure of the Confederacy, it is necessary to look beyond the questions of formation of policy to the more human question of the quality of leadership. At this level, as distinguished from the policy level, there is a great deal of evidence to justify placing a considerable share of the responsibility for the Confederacy's misfortunes directly at the door of Jefferson Davis.

This is not at all the same thing as to say that the strictures of his critics were valid. In fact, the narrowness, pettiness, and lack of realism of men like Alexander Stephens, Brown, and Foote make the narrowness of Davis seem broad-gauge by comparison. Moreover, when these critics assailed him, they usually did so for the wrong reasons. Men who least understood what the South needed were the most vocal in attacking him, while the men who, like Lee and Benjamin, most clearly perceived his real shortcomings were the least vocal because they were also the ones who understood that whatever was to be accomplished must be accomplished through him. With his most acute critics always silent and his most obtuse ones never so, he enjoyed a brand of criticism which, however galling it may have been at the time, has helped his historical reputation, since history must vindicate him if he is measured by some of the accusations brought against him by his critics—accusations of despotism and too much centralization. But if he is measured, instead, by the tests which history itself would apply to the appraisal of leadership, what do we find? We find, it may be argued, a record of personal failure significant enough to have had a bearing on the course of the war.

Davis failed in three important ways—in his relations with other Confederate leaders and with the people, in his fundamental concept of his job as President, and in his specific handling of his politico-military role as commander-in-chief. In every one of these respects, Lincoln offered a striking contrast and presented superlative qualities of leadership.

Concerning Davis' relations with the Confederate leaders, Clifford Dowdey has remarked that he had only two first-rate minds among his advisers—Robert E. Lee and Judah P. Benjamin. Both men had to employ a disproportionate amount of their time and energy in exercising the supreme tact which was necessary in working with Davis. Benjamin was never permitted to bring his originality and resourcefulness into play, and he was forced to forfeit his influence with the public by silently accepting blame for measures which Davis chose not to explain to the people. As for Lee, he was held in peripheral commands or at a desk in Richmond until fourteen of the twenty-seven months during which the South still retained some striking power had passed. Davis never allowed him a post of overall command such as Winfield Scott, George B. McClellan, Henry W. Halleck, and U. S. Grant all enjoyed under Lincoln. When Congress adopted a bill establishing the office of general-in-chief, intended for Lee, Davis vetoed it.

Compare this record with that of Lincoln, who took both William H. Seward and Salmon Chase into his cabinet, who kept Charles Sumner on his side while at the same time holding border state moderates like Edward Bates, who formed a cabinet with four former Democrats and three former Whigs and blandly remarked that he could balance the elements since he was an old Whig himself. Compare, too, Lincoln's forebearance when Seward was trying to run the administration, Chase was conducting a Presidential campaign against Lincoln from his post in the Treasury, and the Blair family was waging its bitter family feuds from the postmaster-general's office.

Again, it is revealing to compare Davis' attitude toward P. G. T. Beauregard when he felt that the Creole general was blaming him for the failure to reap the fruits of First Manassas, and Lincoln's attiude toward Joseph Hooker when he believed that Hooker was saying there ought to be a dictator at Washington. Davis wrote to Beauregard that he was "surprised" at that general's report of the battle "because if we did differ as to the measure and purposes of contemplated campaigns, such fact could have no appropriate place in the report of the battle; further, because it seemed to be an attempt to exalt yourself at my expense." [1]

The accusation was very likely valid, but Lincoln would not have made it. When he wrote to Hooker, it was to say: "I have heard, in such a way as to believe it, of your recently saying that both the army and the government needed a dictator. Of course it was not for this, but in spite of it, that I have given you the command. Only those generals who gain successes can set up dictators. What I now ask of you is military success, and I will risk the dictatorship. The government will support you to the utmost of its ability, which is neither more nor less than it has done and will do for all commanders."

Just as Davis could not really work with other Confederate leaders, so also he could scarcely even communicate with the people of the Confederacy. He seemed to think in abstractions and to speak in platitudes. It is suggestive, I think, to recall his appeal to the men who had fought, suffered, lost their faith, and gone through hell under the command of Braxton Bragg and who wanted no more of their commanding general. Davis' way of dealing with these hard-bitten and badly demoralized soldiers was to praise in flowery language their virtues as fighting men and then, as a climax, to urge

[1] It must be conceded that both Joseph E. Johnston and Beauregard gave Davis great provocation, and that he was sometimes astonishingly patient in replying to them, but he was also capable of being very starchy in his rebukes. When Brigadier General Whiting protested the policy of giving each brigade a commander from its own state, and declined the command of such a brigade himself, and when Johnston forwarded Whiting's letter to Richmond, Secretary Benjamin replied: "The President has read with grave displeasure the very insubordinate letter of General Whiting, in which he indulges in presumptuous censure of the orders of his commander-in-chief and tenders unasked advice to his superiors in command. . . . The President requests me to say that he trusts you will hereafter decline to forward to him communications of your subordinates having so obvious a tendency to excite a mutinous and disorganizing spirit in the army."

them: "Crown these [virtues] with harmony, due subordination, and cheerful support of lawful authority."

One reason for Davis' failure to communicate was that he could seldom admit he was wrong. He used an excessive share of his energy in contentious and even litigious argument to prove he was right. He seemed to feel that if he were right that was enough; that it was more important to vindicate his own rectitude than to get results. When a matter could not be explained without admitting a mistake, as for instance in the case of the loss of Roanoke Island, it simply did not get explained at all, and the people were alienated by the feeling that the administration dared not trust them with the truth. As a critic of Davis, Edward Pollard of the Richmond *Examiner* often displayed rank prejudice, but he came close to the truth when he said that Davis "has not told the people what he needed. As a faithful sentinel, he has not told them what of the night."

The contrast presented by Lincoln shows up clearly in a letter of Lincoln to Grant at the end of the Vicksburg campaign. "When you first reached the vicinity of Vicksburg," said Lincoln, "I never had any faith, except a general hope that you knew better than I, that the Yazoo Pass expedition, and the like, could succeed. When you got below, and took Port Gibson, Grand Gulf, and vicinity, I thought you should go down the river and join General [N. P.] Banks; and when you turned northward east of the Big Black, I feared it was a mistake. I now wish to make the personal acknowledgement that you were right and I was wrong."

This letter has no counterpart in the correspondence of Jefferson Davis.

If Davis failed in his relations with people, he failed also in his concept of his task as President. In April, 1861, history cast him in the role of a revolutionary leader. What such a role requires of a man is that he shall concentrate intensively upon the essentials, with a bold indifference to all that is irrelevant to the cause; that he shall hold to the level of overall leadership, leaving matters of detail to his subordinates; and that he shall have a driving instinct for success and a readiness to adopt the innovations which will bring success. Although Davis possessed talent and intelligence, it would have been hard to find a man more lacking in these qualifications than he.

Davis was a conservative leader, not a revolutionary leader; a man with a strong sense of protocol and convention, but with a weak sense of innovation; a man who was much happier with details than he was with overviews; a man who loved order and logical organization better than he loved results which are achieved by unorthodox methods; above all, a man who thought in terms of principles rather than of possibilities and who cared more about proving he was right than about gaining success.

All these qualities showed up in his handling of his duties as commander-in-chief. In that role, his other weaknesses were accentuated by his firm conviction that he possessed real military talent and that he should give his attention primarily to the close guidance of the operations of all the Confederate armies. Because of this conviction, he ran the war office himself and all six of his war secretaries were either nonentities or transients—even Benjamin seemingly exercised little initiative while in this post. For the same reason the giant, Lee, was never permitted to hold a general command such as even Halleck held under Lincoln. The same irresistible temptation to run military operations himself also led Davis to descend to points of detail where he lost sight of the larger issues with which he should have concerned himself. Consequently, two of the severest criticisms of Davis have come from men who were in the War Department in Richmond. After serving Davis as Secretary of War, George W. Randolph said that, despite all his attention to this area of activities, the President had "no practical knowledge of the workings of our military system in the field." Even more contemptuously, Robert G. H. Kean, an official of the department, said that Davis wasted time on "trash that ought to be dispatched by clerks." [2]

This attention to military detail resulted in something far more serious than the waste of Presidential time. It meant that Davis made decisions in Richmond which should have been made in the field and that he hampered his field commanders by limiting their functions too narrowly and by interfering with their command. Not only did he sometimes visit battlefields and change the disposition of regiments while combat raged, but he sometimes sent orders to subordinate generals without consulting, and even without informing, their field commanders.[3]

A striking contrast to Davis' constant intervention appears in the policy of Lincoln, who was always concerned with military policy and often admonished his generals, but who avoided details and refrained from giving orders. Lincoln's whole philosophy was expressed in a letter to Grant in 1864 in which he said, "The particulars of your plans, I neither know nor seek to know." By this statement Lincoln in no sense ab-

[2] On February 1, 1862, J. E. Johnston wrote to Benjamin: "I have been greatly surprised today to receive an order from the War Office detailing a private for a working party here. I hazard nothing in saying that in time of war, a Secretary of War never before made such a detail."

[3] On February 14, 1862, replying to a protest by J. E. Johnston, Davis said: "While I admit the propriety in all cases of transmitting orders through you to those under your command, it is not surprising that the Secretary of War should, in a case requiring prompt action, have departed from this usual method in view of the fact that he had failed more than once in having his instructions carried out when forwarded to you in the proper manner." This comes close to suggesting that, when a field commander is slow to obey orders, the proper remedy is to bypass him without informing him that he has been bypassed.

dicated his authority as commander-in-chief. Rather, he clearly defined the true division of function between commander-in-chief and field commander. His role was to consider overall questions of military policy. The operational particulars were the business of the generals in the field. Lincoln knew this without learning it by experience. Davis never learned it despite his experience at West Point, in the Mexican War, and as Secretary of War under Pierce.

If Davis had developed a military policy which would produce victory, his compulsion to run everything himself might not have mattered. But his decision to be his own Secretary of War and his own general-in-chief meant that he was the author of Confederate military policy, and that he incorporated into this policy two fatal principles. One was the principle of departmentalization; the other, allied with it, was the principle of dispersion of force for the defense of territory, rather than concentration of force for the defeat of the enemy.

The principle of departmentalization appealed naturally to a man who thought in formal and static terms rather than in functional and dynamic ones. Like the dedicated bureaucrat that he was, Davis loved a symmetrical table of organization. Consequently, he did not hesitate to carry on the peacetime practice of assigning the units of the army to completely separate geographical departments, each one reporting solely to the war office and each operating independently of all the others. Sometimes this led to strange results. For instance, Lee, commanding in a department north of the James, and Beauregard, commanding in a department south of the James, converged in 1864 to defend Petersburg, but they continued to communicate with one another through the War Department in Richmond. But in fact, Lee and Beauregard did cooperate, despite the mechanical awkwardness of their situation. What was more serious was that, in general, the departmental commanders sought reinforcements for their own departments and looked to the defense of them without much regard for the needs of their fellows in other departments. One reason for the loss of Vicksburg was the fact that help had not come from the Trans-Mississippi Department, and Davis had rebuked Secretary Randolph for trying to bring help from that quarter. In June, 1863, Kean wrote: "The fatal notion of making each military department a separate nation for military purposes without subordination, co-operation, or concert—the same on which in point [of fact] the President and General Randolph split—has lost us Mississippi." [4] Dowdey, who also regards this departmentalization as one of the decisive factors in Confederate failure, remarks: "When Lee took over the War office, on hilly North Street, across from Capitol Square [in 1862] Davis had a dispersal of forces in Virginia which, counting subdivisions of armies, had eight separate forces arranged in separate parts of the state. . . . The Confederate forces in Virginia were ready for anything except to fight a battle."

When accused of practicing dispersal, Davis denied that

[4] On July 12, Kean wrote further: "The radical vice of Mr. Davis's whole military system is the separate departmental organization, each reporting only to him. It makes each department depend only on its *own* strength and deprives them of the mutual support and combination which might else be obtained. It appears from a recent report of Richard Taylor that Vicksburg *might* have been relieved from that side; that the whole situation was treated with a levity incomprehensible when the vast stake is considered! Mr. Seddon remarked yesterday that he thought there was more blame on the command on the west than on the east side of the [Mississippi] river for its loss. It was a difference on this very principle of co-operation across the Mississippi, at this very point, Vicksburg, in connection with which General Randolph's resignation was brought about. His instruction to Holmes, who then had the command Smith now has, to cross over when necessary to produce the best results, and by virtue of his rank to take command of the combined force, was the thing of which the President so pointedly disapproved, and *countermanded*."

this was his policy, and he might have claimed, in extenuation, that the state governors exerted great pressure upon him to assign troops for local defense throughout many parts of the South. But he was committed to defensive action by temperament, if not by conviction. He never initiated the daring concentrations which Lee was willing to risk. He always thought in terms of repelling the invader rather than of smashing the enemy, and he was slow to recognize the fearful cost of defending fixed positions, as at Vicksburg. He never showed the compelling urgency of a man who knows that time is on the side of the enemy and that victory must be gained before the enemy's potential strength can be brought into play.

Once again the contrast with Lincoln is illuminating—and damaging to Davis. To my mind, it has been conclusively demonstrated that Lincoln had a sounder concept of the overall military objectives of the Union than any of his generals. He was impatient with the endless maneuvering and seeking of positional objectives which so completely dominated the thought of many of the generals, and he seldom lost sight of the ultimate goal of defeating the enemy's forces. T. Harry Williams quotes his message to Hooker: "I think Lee's Army, and not *Richmond*, is your true objective point. . . . Fight him when opportunity offers. If he stays where he is, fret him and fret him." Many months later, Lincoln wrote again, this time to General Halleck: "To avoid misunderstanding, let me say that to attempt to fight the enemy slowly back into his intrenchments at Richmond, and then to capture him, is an idea that I have been trying to repudiate for quite a year. . . . I have constantly desired the Army of the Potomac to make Lee's army and not Richmond, its objective point. If our army cannot fall upon the enemy and hurt him where he is, it is plain to me it can gain nothing by attempting to follow him over a succession of entrenched lines into a fortified city."

Many passages might be quoted to underscore the extent of the difference between Lincoln and Davis. But it would be hard to find any quotation which focuses the contrast quite as clearly as Lincoln's statement of what he liked about Ulysses S. Grant. I do not mean his curt: "I can't spare this man; he fights," though that is apposite enough. What I am referring to is his observation: "General Grant is a copious worker and fighter but a very meager writer or telegrapher." If Davis was anything, he was a copious writer and telegrapher —so much so that Pollard said he had ink instead of blood in his veins—and what is more to the point, he seemed to cultivate this quality in his commanders. But he was a meager worker and fighter in terms of bringing about results, or even of clearly perceiving the results that needed to be brought about.

Fundamentally, Davis always thought in terms of what was right, rather than in terms of how to win. There is no real evidence in all the literature that Davis ever at any one time gave extended consideration to the basic question of what the South would have to do in order to win the war. He said almost nothing on this subject in his messages to Congress, which abounded in passages designed to prove the iniquity of the North and the rectitude of the South. By contrast, Lincoln wanted victory and wanted it so badly that in order to get it he was willing to cooperate with men who had shown they hated him. As he said, "I need success more than I need sympathy and I have not seen so much greater evidence of getting success from my sympathizers than from those who are denounced as the contrary." Lincoln thought of the war as something to be fought, but Davis thought of it as something to be conducted. There was no instinct for the jugular in Davis.

That is why one seldom finds him pressing his generals to engage the enemy and never finds him striving for the concentration which might make possible a knockout blow.

In the light of Jefferson Davis' conspicuous lack of an instinct for victory, his lack of a drive and thrust for action and results, his failure to define his own office in terms of what needed to be accomplished, it hardly seems unrealistic to suppose that if the Union and the Confederacy had exchanged Presidents with one another, the Confederacy might have won its independence. In this sense, is it not justifiable to doubt that the overwhelming statistical advantages of the North predestined the Confederacy to defeat? Historians have never developed a really satisfactory way of dealing with the relationship between the vast, impersonal, long-range social and economic forces of history and the immediate, close-range, somewhat accidental factors of personality; but here is certainly a case where the factors of personality played an important part in guiding the impact of the impersonal social and economic forces.

A political scientist might well object that it is superficial to emphasize these factors of personality without considering the question of what there was in the political system of the South that prevented the development of any viable alternative to the leadership of Davis. As we all know, any government may occasionally have the bad luck of putting an unsuitable man in a position of leadership. England, in 1939, had her Neville Chamberlain. No system can wholly prevent this from happening. But an effective political system, and especially an effective democratic system, is supposed to contain a mechanism which makes it possible to substitute new leadership when the existing leadership fails. England may have entered the Second World War with Chamberlain at the helm, but she ended with Winston Churchill dominating the scene. Granted there was no mute, inglorious Churchill waiting in the wings of the Confederacy, still there is abundant evidence that before the end of 1862 widespread and deep-seated dissatisfaction with Jefferson Davis was rife in the Confederacy. A great many people—perhaps the majority of informed men—knew that the choice of President had been a mistake. Yet there was no constructive opposition. The petulant, short-sighted, narrow-gauge, negativistic, vindictive quality of the criticisms of Davis made him seem, with all his shortcomings, a better man than most of those who assailed him. The Congress was little better than a bear garden, where Senator Benjamin Hill hit Senator William L. Yancey in the face with an inkwell, where a subordinate clerk of the House shot and killed the chief clerk on the capitol grounds, where a "lady" horsewhipped Senator George G. Vest, and where Senator Foote fought promiscuously with anyone who would fight him. Why did no legislative leader emerge to claim a legislative receivership for the bankrupt office of the executive?

This is a major question which suggests several lines of thought. For one thing, it tempts one to wonder to what extent the long years of defending slavery and building protective legalistic safeguards for the South as a minority section within the Union may have impaired the capacity for affirmative and imaginative action on the part of Southern leaders generally. How much had the vaunted statesmanship of the South suffered in this process? There is another suggestion which comes to mind. This is the possibiilty that the Confederacy may have suffered real and direct damage from the fact that its political organization lacked a two-party system. In the crisis of war, Southerners professed to regard it as a source of strength that they were not divided by party dissensions, but functionally a two-party system has important values. Where parties do not exist, criticism of the administration is likely to remain purely an individual matter; therefore the tone of the criticism is likely to be negative, carping, and petty, as it certainly was in the Confederacy. But where there are parties, the opposition group is strongly impelled to formulate real alternative policies and to press for the adoption of these policies on a constructive basis. In 1863 in the South, new Congressional elections were held, and, though history has neglected these elections most scandalously, we do know that they constituted a sharp rebuke to the administration and its followers.

Alternative leadership at that point, or even earlier, might have found a very substantial backing and might have been able to dominate policy. But the absence of a two-party system meant the absence of any available alternative leadership, and the protest votes which were cast in the election became mere expressions of futile and frustrated dissatisfaction rather than implements of a decision to adopt new and different policies for the Confederacy. Thus, the political leadership could not be altered, and Jefferson Davis continued to the end in his distinctive role—not a role which destiny fatalistically forced upon him, but one for which his qualities and temperament peculiarly fitted him and which he fulfilled in a very functional sense—the role of the leader of a Lost Cause.

The Civil War
in the History of the Modern World:
A Comparative View

The parochialism of American historians has been one of their most unfortunate limitations. We write about liberty without much reference to the French Revolution, about Jacksonian Democracy without reference to the democratic ferment of Europe in the 1830's and 1840's, about American reform without reference to the epic struggles in Britain to halt the slave trade, to free the slave, and to improve the lot of the industrial worker. Some of our worst navel-gazing has occurred in connection with the Civil War—a conflict all our own, as American as apple pie. Yet the Civil War reflected forces at work throughout Western society, and it contributed to the historical direction which those forces took in Western society. When C. Vann Woodward was gathering a volume of essays on how various trends and experiences in the American past related to counterpart trends and experiences in the past of other countries, I was glad that he asked me to try my hand at an essay on the significance of the Civil War in comparative terms.

*I*T HAS BEEN the curious fate of the United States to exert immense influence in the modern world, without itself quite understanding the nature of this influence. Major trends of the modern world—both constructive trends and socially injurious ones—have repeatedly become apparent in the United States before they became evident elsewhere. But though the United States has often been a step ahead in the process of social change, it has frequently been a step behind in its awareness of the meaning of new developments. The

287

shape of things to come often became visible in America earlier than it did elsewhere, but American preconceptions about the frontier, the classless society, and the agrarian basis of democracy prevented Americans from perceiving this shape as realistically as it was perceived by social thinkers in other countries. If Americans have failed effectively to interpret their experience to people in other societies, it is in part because they have not always been able to explain it to themselves. Further, the distinctive qualities of life in America have caused a good many forces which were generically universal to take forms which seemed more restrictively peculiar to the New World than they really were.

Thus in the late eighteenth century, America executed the first democratic political revolution of a democratic age, but American society was already so equalitarian that the revolutionary implication was muted. Without any great social overturn, the American War of Independence seemed conservative when compared with the socially cataclysmic forces released in France a decade later. In the twentieth century the United States developed what was perhaps the first mass society, but the American cult of equality and individualism prevented Americans from analyzing their mass society in realistic terms. Often they treated it as if it were simply an infinite aggregation of Main Streets in Zenith, Ohio. America has witnessed episodes of extreme industrial conflict, but these have not been interpreted in the class terms which a Marxist society would invoke. America has experienced a sweeping revolution in sex behavior, but has not incorporated this change into the system of values by which it explains itself. Ironically, the United States has cherished a belief in its mission to spread a democracy for which it has had difficulty in finding converts, while it has led the world in technological changes which produced social transformations that it had no especial desire to bring about.

The reader need not be astonished, therefore, if the Civil War has been interpreted in terms which disguised its broader meaning. If, as some Americans asserted, its chief importance was in putting an end to chattel slavery, this could hardly be regarded as a leading development in the history of Western civilization; for slavery had disappeared from western Europe, except vestigially, while it still flourished in the Americas, and it had disappeared from most of Latin America, except Cuba and Brazil, while it still persisted in the United States. The American republic was almost destroyed, therefore, in a struggle over an institution which world opinion regarded as an anachronism.

If, on the other hand, the Civil War was, as some other Americans asserted, important chiefly because it preserved the American Union, this statement also was framed in restrictive terms which failed to reveal its broader implications. Beginning with the mystic phrase *E pluribus unum*, the republic had not been able for two generations to resolve the question whether it was, in the last analysis, *pluribus* or *unum*. The Civil War gave *unum* the upper hand, and the importance of this fact became visible in world history in 1917 and again in 1941, when the strength of a consolidated American republic impinged decisively on two world wars. But at the time, in a literal sense, there was not much significance for other nations in the fact that the United States waited for fourscore years and ten to settle a question which other nations settled at their inception. There seemed little universality of significance in a war fought to find, or at least determine, a clear meaning for a cryptic federal system such as no other nation had ever had, and such as was deliberately made ambiguous in the first place in order not to lose the support which it certainly would have lost if its meaning had been clarified.

While the war was in progress, European policy-makers tended to think of it simply in terms of whether it would leave the United States weaker or stronger than before. After it was over, the only people who examined it closely were military historians, looking for the lessons of strategy and tactics that might be derived from the first major conflict in which repeating arms, ironclad vessels, trench warfare, and railroads as supply lines were used on a significant scale.

Thus, while the campaigns of Lee and Grant have fascinated English and European readers, just as the campaigns of Napoleon have fascinated Americans, and while the personality of Lincoln has held an appeal for men everywhere, writers have scarcely asked the question: what was the role of the American Civil War in the history of the modern world? Did it have historical significance for anyone except Americans?

If we are seeking an answer to this question, it may be useful to begin by asking ourselves, simply, what were the prevalent tendencies of the nineteenth century, and what did the Civil War contribute in causing these tendencies to prevail? Historians have neglected the latter part of this question, but have repeatedly given an answer to the first part. They tell us, over and over, that the nineteenth century was an era of liberalism and nationalism. The basis for the generalization is obvious. Nationalism, as we know it in its modern form, scarcely existed before the French Revolution; but by the end of the nineteenth century Britain, France, Germany, Italy, and Japan had become prototypes for modern nationality, sometimes after great travail. Nationalistic forces were fermenting throughout other parts of Europe, and even in the colonial world of Asia and Africa the premonitory stirrings of a latent nationalism could already be detected. The Monroe Doctrine had done its bit to make the Western Hemisphere safe for nationalism, and the Latin Americans had responded by erecting eighteen separate nationalistic republics. Likewise with liberalism. It was scarcely more than an ideology in the minds of British and French rationalists before the French Revolution, but by the beginning of the twentieth century representative government and other liberal institutions prevailed in Britain, France, and Italy, and to some extent even in Germany and Austria-Hungary. The Hapsburgs, the Hohenzollerns, and the Romanoffs were still on their thrones, but they stood on the defensive before the onslaughts of Social Democrats, Social Revolutionaries, and other militant reformers.

All these facts are familiar to the point of triteness and it would be parochial to exaggerate the importance of the American Civil War in connection with them. But if we are to define the place of this war in terms of world history, rather than merely of American history, there are two aspects in which it exercised a crucial effect in shaping the tendencies of world history. These aspects may or may not have served the long-range welfare of human society, and it may be argued that, ultimately, their effect was pernicious. But for good or ill, here are two things which the Civil War did: first, it turned the tide which had been running against nationalism for forty years, or ever since Waterloo; and second, it forged a bond between nationalism and liberalism at a time when it appeared that the two might draw apart and move in opposite directions.

Because of the ultimate triumph of nationalism as a worldwide force by 1900, it is easy to forget how seriously nationalism appeared to have failed at the time when the Civil War occurred. After establishing firm bridgeheads in Britain and France, it had met with disaster after disaster in its efforts to spread into southern and central Europe. Britain had moved successfully to suppress nationalism in Ireland, and Russia had taken the most repressive measures in 1830 to crush it out in Poland. After the galaxy of nationalist revolutions of 1848 the dreams of a united Italy had ended with disaster at Cus-

tozza, those of a united Germany with the anticlimax of the
Frankfurt Parliament, those of Czechoslovakia with the overthrow of the Pan-Slavic Congress, and those of Hungary with
the defeat of Louis Kossuth. Simultaneously, in America, the
steadily rising tensions between North and South seemed increasingly likely to destroy the feeling of national unity which
had appeared completely triumphant during the first two
decades of the century. The forces of nationalism reasserted
themselves successfully in the Italian peninsula in the two
years preceding the American Civil War, but otherwise nationalism and especially liberal nationalism in Europe seemed
a lost cause. Louis Napoleon had made himself emperor of
France in 1852, and within another decade was busily planting a Hapsburg imperialist regime in Mexico.

Viewed from the standpoint of appearances only, the forces
which opposed nationalism in Europe were entirely unlike
those which opposed it in America. In Europe, one might say,
the forces which thwarted nationalism were those of universalism—of the Catholic Church and of the Hapsburg and
Romanoff empires, for which the nationalist impulse seemed
too localizing and disruptive. In America, one might say, the
forces which thwarted it were those of localism and of sectionalism, for which the nationalist impulse seemed too con-
solidating and centralizing. In Europe, imperial forces sought
to stamp out nationalism from above; in America, particular-
istic forces sought to resist it from below. It is perhaps because
the opposition was centripetal in Europe and centrifugal in
America that historians have tended to overlook the parallel
triumphs of national unification, all within a period of twelve
short years, in Italy, the United States, and Germany.

But the contrast between universalism and localism, as the
forces which opposed nationalism, is perhaps more apparent
than real. In both Europe and America, the forces of tradition
and privilege tended to be arrayed against nationalism, while

the forces of liberalism and democracy tended to support it. In America, the secession of the Southern states has been accurately described as a conservative revolt—a revolution by men who were not revolutionists, and who justified their revolution less by a philosophical defense of the right of the self-determination of peoples than by refined, legalistic arguments upon the intent of the Constitution of 1787. These "Rebels," instead of advocating change, were rebelling against it and were the champions of a traditional, relatively static, hierarchical society. They feared, with some reason, as we may now conclude, the transformations that might be wrought by an industrial society. They feared the destruction of a familiar social order and defended the evil institution of slavery less because they believed in human bondage as such than because they could not conceive of their social order without slavery.

In a certain sense, then, the landed planters of the South who opposed American nationalism were not unlike the landed proprietors in central Europe who opposed German or Polish or Italian or Hungarian or Bohemian nationalism. All of them were traditionalists. All feared that nationalism was linked with a democracy which they distrusted. All feared to release from the bottle the genii of manhood suffrage, of democratic equality, of social mobility, of universal education —and in the South, of emancipation for almost four million slaves. In this sense, European and American conservatism shared much in common, and the issue in the war between North and South carried implications considerably beyond the mere question as to whether the American states should form one republic or two.

The uprising of the North in 1861, and its decision to wage a war to preserve the American Federal Union, coming in the same year in which Victor Emmanuel was crowned king of a united Italy, marked a turning of the tide which had been running against nationalism for the preceding forty-five years. For better or worse, the course was set toward a world of sovereign nation-states, subject to no ultimate control in their conduct toward one another. The process of forging additional nations would reach out, within another century, from Europe and the Americas to Asia and Africa, until by 1966 there would be more than 130. As the number of "nations" increased, the beneficial effects of nationalism became increasingly uncertain, for all too many of the new sovereignties regarded the possession of nuclear destructive power as the crowning sanction of their nationhood.

Nationalism today seems something of a curse because of the paradox that while the people of the earth have been growing more and more functionally interdependent socially and economically, they have also simultaneously grown more and more irresponsibly independent of one another politically. The fragmentation of empires and other forms of supranational political authority has proceeded in ironic parallelism with increases in the cohesion of the peoples whose political relationships are being fragmented. At the same time, nationalism has shown that it can have a hideous side, undreamed of by such idealistic nationalists as Mazzini, and Lamartine, and Daniel Webster. Hitler is the supreme example, but even at the present moment a number of tyrants whose authority would command no more respect than that of a gangster if it were not sanctified by the mystique of national inviolability—a number of such tyrants have given us cause to doubt that the advancement of nationalism is necessarily a contribution to human progress. Suppose Lincoln did save the American Union, did his success in keeping one strong nation where there might have been two weaker ones really entitle him to a claim to greatness? Did it really contribute any constructive values for the modern world?

To answer this question, it may be necessary to recognize

not only that Lincoln sought to save American nationalism, but also why he sought to save it. To him, as to other idealistic nationalists, the Union—that is, the nation—was not an end in itself but a means to an end. He might affirm that "my paramount object . . . is to save the Union," and he might wage one of the most deadly wars ever fought up to that time to achieve his object. But he thought of the Union primarily as a context within which freedom might be preserved and extended. Moreover, he thought that survival of a liberal nation in America was vital as a test of the survival capacity of liberal nationalism anywhere. Thus, although personally he was distinctively and uniquely and even restrictively American —the only one of the great Presidents who never went outside the United States—he thought of American democracy in the least restrictive of terms. Many years before his Presidency, he eulogized Henry Clay as one who "loved his country partly because it was his own country but mostly because it was a free country." When the Civil War came, he asserted that it involved "more than the fate of these United States" and was of concern "to the whole family of man." The Union mattered to him not because of the question of authority at Washington, but because of the "necessity that is upon us of proving that popular government is not an absurdity." In his supreme moment at Gettysburg, this American nationalist did not once use the word American, or United States. He spoke, to be sure, of the nation "which our fathers brought forth," but this one nation conceived in liberty and dedicated to equality was linked in his thought with "any other nation so conceived and so dedicated." He wanted the war to result, for his own nation, in a "new birth of freedom," but this goal was not for America alone; it was to assure "men everywhere" that "government of the people, by the people, and for the people shall not perish from the earth."

It has been well said that Lincoln fused the cause of union

with the cause of freedom, which is equivalent to saying that he fused the cause of nationalism with the cause of liberalism. A number of idealistic nationalists of the nineteenth century made this same equation, and impressed it upon the public mind so vigorously that, even a century later, when we have had fairly numerous as well as traumatic illustrations of how completely antagonistic liberalism and nationalism can sometimes be, most of us respond affirmatively to claims made in the name of national integrity. We do so because our own thought still moves in the grooves cut by the great liberal nationalists of the nineteenth century.

This equation of liberalism and nationalism is not, of course, without logical foundations. Nationalism and liberalism both share certain common assumptions. Both depend upon the awakening self-consciousness of the individual—in the one case awakening to his membership in the political community, in the other awakening to his rights to participate in the decisions of the community and to enjoy its advantages. But while logic might impel nationalism and liberalism to go hand in hand, history often violates logic, and today we have copious proof that nationalism can flourish in separation from any liberal counterpart. It did so in Fascist Italy and Nazi Germany. It does so in Red China and in Soviet Russia (though these countries theoretically reject nationalism), and it is doing so in various dictatorships in the "emerging" nations. But if one kind of logic would prove nationalism and liberalism to be twin offspring of the idea of the free individual as patriot and as citizen, there is another logic which declares liberalism and nationalism to be opposites, since liberalism regards the state as existing for the individual and nationalism regards the individual as existing for the state.

This is only to say that the nineteenth-century conjunction of nationalism and liberalism was by no means inevitable. To regard it as inevitable is to lose the larger meaning of the

Civil War, for the war was one of the important historic developments contributing to a conjunction which, in other circumstances, might never have occurred. Lincoln's dedication of nationalistic means to liberal ends went far to produce this conjunction in the cosmos of American values. But at the same time when Lincoln was fusing nationalism with liberalism in America, another of the great figures who made the nineteenth century a century of nationalism, Count Otto von Bismarck, was carefully disassociating liberalism from nationalism in Germany. Having watched how the debacle of liberalism wrecked all hopes of German unification at Frankfurt in 1848, Bismarck wedded his nationalism to a concept of power and not to ideas of freedom or popular government. He signalized this position by publicly embracing a policy of "blood and iron" when he came to the head of the Prussian ministry in the year of Lincoln's Emancipation Proclamation. Nine years and three wars later, while President Grant, as the head of an imperfectly reunited nation, was struggling to reconcile the liberal principle of home rule for the South with the liberal principle of citizenship rights for the Negro, Bismarck made his monarch emperor of a Germany which was at last firmly united under authoritarian controls.

Bismarck and Lincoln were, perhaps, the two foremost exponents of nineteenth-century nationalism, after Napoleon. No two exemplars of the same force could have been more dissimilar, and no dramatist could have designed two figures better suited to point up contrasting styles of nationalism. The Gettysburg Address would have been as foreign to Bismarck as a policy of "blood and iron" would have been to Lincoln.

The contrast, perhaps, points the way to what was significant, in world perspective, about the American Civil War. The significance lay not in the fact that it was a triumph for nationalism (though the war forged the North as well as the

South into a nation larger than any in western Europe), not in the fact that it was a triumph of liberalism (though Lincoln vindicated government of the people, by the people, and for the people, and proved that democracy, with all its weaknesses, can withstand the shocks of war). The significance lay rather in the fact that the Civil War, more perhaps than any event in Europe, fused the two great forces of the nineteenth century—liberalism and nationalism. It fused them so thoroughly that their potential separateness was lost from view. The fusion gave to nationalism a sanction which, frequently since then, it has failed to deserve, and gave to liberalism a strength which, since then, it has frequently not known how to use.

Meanwhile, Americans remained in confusion as to what their war had signified for the world. Some thought they had proved the strength of democracy, forgetting that the Confederacy which they defeated was also democratic and shared democracy's weaknesses. Others thought that they had vindicated the principle of nationalism, forgetting that the loyalty which Southerners gave to the Confederacy was no less nationalistic than the loyalty which Yankees gave to the Union. Few perceived that one of the most sweeping consequences of the war was to identify with one another these two forces which were not necessarily linked. This partially fictitious identification may, in the final analysis, have done great harm by giving a spurious sanction to modern nationalism, with all its potential dangers for the larger human society. But in a more immediate sense, it was perhaps the most constructive identification made during the nineteenth century, for it gave significant moral purpose to the force of nationalism, which, without such purpose, was always in danger of degenerating into mere group egocentrism or chauvinism. At the same time, it also gave significant institutional support to

the principle of freedom, which without such support would
have had only the ideals of reformers to sustain it.

BIBLIOGRAPHY

While the bibliography of the American Civil War is, of course,
enormous, the bibliography strictly applicable to this essay is composed largely of books that are yet to be written. It is in fact one
point of the essay that the significance of the Civil War for world
history, and particularly for the history of nationalism, has been
generally neglected by historians.

A good bibliography of the general literature on nationalism up
to the date of its publication is Koppel S. Pinson, A *Bibliographical Introduction to Nationalism* (New York, 1934). An interesting interpretative treatment is Boyd C. Shafer, *Nationalism: Myth
and Reality* (New York, 1955), and a somewhat older one is Hans
Kohn, *The Idea of Nationalism: A Study of its Origins and Background* (New York, 1943). Carlton J. H. Hayes, *Essays on Nationalism* (New York, 1926) and *The Historical Evolution of
Modern Nationalism* (New York, 1931) are still of interest.

The theme of nationalism in American history is treated in Hans
Kohn, *American Nationalism: An Interpretative Essay* (New
York, 1957). On the impact of nationalism on the historiography
of the American Civil War see David M. Potter, "The Historian's
Use of Nationalism and Vice Versa," in this volume. For rather
random samples of foreign views of the Civil War see Belle B.
Sideman and Lillian Friedman (eds.), *Europe Looks at the Civil
War* (New York, 1960).

A good critical assessment and analysis of Civil War historiography is Thomas J. Pressly, *Americans Interpret Their Civil War*
(Princeton, 1954). Of the thousands of works on the subject, two
of the most important are J. G. Randall, *Lincoln the President*
(4 vols.; New York, 1945–1955; Vol. IV completed by Richard N.
Current) and Allan Nevins, *The Emergence of Lincoln* (2 vols.;
New York, 1950) and *The War for the Union* (2 vols.; 1959–60,
with more to come).

For the idea of the comparison of Lincoln and Bismarck,
I am indebted to Sir Denis Brogan, *The Free State* (London,
1945).

Index

Aaron, Daniel, 125n
Abernethy, Thomas P., 183
Abolitionists: Beveridge on historiography of, 92; Barnes on, 93; Craven and Randall on, 96; blamed for causing war, 106–107, 110; anti-Negro attitudes among, 110; biographies of antislavery figures, 110–11, 113; reaction in favor of, 108, 111–12; Donald, analysis of, in terms of status politics, 111; record of, after Civil War, 113; Attacks of, upon Lincoln, 157–58; ambivalent attitude of, toward Negroes, 203–204; belief of, in slave insurrection, 204, 213–15
Abrams, Richard M., viii
Adams, James Truslow, 222n
Adams, Charles Francis (1807–1886): biography of, by Duberman, 136, 145–46; New Mexico bill of, 248
Adams, Charles Francis (1835–1915), 90–91
Adams, John Quincy, 109, 134
Agrarianism: Concept of, advanced as key to southern distinctiveness, 6–7; theme of, used to minimize biracial factors, 7; critique of, as inapplicable to South, 9, 15, 118; reasons for appeal of concept of, to Southerners, 12–14; as social concept, 12–13; rejected or attacked, 10, 14; clash of, with industrialism, advanced as key to sectional clash, 72–74; this interpretation rejected, 118; *see also* Sectionalism
Agriculture in South: historical studies of, 121, 128n, 147, 183
Alabama: studies relating to, 121n, 128, 183, 184
Alcorn, James L., 145
Alden, John R., 122
Alexander, Thomas B., 131, 187
Allston, Robert F. W., 128n
Ambler, Charles H., 183
American historical experience: ideological obstacles to understanding of, by Americans, 287–88
Anderson, Osborn P., 209
Angle, Paul M., 141, 167, 173
Antislavery: lack of full support for, in North, 97, 114–16, 118;

Comparative History: lack of, in American historical studies, 287

Compromise, during sectional crisis: hostility to, primary motive of Greeley, 233–35, 242; tends to strengthen Southern fire-eaters, 253; not necessarily supportive to Union, 254; rejected in part to weaken Southern disunionists and strengthen unionists, 254; rejection of, not necessarily equivalent to acceptance of disunion or war, 254; status of as alternative to secession or war, 255

Compromise of 1850, 137–38

"Compromise of 1877," 188

Confederate States: as expression of Southern nationalism, 63; majority of slave states originally refuse to join, 143; titles of studies on, 184;

—Defeat of, explanation for; Southern economic handicaps as causes, 264–65; results of war not necessarily determined by quantity of assets, 265–66; situations in which South apparently might have won, 265–66; differential in military performance in favor of South, 266; differential in political performance questionable, 266; failure to raise revenue by taxation, 267; failure of policy for use of cotton, 268–70; disastrous economic effects of impressment system, 271; failure to use Negro manpower, 271–72; failures of Davis as leader, 274–84; lack of political party mechanism, 284–86; poor quality of Congress, 285; long conditioning to defensive, negative policies, 285; *see also* Davis, Jefferson

Conrad, Alfred H., 128n

Cook, John E., 210, 216

Cook, Thomas I., 125n

Cotton: policy of Confederacy concerning export and trading, 268–70

Cotton culture: studies of, 128n

Coulter, Ellis Merton, 122, 184

Cox, LaWanda and John H., 188

Craven, Avery O.: his view on causes of the Civil War, 94–95; compared with Randall, 96–98; later modification of views of, 101; studies by, 69n, 122, 124, 183; review of his *An Historian and the Civil War*, 147–50; on Kansas-Nebraska Act, 138n; on "Bleeding Kansas," 140n; on John Brown's raid, 141; mentioned, 102, 243

—Analysis of his views of coming of Civil War: 148–50; problem not to explain antagonism, but to explain failure to solve antagonisms without war, 148; transition from emphasis upon unrealistic emotions to exphasis upon differential impact of industrialization upon two societies, 148–49; latter concept neglected by his critics, 149; persisting concepts in the two phases of his interpretation, 149; "revisionist" label not applicable to his later views, 150

Crenshaw, Ollinger, 137n, 142

Crèvecoeur, Hector St. John de, 56

Crippen, Lee, 145

Crittenden, John J., 143, 247

Culture: concept of homogeneity

of, as basis of nationality, 37,
50; concept of cultural differences between North and South
used by historians in analysis
of sectionalism, 68–69, 131–
32; pitfalls of cultural approach,
132; shared qualities overlooked, 70; differential qualities
exaggerated, 68–69, 118; analysis influenced by motive to
justify or discredit separatist
movement, 68–69, 70; historical method conducive to exaggeration, 70; *see also* Economic
interests, Sectionalism
Current, Richard N.: on Calhoun,
125n; on Webster, 135; on
crisis at Fort Sumter, 143; on
Lincoln, 144n; believes Lincoln
accepted alternative of war,
259; mentioned, 263
Currie, Brainerd, viii
Curry, Richard O., 183
Curti, Merle: 48, 55, 66n, 69;
quoted, 48n, 66n
Curtis, Benjamin R., 141

Davenport, F. Garvan, 128n
Davis, Charles S., 121n, 183
Davis, Curtis Carroll, 69, 126
Davis, David Brion, 115
Davis, Edwin A., 183
Davis, Jefferson: as symbol of
hierarchical South, 5; Vandiver
on, 22; biography cited, 144
—Qualities of, significant in
Confederate defeat: 267; prevents trade in cotton, 269; his
recognition of need to use
Negro labor as an exception to
his general poor judgment, 273;
contemporary criticism of, usually on wrong grounds, 274,
285; his failures—in relations

with Confederate leaders and
people, 274–77; unwilling to
admit error, 277; lacked drive
to win, 278, 282–84; errors as
Commander-in-chief, 278–83;
departmentalization, 280–81;
opposition to, could not ex-
press itself politically, 285–86
Davis, Richard Beal, 127
Dana, Charles A., 225n
De Bow, J. D. B., 18, 31, 67
Degler, Carl N., 189
Delap, Simeon A., 184
Democratic Party: impact of sec-
tionalism upon, 98; division in,
in 1844, 136
Denman, Clarence P., 121n, 184
Desegregation: as theme for his-
torical study, 194–95
Deutsch, Karl W., 42, 54
DeVoto, Bernard, 100, 137n
Dillon, Merton L., 113
Disunion: danger of, in 1850,
137–38; *see also* Secession
Dodd, William E., devices of, for
creating image of democratic
South, 5–7, 25; as pioneer his-
torian of South, 124; on intel-
lectual history of South, 124
Doherty, Herbert: on historian's
use of other disciplines, 195–
96; mentioned, 87
Donald, David: biography of
Sumner, 107, 136, 146n; attacked for treatment of Sumner,
108; analysis of abolitionists,
110–11; on Lincoln, 144n; on
Reconstruction, 188; men-
tioned, viii, 87, 263
Douglas, Stephen A.: treated historiographically as foil to Lincoln, 92; Beveridge on, 92, 172;
G. F. Milton on, 93; Jaffa on,
101; his importance in Com-

to, as a world force, 290; Lincoln links cause of, with cause of Union, 295–96; and nationalism not necessarily linked, 296; and nationalism linked in Civil War, 295, 297–98

Lieber, Francis, 145

Lincoln, Abraham: Belief of, in primacy of cause of Union, 65; not an advocate of racial equality, 75; antislavery position of, regarded by some historians as equivocal, 110; Beveridge's biography of, 92–93; revisionists minimize distinction between his position and that of Douglas, 106; Jaffa and Fehrenbacher emphasize this distinction, 101, 106; his election to presidency, 142; his policy in crisis at Fort Sumter, 142–43, 168, 174, 257–58, 258–60; literature on, 144, 153–76

—Historical treatment of, as reflection of all major themes of American historiography, 153–76; as a folk hero, 154–55; martyrdom, analogous with sacrifice of Jesus, 154; apochrypha concerning, 155; nationalist background for interpretation of Lincoln's career, 155–56; image of, as great emancipator, 156–57; recognition by early writers of Lincoln's reluctance as emancipator, 157–58, 159–60; development of stereotype of emancipator, 158–60; relation of emancipation theme to theme of exalted nationalism, 160; frontier theme, 160; development of stereotype of Lincoln as a frontiersman, 161–65; legiti-

macy of birth questioned, 163; legitimacy proved by Barton, 173; beginning of full documentary study of, in work of Nicolay and Hay, 165–68; first critical study of, by Charnwood, 168–70; phase of harsh self-criticism in historiography, and criticism of Lincoln, 171; Freudianism in historiography and Freudian treatment of Lincoln, 171; intensive scholarship in historiography, and intensive scholarly studies of Lincoln, 172–74; final restatement of the legend by Sandburg, 174; cumulative restatement of monographic findings, by Randall, 174–75

—Universality of, 174–75; links ideas of nationalism with idea of freedom, 175, 295–97; his nationalism contrasted with that of Bismarck, Napoleon, Cavour, 176, 297

—His appraisal of John Brown's raid, 217; his reaction to secession, 220; his faith in Southern unionism, 254–56, 259; policy of inactivity in secession crisis, 257

—Leadership of, significant in Union victory, 267; comparison of, with Davis, 275–83; effectiveness of, in dealing with leaders, 275, 277; willing to admit error, 277; sound concept of role of Commander-in-Chief, 279, 282–83; instinct of, for victory, 283

Lincoln, Robert Todd, 165
Lincoln, Thomas, 163, 173
Lincoln-Douglas debates, 141
Linden, Fabian, 123, 191

with, 65–66; dubious value of, in modern world, 152–56, 294; cult of, by Bancroft, 156 —Relation of Civil War to: dominance of nationalism in twentieth century, 290; precarious condition of, in mid-nineteenth century, 291–92; comparison of forces in Europe and in America opposing, 292–93; Civil War and unification of Italy in 1861 as a turning point in history of, 293; debatable value of saving, 294; the nation as a means to the end of perpetuating liberal values, 295; nationalism and liberalism linked in Civil War, 175–76, 296; *see also* Nationality, Sectionalism, Culture

Nationality: concept of, as device for structuring historians' view of modern world, 35–36; distinctive culture as basis for, 37, 50; group interest as basis for, 54–55; historians' tendency to overestimate culture as basis for, 68–70; analysis of, warped by fact that attribution of nationality sanctions the group to which it is attributed, 43–47; psychological versus institutional concepts of, 36–38; implications of the psychological concept, 37–47; tendency of political and cultural aspects to converge, 42; concept in terms of attribution of group identity versus sanction for group autonomy, 64–65; *see also* Nationalism

Negro Revolution, effect of, on historiography of antislavery movement and Civil War, 116

Negroes: folk culture of, 15–16; relative importance of legal status as slaves and economic status as cotton cultivators in determining condition of, 94; prejudice against, in free states, 114–16, 118; opportunities for research in history of, 195; lack of opportunity to choose their leaders, 201–203; means by which leaders of, have emerged, 202–203; failure of Confederacy to claim right to use labor of, 271–73; *see also* Biracial system, Racial prejudice, Segregation, Slavery

Nevins, Allan: on causes of the Civil War, 103–105; on Kansas-Nebraska Act, 138; on Dred Scott Case, 141; on John C. Frémont, 145; on question of sanity of John Brown, 212; mentioned, 88, 98, 100, 108

New England Emigrant Aid Society, 140

Nichols, Alice, 140n

Nichols, Roy F.: on political party practices as cause of Civil War, 98; on historiography of Kansas-Nebraska Act, 139; mentioned, 102, 243

Nicolay, John G., 144, 165–68

Noblin, Stuart, 184

North: majority position of, permits coordination of sectional and national interests, 66; *see also* Union, causes of victory of, and Sectionalism

North Elba, New York: community for Negroes at, 205

North Carolina: studies relating to, 121n, 128n, 183, 184; defeat of secession in, 255

Northrop, Lucius B., 268

20, 122; early history of, 122; development of, 124–33; in the churches, 131; in political parties, 131

Seddon, James A., 281n

Segregation: liberals' unwillingness to understand in historical terms, 29; problems in understanding of, 196–97

Sellers, Charles G., 19, 31, 131n

Sellers, James B., 128n, 183

Semmes, Raphael, 177–78

Separation as an Alternative in 1861: not perceived by many Republicans as alternative to compromise or war, 255

Seward, William H.: studies of, 145–46; learns of plan by John Brown, 207; reaction to secession, 220; belief in Southern unionism, 255–56; relationship with Lincoln, 275

Sewell, Richard H., 113

Shafer, Boyd C., 50n, 55, 57n

Shanks, Henry T., 121n, 184

Sheldon, William D., 184

Shenton, James P., 146n

Sherwin, Oscar, 111

Shugg, Roger, 121n, 187

Silbey, Joel H., 131

Silver, James W.: on Southern distinctiveness, 18–19; on Faulkner's view of race relations, 23n; on Mississippi in Confederacy, 184

Simkins, Francis B.: view of liberals' distortion of Southern history, 25–26; on racial segregation, 26–29; revises traditional view of Reconstruction, 187; mentioned, 17, 19, 120n

Simms, William Gilmore, 126

Sindler, Allen P., 184

Singletary, Otis A., 137n

Sitterson, Joseph Carlyle, 121n, 128n, 183–84

Skotheim, Robert A., 111n

Slave insurrection: abolitionists' belief in, 204, 213–15; John Brown's plan for and faith in, 209, 210, 213; Northern belief in, 213–15; Southerners' fear of, 215; abstractness of Brown's idea, 216

Slave society, contrast of, with bourgeois society, 117–18

Slaveholding: regional differences in as factor in sectional conflict, 73, 75; distribution of, in South, 94

Slavery: interpretation of, by U. B. Phillips, 10; by Kenneth Stampp, 11, 129; by Stanley Elkins, 129; by Eugene Genovese, 130, 191–93; literature on, 120–21, 128–29, 183; changing emphasis in historiography of, 186; unsettled questions concerning, 190

—As an economic interest, 81, 128n, 129; belief that it would have disappeared, not valid, 118

—relation of, to capitalism, 117–18; dispute as to agrarian or capitalistic nature of, 192–93

—Southern defense of, 125; resistance of slaves to, 130. *See also* Slavery as a cause of Civil War

Slavery as Cause of Civil War: discussed, 65, 90, 91, 94, 97, 102, 106–107, 113–14, 115–16, 118; questioned by Craven, 95; significance as an institution and as an issue, 97; affirmed by Schlesinger, Jr., 99; relation of, as issue, to broader issue of racial subordination, 116

on neglected topics in Southern
history, 195–96
Tobacco culture: studies of, 128n,
183
Toombs, Robert, 145
Toussaint L'Ouverture, Francois
Dominique: compared to John
Brown, 217
Tracy, Gilbert, 167
Transcontinental Railroad: as is-
sue of sectional contention, 132
Trefousse, Hans L., 146n
Treitschke, Heinrich von, 56
Trexler, Harrison A., 121n, 183
Tribune, New York, explains pol-
icy of inactivity in secession
crisis, 257–58; *see also* Greeley,
Horace
Trumbull, Lyman, 145–46
Tucker, Glenn, 145
Tyler, Alice Felt, 109
Tyler, John, 134
Turner, Frederick J.: on sectional-
ism, 60; applicability of theo-
ries to South, 147; frontier the-
sis, 160–61; concept of sec-
tions, 178, 179, 190

Underground railroad: study of,
113; as white man's legend, 203
Union, value of, as justification of
war, 65; as an issue of the Civil
War, 102, 103, 116
Union, causes of victory of the:
economic factors as explanation, 264; factors of leadership
as explanation, 275–83; *see also*
Confederate states, defeat of,
explanations for; Lincoln, Abraham; Davis, Jefferson
Unionism in South: defeated but
retained vitality to return after
war, 78; prominent but widely
misunderstood in Feb. and

Mar., 1861, 255; quality of,
256
Universal Negro Improvement Association, 202
Urban, C. Stanley, 137n

Van Buren, Martin, 135
Vance, Rupert B., 179, 191
Vance, Zebulon B., 145
Van Deusen, Glyndon G.; on
Clay, 135; on Jackson period,
135; on Weed, 145; on Greeley,
145; on Seward, 146n; men-
tioned, 243
Van Deusen, John G., 132n
Vandiver, Frank E., 17, 19–20
Venable, Austin, on secession in
Alabama, 184
Vesey, Denmark: compared to
John Brown, 217
Vest, George G., 285
Vicksburg: policy of Davis as fac-
tor in Confederate loss of, 281–
82
Virginia: studies relating to, 114,
121n, 124, 127, 128n, 183,
184; defeat of secession in, 255
Vogel, Robert W., 128n
Voltaire, Francois Marie Arouet
de, 54
Von Abele, Rudolph, 144

Wade, Benjamin F., 146
Wade, Richard C., 186
Walker, Robert J., 145, 206
Wall, Bennett H.: 87, 195–96
War, preventability of, 96; irra-
tional factors as causes of, 96–97
War, avoidance of: as a value in
sectional crisis, 102
Warren, Louis A., 173
Warren, Gouverneur, 265
Washington, Booker T., 30, 196,
201, 202